BUSINESS ISSUES, COMPETITION AND ENTREPRENEURSHIP

BUSINESS TRENDS IN THE 21ST CENTURY

REGULATIONS AND LEGISLATION

Business Issues, Competition and Entrepreneurship

Additional books and e-books in this series can be found on Nova's website under the Series tab.

BUSINESS ISSUES, COMPETITION AND ENTREPRENEURSHIP

BUSINESS TRENDS IN THE 21ST CENTURY

REGULATIONS AND LEGISLATION

CRUZ OMAR CLEMENTE ESCAMILLA
EDITOR

snova
New York

Additional color graphics may be available in the e-book version of this book.

Library of Congress Cataloging-in-Publication Data

ISBN: 978-1-53614-260-0

Published by Nova Science Publishers, Inc. † New York

CONTENTS

PREFACE

This book opens with an examination of the economic circumstances of veteran-owned business. It provides a brief overview of veterans' employment experiences, comparing unemployment and labor force participation rates for veterans, veterans who have left the military since September 2001 and nonveterans. The next chapter provides a historical examination of the SBA (Small Business Administration's) size standards and assesses competing views concerning how to define a small business. The third chapter is a 3-page CRS report on business capital investment spending, its components and causes of the recent slowdown. The fourth chapter of this book examine the SB OIG (offices of inspector general) funding in Fiscal Year 2018, its impact on monetary saving, SBA programs and operations and legislation affecting the agency. It concludes with observations concerning the SBA OIG's relationship with Congress. The last chapter opens with a discussion of the rationale provided for having a Microloan program, describes the program's eligibility standards and operating requirements for lenders and borrowers, and examines the arguments presented by the program's critics and advocates.

Chapter 1 - Several federal agencies, including the Small Business Administration (SBA), provide training and other assistance to veterans seeking civilian employment. For example, the Department of Defense (DOD), in cooperation with the SBA, Department of Labor, Department of

Veterans Affairs, and several other federal agencies, operates the Transition Goals Plans Success program (Transition GPS), which provides employment information and entrepreneurship training to exiting military servicemembers to assist them in transitioning from the military to the civilian labor force.

In recent years, the unemployment rate among veterans as a whole has generally been similar to or lower than the unemployment rate for nonveterans 18 years and older. However, veterans who have left the military since September 2001 have experienced higher unemployment than other veterans and nonveterans. As a result, Congress has focused much of its attention on finding ways to assist veterans who have left the military since September 2001.

The SBA provides management and technical assistance services to more than 100,000 veterans each year through its various management and technical assistance training partners (e.g., Small Business Development Centers, Women's Business Centers [WBCs], Service Corps of Retired Executives [SCORE], and Veterans Business Outreach Centers [VBOCs]). The SBA's Office of Veterans Business Development (OVBD) also administers several programs to assist veterans, including the Operation Boots to Business: From Service to Startup initiative which is part of DOD's Transition GPS program.

The expansion of federal employment training programs targeted at specific populations, such as women and veterans, has led some Members and organizations to ask if these programs should be consolidated. In their view, eliminating program duplication among federal business assistance programs across federal agencies, and within the SBA, would result in lower costs and improved services. Others argue that keeping these business assistance programs separate enables them to offer services that match the unique needs of various underserved populations, such as veterans. In their view, instead of considering program consolidation as a policy option, the focus should be on improving communication and cooperation among the federal agencies providing assistance to entrepreneurs.

This chapter opens with an examination of the economic circumstances of veteran-owned businesses drawn from the Bureau of the Census's 2012 Survey of Business Owners (SBO). It then provides a brief overview of veterans' employment experiences, comparing unemployment and labor force participation rates for veterans, veterans who have left the military since September 2001, and nonveterans. The chapter also describes the employment assistance programs offered by several federal agencies to assist veterans in their transition from the military to the civilian labor force and examines, in greater detail, the SBA's veteran business development programs, the SBA's efforts to assist veterans' access to capital, and the SBA's veteran contracting programs. It also discusses the SBA's Military Reservist Economic Injury Disaster Loan program and P.L. 114-38, the Veterans Entrepreneurship Act of 2015, which authorized and made permanent the SBA's recent practice of waiving the SBAExpress loan program's one time, upfront loan guarantee fee for veterans (and their spouse).

Chapter 2 - Small business size standards are of congressional interest because the standards determine eligibility for receiving Small Business Administration (SBA) assistance as well as federal contracting and tax preferences. Although there is bipartisan agreement that the nation's small businesses play an important role in the American economy, there are differences of opinion concerning how to define them. The Small Business Act of 1953 (P.L. 83-163, as amended) authorized the SBA to establish size standards for determining eligibility for federal small business assistance. The SBA currently uses two types of size standards to determine SBA program eligibility: industry-specific size standards and alternative size standards based on the applicant's maximum tangible net worth and average net income after federal taxes.

The SBA's industry-specific size standards determine program eligibility for firms in 1,037 industrial classifications in 19 sub-industry activities described in the 2017 North American Industry Classification System (NAICS). The size standards are based on one of four measures: (1) number of employees, (2) average annual receipts in the previous three years, (3) average asset size as reported in the firm's four quarterly financial statements for the preceding year, or (4) a combination of number of employees and barrel per day refining capacity. Overall, the SBA currently classifies about 97% of all employer firms as small. These firms represent about 30% of industry receipts.

The SBA has always based its size standards on economic analysis of each industry's overall competitiveness and the competitiveness of firms within each industry. However, in the absence of precise statutory guidance and consensus on how to define small, the SBA's size standards have often been challenged, typically by industry representatives seeking to increase the number of firms eligible for assistance and by Members concerned that the size standards may not adequately target assistance to firms that they consider to be truly small.

During the 111th Congress, P.L. 111-240, the Small Business Jobs Act of 2010:

- authorized the SBA to establish an alternative size standard using maximum tangible net worth and average net income after federal taxes for both the 7(a) and 504/CDC loan guaranty programs;
- established, until the SBA acted, an interim alternative size standard for the 7(a) and 504/CDC programs of not more than $15 million in tangible net worth and not more than $5 million in average net income after federal taxes (excluding any carry-over losses) for the two full fiscal years before the date of the application; and
- required the SBA to conduct a detailed review of not less than one-third of the SBA's industry size standards every 18 months beginning on the new law's date of enactment (September 27, 2010) and ensure that each size standard is reviewed at least once every five years.

This chapter provides a historical examination of the SBA's size standards and assesses competing views concerning how to define a small business. It also discusses

- P.L. 112-239, the National Defense Authorization Act for Fiscal Year 2013, which requires the SBA to make available a justification when establishing or approving a size standard that the size standard is appropriate for each individual industry classification. It addresses the SBA's recent practice of combining size standards within industrial groups as a means to reduce the complexity of its size standards and to provide greater consistency for industrial classifications that have similar economic characteristics.
- P.L. 114-328, the National Defense Authorization Act for Fiscal Year 2017, which authorizes the SBA to establish different size standards for agricultural enterprises using existing methods and appeal processes. Previously, the small business size standard for agricultural enterprises was set in statute as having annual receipts not in excess of $750,000.
- Legislation introduced during the 112th Congress (H.R. 585, the Small Business Size Standard Flexibility Act of 2011), 113th Congress (H.R. 2542, the Regulatory Flexibility Improvements Act of 2013, and included in H.R. 4, the Jobs for America Act), 114th Congress (H.R. 527, the Small Business Regulatory Flexibility Improvements Act of 2015, and its Senate companion bill, S. 1536), and 115th Congress (H.R. 33, the Small Business Regulatory Flexibility Improvements Act of 2017, and its Senate companion bill, S. 584, and included in H.R. 5, the Regulatory Accountability Act of 2017) to authorize the SBA's Office of Chief Counsel for Advocacy to approve or disapprove a size standard requested by a federal agency for purposes other than the Small Business Act or the Small Business Investment Act of 1958. The SBA's Administrator currently has that authority.

Chapter 3 - Business capital investment spending is composed of private spending on nonresidential structures (e.g., factories), equipment (e.g., machinery), and intellectual property products (e.g., software). Business investment is a key determinant of economic growth. When businesses add to the capital stock, the value of goods and services (i.e., gross domestic product [GDP]) the economy can produce increases. One reason that economic growth has been lower in the last decade is because business investment spending has grown more slowly. Boosting investment spending was one of the key goals of the 2017 tax cuts.

Chapter 4 - Congress created offices of inspector general (OIGs) to assist in its oversight of the executive branch. OIGs provide independent, nonpartisan analysis, conducted in accordance with generally accepted government auditing standards, to identify and recommend ways to limit waste, fraud, and abuse in federal programs and enhance program and operational efficiency and effectiveness. OIGs' activities supplement and complement those of the Government Accountability Office (GAO), which serves a similar, though not identical, role in assisting congressional oversight of the executive branch. Together, OIGs and GAO provide Congress with information and analysis needed to conduct effective oversight and, in the process, help Congress maintain its balance of power with the presidency.

OIGs exist in more than 70 federal agencies, including all departments and larger agencies, numerous boards and commissions, and other entities. The U.S. Small Business Administration's Office of Inspector General (SBA OIG) was created under authority of the Inspector General Act of 1978 (P.L. 95-452, as amended). Its three primary statutory purposes are to

- conduct and supervise audits and investigations of the SBA's programs and operations;
- recommend policies designed to promote the economy, efficiency, and effectiveness of the SBA's programs and operations and to prevent and detect fraud and abuse; and

- keep both the SBA Administrator and Congress "fully and currently informed about problems and deficiencies relating to the administration of such programs and operations and the necessity for and progress of corrective action."

During FY2017, the SBA OIG issued 19 audit reports containing 72 recommendations for improving the SBA's programs and operations, and its investigations resulted in 35 indictments or informations and 25 convictions. The SBA OIG claimed that its recommendations resulted in monetary savings and recoveries of nearly $82.1 million in FY2017. In addition, the SBA OIG's annual *Report on the Most Serious Management and Performance Challenges Facing the SBA* focuses attention "on areas that are particularly vulnerable to fraud, waste, error, and mismanagement, or otherwise pose a significant risk and generally have been subject to one or more OIG or GAO reports."

This chapter examines the SBA OIG's statutory authorities; reporting requirements; funding ($26.9 million in FY2018, including $7 million in supplemental appropriations for overseeing SBA disaster assistance); staffing and organizational structure; and recent activities (audits, investigations, etc.). It also examines the SBA OIG's impact on monetary savings, SBA programs and operations, and legislation affecting the agency. The chapter concludes with observations concerning the SBA OIG's relationship with Congress.

Some areas of possible congressional interest, other than SBA OIG funding and staffing issues, include exploring ways to more accurately quantify the SBA OIG's claims of monetary savings and to determine if the SBA OIG should undertake additional tracking and monitoring activities to more accurately quantify the office's impact on SBA programs, operations, and legislation.

Chapter 5 - The Small Business Administration's (SBA's) Microloan program provides direct loans to qualified nonprofit intermediary lenders who, in turn, provide "microloans" of up to $50,000 to small businesses and nonprofit child care centers. It also provides marketing, management, and technical assistance to microloan borrowers and potential borrowers. Authorized in 1991 as a five-year demonstration project, it became operational in 1992, and was made permanent, subject to reauthorization, in 1997.

The Microloan program is designed to assist women, low-income, veteran, and minority entrepreneurs and small business owners by providing them small-scale loans for working capital or the acquisition of materials, supplies, or equipment. In FY2017, Microloan intermediaries provided 4,992 microloans totaling $69.3 million. The average Microloan was $13,884 and had a 7.5% interest rate.

Critics of the SBA's Microloan program argue that it is expensive relative to alternative programs, duplicative of the SBA's 7(a) loan guaranty program, and subject to administrative shortfalls. The program's advocates argue that it assists many who otherwise would not be served by the private sector and is an important source of capital and training assistance for low-income, women, and minority business owners.

Congressional interest in the Microloan program has increased in recent years, primarily because microloans are viewed as a means to assist very small businesses, especially women- and minority-owned startups, to get loans that enable them to create and retain jobs. Job creation, always a congressional interest, has taken on increased importance given continuing concerns about job growth during the current economic recovery.

This chapter opens with a discussion of the rationale provided for having a Microloan program, describes the program's eligibility standards and operating requirements for lenders and borrowers, and examines the arguments presented by the program's critics and advocates. It then discusses P.L. 111-240, the Small Business Jobs Act of 2010, which increased the Microloan program's loan limit for borrowers from $35,000 to $50,000, and the aggregate loan limit for intermediaries after their first year of participation in the program from $3.5 million to $5 million.

It also discusses P.L. 115-141, the Consolidated Appropriations Act, 2018, which, among other provisions, relaxed requirements on Microloan intermediaries that prohibited them from spending more than 25% of their technical assistance grant funds on prospective borrowers and more than

25% of those grant funds on contracts with third parties to provide that technical assistance. The act increased those percentages to 50% (originally in H.R. 2056, the Microloan Modernization Act of 2017, and S. 526, its companion bill in the Senate).

In: Business Trends in the 21st Century ISBN: 978-1-53614-260-0
Editor: C. O. Clemente Escamilla

Chapter 1

SBA Veterans Assistance Programs: An Analysis of Contemporary Issues (Updated)*

Robert Jay Dilger and Sean Lowry

Abstract

Several federal agencies, including the Small Business Administration (SBA), provide training and other assistance to veterans seeking civilian employment. For example, the Department of Defense (DOD), in cooperation with the SBA, Department of Labor, Department of Veterans Affairs, and several other federal agencies, operates the Transition Goals Plans Success program (Transition GPS), which provides employment information and entrepreneurship training to exiting military servicemembers to assist them in transitioning from the military to the civilian labor force.

In recent years, the unemployment rate among veterans as a whole has generally been similar to or lower than the unemployment rate for nonveterans 18 years and older. However, veterans who have left the

* This is an edited, reformatted and augmented version of a Congressional Research Service report, R42695, dated April 27, 2018.

military since September 2001 have experienced higher unemployment than other veterans and nonveterans. As a result, Congress has focused much of its attention on finding ways to assist veterans who have left the military since September 2001.

The SBA provides management and technical assistance services to more than 100,000 veterans each year through its various management and technical assistance training partners (e.g., Small Business Development Centers, Women's Business Centers [WBCs], Service Corps of Retired Executives [SCORE], and Veterans Business Outreach Centers [VBOCs]). The SBA's Office of Veterans Business Development (OVBD) also administers several programs to assist veterans, including the Operation Boots to Business: From Service to Startup initiative which is part of DOD's Transition GPS program.

The expansion of federal employment training programs targeted at specific populations, such as women and veterans, has led some Members and organizations to ask if these programs should be consolidated. In their view, eliminating program duplication among federal business assistance programs across federal agencies, and within the SBA, would result in lower costs and improved services. Others argue that keeping these business assistance programs separate enables them to offer services that match the unique needs of various underserved populations, such as veterans. In their view, instead of considering program consolidation as a policy option, the focus should be on improving communication and cooperation among the federal agencies providing assistance to entrepreneurs.

This chapter opens with an examination of the economic circumstances of veteran-owned businesses drawn from the Bureau of the Census's 2012 Survey of Business Owners (SBO). It then provides a brief overview of veterans' employment experiences, comparing unemployment and labor force participation rates for veterans, veterans who have left the military since September 2001, and nonveterans. The chapter also describes the employment assistance programs offered by several federal agencies to assist veterans in their transition from the military to the civilian labor force and examines, in greater detail, the SBA's veteran business development programs, the SBA's efforts to assist veterans' access to capital, and the SBA's veteran contracting programs. It also discusses the SBA's Military Reservist Economic Injury Disaster Loan program and P.L. 114-38, the Veterans Entrepreneurship Act of 2015, which authorized and made permanent the SBA's recent practice of waiving the SBAExpress loan program's one time, upfront loan guarantee fee for veterans (and their spouse).

SBA ASSISTANCE FOR VETERANS

The Small Business Administration (SBA) administers several programs to support small business owners and prospective entrepreneurs. For example, it provides education programs to assist with business formation and expansion; loan guaranty programs to enhance small business owners' access to capital; and programs to increase small business opportunities in federal contracting, including oversight of the service-disabled veteran-owned small business federal procurement goaling program.[1] The SBA also provides direct loans for owners of businesses of all sizes, homeowners, and renters to assist their recovery from natural disasters.

The Military Reservist Economic Injury Disaster Loan (MREIDL) program is also of interest to veterans. It provides direct loans of up to $2 million to small business owners who are not able to obtain credit elsewhere meet ordinary and necessary operating expenses that they could have met but are not able to because an essential employee has been called up to active duty in his or her role as a military reservist or member of the National Guard due to a period of military conflict.[2]

The SBA provides management and technical assistance to more than 100,000 veterans each year through its various training partners (e.g., Small Business Development Centers, Women's Business Centers, SCORE [formerly the Service Corps of Retired Executives], and Veterans Business Outreach Centers [VBOCs]). In addition, the SBA's Office of

---

[1] For further information and analysis concerning the Small Business Administration's (SBA's) entrepreneurial education programs, see CRS Report R41352, *Small Business Management and Technical Assistance Training Programs*, by Robert Jay Dilger. For further information and analysis concerning the SBA's access to capital programs, see CRS Report R41146, *Small Business Administration 7(a) Loan Guaranty Program*, by Robert Jay Dilger and CRS Report R41184, *Small Business Administration 504/CDC Loan Guaranty Program*, by Robert Jay Dilger.

[2] SBA, "Disaster Assistance Program: SOP 50-30-7," May 13, 2011, p. 48, at https://www.sba.gov/sites/default/files/ sops/SOP%2050%2030%207.pdf; and 13 C.F.R. §123.508. For further information and analysis concerning the SBA's disaster assistance loan program, see CRS Report R41309, *The SBA Disaster Loan Program: Overview and Possible Issues for Congress*, by Bruce R. Lindsay.

Veterans Business Development (OVBD) administers several programs to assist veteran-owned small businesses.[3]

The SBA's OVBD received an appropriation of $12.3 million for FY2018.[4]

The SBA has always assisted veteran small business owners and aspiring veteran entrepreneurs. In recent years, they have focused increased attention on assisting veterans' transition from the military to the civilian labor force. For example, the SBA's OVBD, in partnership with Syracuse University, launched the Operation Boots to Business: From Service to Startup initiative for transitioning servicemembers in July 2012. The program consists of a two-day introductory course on entrepreneurship followed by an eight-week, on-line course to prepare servicemembers and military spouses "for post-service career success as business owners."[5]

Congress provided the SBA's OVBD an additional $7 million in FY2014 to expand the Boots to Business initiative "nationwide to the 250,000 yearly transitioning servicemembers in all branches of the military."[6] The initiative's two-day Introduction to Entrepreneurship course is currently offered at 213 military institutions worldwide and is "a standard portion of the curricula offered at the revised Transition

---

[3] SBA, "FY2019 Congressional Budget Justification and FY2017 Annual Performance Report," pp. 91-96, at https://www.sba.gov/sites/default/files/aboutsbaarticle/SBA_FY_19_508-Final-FINAL.PDF.

[4] The SBA anticipates that it will spend $25.9 million on the Office of Veterans Business Development (OVBD) in FY2018, using funds from its salaries and expenses account to supplement OVBD's appropriation. See ibid., p. 91.

[5] SBA, "Operation Boots to Business: From Service to Startup," at http://www.sba.gov/bootstobusiness; and Institute for Veterans and Military Families, Syracuse University, "White Paper: Operation Boots to Business Veteran Entrepreneurship Assessment," June 2016, p. 2, at https://www.sba.gov/sites/default/files/b2b_vet_entrepreneurship_assessment.pdf. The eight-week, on-line course provides instruction on the "elements of a business plan, evaluating venture ideas, identifying components of business venture strategies and interrelations of marketing, accounting/finance, operations/production, and human resources." See ibid., p. 15.

[6] SBA, "FY2014 Congressional Budget Justification and FY2012 Annual Performance Report," p. 52, at https://www.sba.gov/sites/default/files/files/1-508-Compliant-FY-2014-CBJ%20FY%202012%20APR.pdf. Recommended FY2014 funding levels for the SBA's non-credit programs are in the Explanatory Statement accompanying the Consolidated Appropriations Act, 2014 (Division E-Financial Services and General Government Appropriations Act, 2014), pp. 37-39, at http://docs.house.gov/billsthisweek/20140113/113-HR3547-JSOM-D-F.pdf.

Assistance Program (TAP) to servicemembers."[7] TAP is administered by the Department of Defense (DOD) in cooperation with the Department of Labor (DOL), Department of Veterans Affairs (VA), Department of Education (DOE), Department of Homeland Security (DHS), Office of Personnel Management (OPM), and the SBA.[8]

Congress has approved additional appropriations to continue the initiative, and it was expanded in 2014 to include veterans of all eras, active duty servicemembers (including National Guard and Reserves), and their partner or spouse via the Boots to Business: Reboot initiative.[9] In FY2017, 17,320 servicemembers participated in the Boots to Business program.[10]

During the 114th Congress, legislation was introduced and reported favorably by the Senate Committee on Small Business and Entrepreneurship to provide the Boots to Business initiative statutory authorization (S. 1866, the Veterans Small Business Ownership Improvements Act of 2015). Similar legislation has been introduced during the 115th Congress (S. 121, the Veterans Small Business Ownership Improvements Act, and H.R. 5193, the Veteran Entrepreneurship Training

---

[7] Institute for Veterans and Military Families, Syracuse University, "White Paper: Operation Boots to Business Veteran Entrepreneurship Assessment," June 2016, p. 13, at https://www.sba.gov/sites/default/files/b2b_vet_entrepreneurship_assessment.pdf.

[8] The Department of Defense introduced a redesigned curriculum for the TAP program, called the Transition Goals Plans Success pilot program (Transition GPS), at seven military bases in the summer of 2012. Transition GPS is now offered nationwide. It includes a five-day core program intended to ensure that servicemembers are "career ready" when they leave military service. The core curriculum includes the following modules: pre-separation counseling (4 hours), Department of Veterans Affairs benefits (6 hours), employment workshop (24 hours), financial planning (4 hours), resilient transition (1 hour), and a crosswalk between military and civilian skills that includes a "skills gap" analysis (2 hours). Transition GPS is mandatory for nearly all exiting servicemembers. See U.S. Department of Defense, "Turbo Tap," at http://www.turbotap.org/register.tpp.

[9] Institute for Veterans and Military Families, Syracuse University, "White Paper: Operation Boots to Business Veteran Entrepreneurship Assessment," June 2016, p. 2, at https://www.sba.gov/sites/default/files/b2b_vet_entrepreneurship_assessment.pdf.

[10] The SBA reports that the Boots for Business program had 4,514 participants in FY2013, 14,684 participants in FY2014, 14,457 participants in FY2015, and 17,966 participants in FY2016. See SBA, "FY2019 Congressional Budget Justification and FY2017 Annual Performance Report," p. 92, at https://www.sba.gov/sites/default/files/aboutsbaarticle/SBA_FY_19_508-Final-FINAL.PDF.

Act of 2018). To date, nearly 70,000 servicemembers have participated in the initiative.[11]

The expansion of federal employment training programs targeted at specific populations, such as women and veterans, has led some Members and organizations to ask if these programs should be consolidated. In their view, eliminating program duplication among federal business assistance programs across federal agencies, and within the SBA, would lower costs and improve services. Others argue that keeping these business assistance programs separate enables them to offer services that match the unique needs of underserved populations, such as veterans. Instead of consolidating these programs, their focus is on improving communication and cooperation among the federal agencies providing assistance to entrepreneurs.

This chapter examines the economic circumstances of veteran-owned businesses drawn from the Bureau of the Census's 2012 Survey of Business Owners (SBO). It also provides a brief overview of veterans' employment experiences, comparing unemployment and labor force participation rates for veterans, veterans who have left the military since September 2001, and nonveterans. The chapter also describes the employment assistance programs offered by several federal agencies to assist veterans transitioning from the military to the civilian labor force and examines, in greater detail, the SBA's veteran business development programs, the SBA's efforts to enhance veterans' access to capital, and the SBA's veteran contracting programs.

It also discusses the SBA's Military Reservist Economic Injury Disaster Loan program and P.L. 114-38, the Veterans Entrepreneurship Act of 2015, which authorized and made permanent the SBA's recent practice of waiving the SBAExpress loan program's one time, up-front loan guarantee fee for veterans (and their spouse).

[11] Ibid.

AN ECONOMIC PROFILE OF VETERAN-OWNED BUSINESSES

Every five years since 1972, for years ending in "2" and "7," the U.S. Bureau of the Census has sent a questionnaire to a stratified random sample of nonfarm businesses in the United States that file Internal Revenue Service tax forms as individual proprietorships, partnerships, or any type of corporation, and with receipts of $1,000 or more.[12] The questionnaire asks for information about the characteristics of the businesses and their owners. About 66% of the 1.75 million businesses that received the 2012 SBO responded.[13] The SBO "provides the only comprehensive, regularly collected source of information on selected economic and demographic characteristics for businesses and business owners by gender, ethnicity, race, and veteran status."[14]

The SBO provides estimates of the number of employer and nonemployer firms and their sales and receipts, annual payroll, and employment. Data aggregates are provided by gender, ethnicity, race, and veteran status for the United States by North American Industry Classification System (NAICS) classification; the kind of business; and state, metropolitan and micropolitan statistical area, and county. This information is combined with data collected through the Census Bureau's main economic census and administrative records to provide a variety of searchable data products on Census's website, http://www.census.gov/econ/sbo/, including the most detailed economic information available on veterans and veteran-owned firms.

---

12 U.S. Bureau of the Census, "Methodology – 2007 Survey of Business Owners," at http://www.census.gov/econ/sbo/methodology.html?2007; and U.S. Bureau of the Census, "Methodology - 2012 Survey of Business Owners," at http://www.census.gov/econ/sbo/methodology.html.

13 U.S. Bureau of the Census, "Methodology - 2012 Survey of Business Owners," at http://www.census.gov/econ/sbo/ methodology.html.

14 U.S. Bureau of the Census, "Survey of Business Owners (SBO)," at https://www.census.gov/econ/overview/ mu0200.html.

Demographics

The Bureau of the Census estimates that in 2012 about 9.2% of nonfarm firms in the United States (2.54 million of 27.62 million) were owned by veterans.[15] Four states had more than 100,000 veteran-owned firms: California (254,873), Texas (215,217), Florida (187,074) and New York (138,670). Of the 2.54 million veteran-owned, nonfarm firms in 2012,

- 82.3% (2.09 million) had no paid employees and 17.7% (450,807) had paid employees. This ratio is similar to comparable national figures of 80.4% (22.20 million) with no paid employees and 19.6% (5.42 million) with paid employees.[16]
- 84.3% (2.14 million) were owned by a male, 15.1% were owned by a female (384,549), and 0.6% (14,035) were owned equally by a male and a female. Veteran-owned firms were more likely than other firms in 2012 to be owned by a male. The comparable national figures are 54.3% (14.99 million) were owned by a male, 36.0% (9.93 million) were owned by a female, and 9.0% (2.50 million) were owned equally by a male and a female.[17]
- 85.1% (2.16 million) were owned by a Caucasian, 10.7% (270,702) were owned by an African American, 2.1% (52,933) were owned by an Asian, 1.3% (34,174) were owned by an

[15] An additional 599,335 nonfarm U.S. firms (about 2.2% of all nonfarm U.S. firms) were owned equally (50%-50%) by veterans and nonveterans. See U.S. Bureau of the Census, "Preliminary Statistics for All U.S. Firms by Sector, Veteran Status, and Gender for the U.S. and States: 2012," at http://factfinder.census.gov/faces/tableservices/jsf/pages/productview.xhtml?pid=SBO_2012_00CSA02&prodType=table. Veteran status was based on self-identification. Respondents were asked to report if a business owner is a veteran of the U.S. military service including the Coast Guard. Businesses could be categorized as: veteran-owned (U.S. military service veterans own 51% or more of the equity, interest, or stock of the business); equally veteran/nonveteran-owned (50% veteran and 50% nonveteran ownership of the equity, interest, or stock of the business); or nonveteran-owned (nonveterans own 51% or more of the equity, interest, or stock of the business).

[16] U.S. Bureau of the Census, "Preliminary Statistics for All U.S. Firms by Sector, Veteran Status, and Gender for the U.S. and States: 2012," at http://factfinder.census.gov/faces/tableservices/jsf/pages/productview.xhtml?pid=SBO_2012_00CSA02&prodType=table.

[17] Ibid.

American Indian or Alaska Indian, 0.3% (7,011) were owned by a native Hawaiian or other Pacific Islander, and 2.2% (56,091) were owned by "some other race." Veteran-owned firms were somewhat more likely than other firms in 2012 to be owned by a Caucasian and somewhat less likely to be owned by an Asian. The comparable national figures for 2012 are 78.7% (21.74 million) were owned by a Caucasian, 9.4% (2.59 million) were owned by an African American, 7.0% (1.94 million) were owned by an Asian, 1.0% (274,238) were owned by an American Indian or Alaska Indian, 0.2% (55,077) were owned by a native Hawaiian or other Pacific Islander, and 4.3% (1.18 million) were owned by "some other race."[18]

- 3.3% (76,250 of the 2,299,501 reporting) were owned by an individual under the age of 35, 22.6% (520,472) were owned by an individual aged 35 to 54, and 74.5% (1,712,779) were owned by an individual aged 55 or older. Veteran-owned firms were more likely than other firms in 2012 to be owned by an individual aged 55 or older. The comparable national figures (minus veterans) for 2012 are 14.7% (2,943,446 of the 19,990,309 reporting) of nonfarm firms were owned by an individual under the age of 35; 48.1% (9,613,854) were owned by an individual aged 35 to 54; and 37.2% (7,433,009) were owned by an individual aged 55 or older.[19]
- 7.3% (167,052 of the 2,292,035 reporting) were owned by an individual who reported that he or she had a service-connected disability.[20]

---

[18] The total percentage exceeds 100 because each owner had the option of selecting more than one race and was included in each race selected. See U.S. Bureau of the Census, "American Fact Finder: Preliminary Statistics for All U.S. Firms by Sector, Veteran Status, and Race for the U.S. and States: 2012," at http://factfinder.census.gov/faces/ tableservices/jsf/pages/ productview.xhtml?pid=SBO_2012_00CSA04&prodType=table.

[19] U.S. Bureau of the Census, "American Fact Finder: Statistics for Owners of Respondent Firms by Owner's Age by Gender, Ethnicity, Race, and Veteran Status for the U.S.: 2012," at http://factfinder.census.gov/faces/tableservices/jsf/pages/productview.xhtml?pid=SBO_2012_00CSCBO08&prodType=table.

[20] U.S. Bureau of the Census, "American Fact Finder: Statistics for Veteran Owners of Respondent Firms by Owner's Service-Disabled Veteran Status and Gender for the U.S.:

In addition, 99.8% of veteran-owned employer firms (441,799) had fewer than 500 employees and 0.2% (686) had at least 500 employees. This ratio is similar to comparable national figures for 2012, according to which 99.7% (5.41 million) had fewer than 500 employees and 0.3% (17,724) had at least 500 employees.[21]

Employment, Payroll, and Sales/Receipts

In 2012, veteran-owned firms employed more than 5.5 million persons, reported a total payroll of $220.8 billion, and generated more than $1.47 trillion in total sales/receipts.[22]

Veteran-owned employer firms

- employed 5.5 million persons (about 4.8% of total U.S. employment);
- reported a total payroll of $220.8 billion (about 4.2% of total U.S. payroll);
- generated $1.375 trillion in total sales/receipts (about 4.2% of total U.S. receipts); and
- had average sales/receipts of $3.1 million.[23] Veteran-owned nonemployer firms
- generated 6.4% ($94.5 billion) of the total sales/receipts generated by veteran-owned firms; and
- had average sales/receipts of $45,198.

2012," at http://factfinder.census.gov/faces/tableservices/jsf/pages/productview.xhtml?pid=SBO_2012_00CSCBO12&prodType=table.

[21] U.S. Bureau of the Census, "American Fact Finder: Statistics for All U.S. Firms With Paid Employees by Industry, Veteran Status, and Employment Size of Firm for the U.S. and States: 2012," at http://factfinder.census.gov/faces/tableservices/jsf/pages/productview.xhtml?pid=SBO_2012_00CSA12&prodType=table.

[22] U.S. Bureau of the Census, "Preliminary Statistics for All U.S. Firms by Sector, Veteran Status, and Gender for the U.S. and States: 2012," at http://factfinder.census.gov/faces/tableservices/jsf/pages/productview.xhtml?pid=SBO_2012_00CSA02&prodType=table.

[23] Ibid.

Access to Capital

Table 1. Source of Capital for Veteran Business Owners Starting or Acquiring Their Businesses, 2012

Source of Capital	Number of Veteran Responses	Percentage of Veteran Respondents
Personal or Family Savings	886,471	59.4%
Personal or Business Credit Card	148,856	10.0
Business Loan from a Bank or Financial Institution	116,045	7.8
Personal or Family Assets Other Than the Owner's Savings	92,748	6.2%
Personal or Family Home Equity Loan	39,014	2.6
Business Loan or Investment from Family or Friends	20,882	1.4
Government-Guaranteed Business Loan from a Bank or Financial Institution	9,869	0.7
Investment from Venture Capitalists	2,707	0.2
Business Loan from a Federal, State, or Local Government	2,002	0.1
Grant	1,478	0.1
Other Source(s) of Capital	28,686	1.8
Did Not Need Any Capital to Start or Acquire Their Business	353,917	17.9
Did Not Recall Where They Received the Capital to Start or Acquire Their Business	83,047	5.6
Total Responses/Respondents	1,785,722 responses	112.5%
	(1,492,583 respondents)	(100.0%)

Source: U.S. Bureau of the Census, "American Fact Finder: Statistics for All U.S. Firms by Sources of Capital Used to Start or Acquire the Business by Industry, Gender, Ethnicity, Race, and Veteran Status for the U.S.: 2012," at http://factfinder.census.gov/faces/tableservices/jsf/pages/productview.xhtml?pid=SBO_2012_00CSCB13&prodType=table.

Note: The sum of the number of responses for each source of capital exceeds the total number of respondents and the sum of the percentages for each source of capital exceeds 100.0% because each owner had the option of selecting more than one source of capital.

The comparable national figures for sales/receipts in 2012 were $6.0 million for employer firms and $47,679 for nonemployer firms.[24]

[24] Ibid.

Table 2. Source of Capital for Veteran Businesses Owners Expanding or Making Capital Improvements to Their Businesses, 2012

Source of Capital	Number of Veteran Responses	Percentage of Veteran Respondents
Personal or Family Savings	313,296	20.8%
Personal or Business Credit Card	114,815	7.6
Business Profits or Assets	82,182	5.5
Government-Guaranteed Business Loan from a Bank or Financial Institution	64,499	4.3
Personal or Family Assets Other Than the Owner's Savings	35,220	2.3
Personal or Family Home Equity Loan	20,173	1.3
Business Loan or Investment from Family or Friends	5,923	0.4
Business Loan from a Federal, State, or Local Government	3,062	0.2
Business Loan from a Bank or Financial Institution	1,324	0.1
Investment from Venture Capitalists	1,200	0.1
Grant	1,369	0.1
Other Source(s) of Capital	9,65 1	0.6
Did Not Expand or Make Capital Improvements	931,199	61.8
Wanted To Expand or Make Capital Improvements But Could Not Obtain Funding	18,840	1.3
Did Not Recall Where They Received the Capital to	101,230	6.7
Expand or Make Capital Improvements to Their Business		
Total Responses/Respondents	1,703,983 responses	113.8%
	(1,505,631 respondents)	(100.0%)

Source: U.S. Bureau of the Census, "American Fact Finder: Statistics for All U.S. Firms by Sources Used to Finance Expansion or Capital Improvements by Industry, Gender, Ethnicity, Race, and Veteran Status for the U.S.: 2012" at http://factfinder.census.gov/faces/tableservices/jsf/pages/productview.xhtml?pid=SBO_2012_00CSCB28&prodType=table.

Note: The sum of the number of responses for each source of capital exceeds the total number of respondents and the sum of the percentages for each source of capital exceeds 100.0% because each owner had the option of selecting more than one source of capital.

As shown in Table 1, in 2012, veterans most frequently used personal or family savings to start or acquire a business (886,471 veterans, or 59.4% of respondents), followed by a personal or business credit card (148,856 veterans, or 10.0% of respondents), a business loan from a bank or financial institution (116,045 veterans, or 7.8% of respondents), and personal or family assets other than the owner's savings (92,748 veterans, or 6.2% of respondents).

As shown in Table 2, the source of capital most frequently used by veterans to expand or make capital improvements to an existing business in 2012 was personal or family savings (313,296 veterans, or 20.8% of respondents). The next most frequently used source of capital to expand or make capital improvements to an existing business was a personal or business credit card (114,815 veterans, or 7.6% of respondents), followed by business profits or assets (82,182 veterans, or 5.5% of respondents), and a government-guaranteed business loan from a bank or financial institution (64,499 veterans, or 4.3% of respondents).

VETERANS' EMPLOYMENT DATA

The Department of Labor's Bureau of Labor Statistics (BLS) provides monthly updates of the employment status of the nation's veterans. The BLS reports that as of March 2018, there were about 19.3 million veterans.[25] There were 9.6 million veterans in the civilian labor force (i.e., they were either employed or unemployed and available for work, except for temporary illness, and had made specific efforts to find employment sometime during the four-week period ending with the reference week). Of those veterans in the civilian labor force, about 9.22 million were employed and about 392,000 were unemployed.[26]

In recent years, the unemployment rate among veterans as a whole has generally been similar to or lower than the unemployment rate for nonveterans 18 years and older. However, veterans who have left the military since September 2001 have experienced higher unemployment than other veterans and nonveterans. For example, in March 2018, the

---

[25] DOL, Bureau of Labor Statistics, "Table A-5. Employment status of the civilian population 18 years and over by veteran status, period of service, and sex, not seasonally adjusted," at http://www.bls.gov/news.release/empsit.t05.htm.

[26] Ibid.

unemployment rate for nonveterans 18 years and older was 4.0%, which was similar to the unemployment rate for veterans as a whole (4.1%). However, the unemployment rate for veterans who have left the military since September 2001 was 5.0%, which was higher than the unemployment rate for other veterans (3.6%) and nonveterans 18 years and older (4.0%).[27]

Veterans who have left the military since September 2001 also have a higher labor force participation rate (82.2%) than other veterans (41.1%) and nonveterans aged 18 and older (65.5%).[28] The higher labor force participation rate for veterans who left the military since September 2001 was not wholly unexpected. They entered the civilian workforce more recently and have had less time to develop a reason (e.g., health issue, family responsibility, discouragement, retirement) to withdraw from the civilian workforce than other veterans and nonveterans aged 18 and older.

The lower labor force participation rate for other veterans was also not wholly unexpected. They entered the civilian workforce earlier and have had more time to develop a reason to withdraw from the civilian workforce than veterans who left the military since September 2001 and nonveterans aged 18 and older.[29]

VETERANS' EMPLOYMENT AND BUSINESS DEVELOPMENT PROGRAMS

Several federal agencies, including the SBA, sponsor employment and business development programs to assist veterans in their transition from

---

[27] Ibid.

[28] Ibid.

[29] A report by the Council of Economic Advisers and the National Economic Council attributed lower labor force participation for veterans to several factors, including the difficulty many civilian employers have in understanding a military resume and how military job titles translate into civilian job skills, the presence of a service-connected disability, especially among the post-9/11 veteran population, and the number of post-9/11 veterans (about 217,000) who have been diagnosed with post-traumatic stress disorder. See Executive Office of the President, Council of Economic Advisers and the National Economic Council, "Military Skills for America's Future: Leveraging Military Service and Experience to Put Veterans and Military Spouses Back to Work," May 31, 2012, pp. 4-6, at http://www.whitehouse.gov/sites/default/files/docs/veterans_report_5-31-2012.pdf.

the military into the civilian labor force. As discussed, the expansion of federal employment and business development training programs targeted at specific populations, such as women and veterans, has led some Members and organizations to ask if these programs should be consolidated. Others question if the level of communication and coordination among federal agencies administering these programs has been sufficient to ensure the programs are being administered in the most efficient and effective manner.

The SBA's Veterans Business Development Programs

In an effort to assist veteran entrepreneurs, the SBA has either provided or supported management and technical assistance training for veteran-owned small businesses since its formation as an agency.[30] The SBA provides management and technical assistance to more than 100,000 veterans each year through its various training partners (e.g., Small Business Development Centers, Women's Business Centers, SCORE [formerly the Service Corps of Retired Executives], and Veterans Business Outreach Centers [VBOCs]).[31]

In addition, the SBA's OVBD administers several programs to assist veteran-owned businesses, including

- the Entrepreneurship Bootcamp for Veterans with Disabilities Consortium of Universities, which provides "experiential training in entrepreneurship and small business management to post-9/11 veterans with disabilities" at eight universities;[32]

[30] U.S. Congress, Senate Committee on Banking and Currency, *Extension of the Small Business Act of 1953*, report to accompany S. 2127, 84th Cong., 1st sess., July 22, 1955, S.Rept. 84-1350 (Washington: GPO, 1955), p. 17.

[31] SBA, "FY2019 Congressional Budget Justification and FY2017 Annual Performance Report," pp. 91-96, at https://www.sba.gov/sites/default/files/aboutsbaarticle/SBA_FY_19_508-Final-FINAL.PDF.

[32] Syracuse University, "About the EBV," Syracuse, NY, at http://whitman.syr.edu/ebv/about/.

- the Veteran Women Igniting the Spirit of Entrepreneurship (V-WISE) program, administered through a cooperative agreement with Syracuse University, which offers women veterans a 15-day, online course focused on entrepreneurship skills and the "language of business," followed by a 3-day conference (offered twice a year at varying locations) in which participants "are exposed to successful entrepreneurs and CEOs of Fortune 500 companies and leaders in government" and participate in courses on business planning, marketing, accounting and finance, operations and production, human resources, and work-life balance;[33]
- the Operation Endure and Grow Program, administered through a cooperative agreement with Syracuse University, which offers an eight-week online training program "focused on the fundamentals of launching and/or growing a small business" and is available to National Guard and reservists and their family members;[34]
- the Boots to Business initiative, which is "an elective track within the Department of Defense's revised Training Assistance Program called Transition Goals, Plans, Success (Transition GPS) and has three parts: the *Entrepreneurship Track Overview*—a 10-minute introductory video shown during the mandatory five-day Transition GPS course which introduces entrepreneurship as a post-service career option; *Introduction to Entrepreneurship*—a two-day classroom course on entrepreneurship and business fundamentals offered as one of the three Transition GPS elective tracks; and *Foundations of Entrepreneurship*—an eight-week, instructor-led online course that offers in-depth instruction on the elements of a business plan and tips and techniques for starting a business";[35]

---

33 Syracuse University, "Women Veterans Igniting the Spirit of Entrepreneurship (V-WISE)," Syracuse, NY, at http://whitman.syr.edu/vwise/about.aspx.

34 Syracuse University, "About Operation Endure and Grow," Syracuse, NY, at http://vets.syr.edu/education/enduregrow/.

35 SBA, "Operation Boots to Business: From Service to Startup," at https://www.sba.gov/offices/headquarters/ovbd/ resources/160511; SBA, "Operation Boots to Business: Fact Sheet," at https://www.sba.gov/sites/default/files/files/ B2B_Fact%20Sheet.pdf; and SBA, "SBA Awards Funding to Nonprofit Organizations Providing "Boots to Business"

- the Boots to Business: Reboot initiative, which expanded the Boots to Business initiative in 2014 to include veterans of all eras, active duty servicemembers (including National Guard and Reserves), and their partner/spouse;
- the Veterans Institute for Procurement (VIP) program, which is designed to increase the ability of veteran-owned businesses to win government contracts by providing "an accelerator-like, in-residence educational training program for owners, principals, and executives of veteran-owned businesses, consisting of a three-day comprehensive certification program instructed by professional service experts, government officials, and agency representatives";[36] and
- the VBOC program, which provides veterans and their spouses management and technical assistance training at 21 locations, including assistance with the Boots to Business initiatives, the development and maintenance of a 5-year business plan, and referrals to other SBA resource partners when appropriate for additional training or mentoring services.[37]

Entrepreneurship Training," at https://www.sba.gov/about-sba/sba-newsroom/press-releases-media-advisories/sbaawards-funding-nonprofit-organizations-providing-boots-business-entrepreneurship-training.

[36] SBA, "FY2018 Congressional Budget Justification and FY2016 Annual Performance Report," p. 98, at https://www.sba.gov/sites/default/files/aboutsbaarticle/FINAL_SBA_FY_2018_CBJ_May_22_2017c.pdf.

[37] SBA, Office of Veterans Business Development, "Resources: Veterans Business Outreach Center (VBOC) Program," at https://www.sba.gov/offices/headquarters/ovbd/resources/1548576. VBOC grants, starting at $180,000, "are made for up to a three-year period of performance, consisting of a base period of 12 months from the date of award and up to two renewal option periods of 12 months each. Exercise of the option periods will be solely at SBA's discretion and is subject to continuing program authority, the availability of funds, and the recipient's continued satisfactory performance and compliance." Also, "funding per VBOC will vary based on proposed Boots to Business (B2B) program delivery and associated outreach." See SBA, Office of Veterans Business Development, "FY 2015 Program Announcement No. VBOC-2015-02," pp. 6-7, at https://www.sba.gov/offices/headquarters/ovbd/spotlight. In FY2013, the Veterans Business Outreach Centers Program conducted its ninth annual "Customer Satisfaction Survey." The FY2013 survey found that 91% of the clients using the centers were satisfied or highly satisfied with the quality, relevance, and timeliness of the assistance provided. See SBA, "FY2015 Congressional Budget Justification and FY2013 Annual Performance Report," p. 81, at https://www.sba.gov/sites/default/files/files/FY%202015%20CBJ%20FY%202013%20APR%20FINAL%20508(1).pdf.

The SBA also continues to work closely with the Interagency Task Force for Veterans Small Business Development, which was established by executive order on April 26, 2010, held its first public meeting on October 15, 2010, and issued its first report on November 1, 2011, to identify "gaps in ensuring that transitioning military members who are interested in owning a small business get needed assistance and training."[38] The task force's second report, issued on November 29, 2012, focused on progress made since the initial report.[39] The task force continues to meet on a quarterly basis to foster communication and monitor agency progress in assisting transitioning servicemembers.

Congressional Issues: Duplication of Services

The SBA's OVBD, which serves as the SBA's focal point for its veteran assistance programs, was created by P.L. 106-50, the Veterans Entrepreneurship and Small Business Development Act of 1999. The act addressed congressional concerns that the United States generally, and the SBA in particular, was not, at that time, doing enough to meet the needs of veteran entrepreneurs, especially service-disabled veteran entrepreneurs.[40]

---

[38] SBA, Office of Veterans Business Development, "Interagency Task Force," at https://www.sba.gov/offices/ headquarters/ovbd/resources/14372; and The Interagency Task Force on Veterans Small Business Development, "Report to the President: Empowering Veterans Through Entrepreneurship," November 1, 2011, at https://www.sba.gov/sites/default/files/FY2012-Final%20Veterans%20TF%20Report%20to%20President.pdf.

[39] The Interagency Task Force on Veterans Small Business Development, "Heroes on the Home Front: Supporting Veteran Success as Small Business Owners," November 29, 2012, at https://www.sba.gov/sites/default/files/files/ Veterans_Report_FINAL.pdf. The Interagency Task Force on Veterans Small Business Development includes senior-level representatives of the SBA, the Departments of Defense, Labor, Treasury, and Veterans Affairs, the General Services Administration, the Office of Management and Budget, and four representatives from veterans' service or military organizations appointed by the SBA administrator. SBA Acting Associate Administrator Barbara Carson serves as its chair. See Executive Order 13540, "Interagency Task Force on Veterans Small Business Development," 75 *Federal Register* 22497-22498, April 29, 2010; and U.S Small Business Administration, "Inter-Agency Task Force on Veterans Small Business Development: Kick Off Meeting Wednesday, September 15, 2010," at https://www.sba.gov/offices/headquarters/ovbd/resources/14368.

[40] P.L. 106-50, the Veterans Entrepreneurship and Small Business Development Act of 1999, Section 101. Findings.

At that time, several Members of Congress argued that "the needs of veterans have been diminished systematically at the SBA" as evidenced by the agency's elimination of direct loans, including direct loans to veterans, in 1995; and a decline in the SBA's "training and counseling for veterans ... from 38,775 total counseling sessions for veterans in 1993 to 29,321 sessions in 1998."[41] To address these concerns, the act authorized the establishment of the federally chartered National Veterans Business Development Corporation (known as the Veterans Corporation and reconstituted, without a federal charter, in 2012 as Veteranscorp.org).[42] Its mission is to

> (1) expand the provision of and improve access to technical assistance regarding entrepreneurship for the Nation's veterans; and (2) to assist veterans, including service-disabled veterans, with the formation and expansion of small business concerns by working with and organizing public and private resources, including those of the Small Business Administration, the Department of Veterans Affairs, the Department of Labor, the Department of Commerce, the Department of Defense, the Service Corps of Retired Executives..., the Small Business Development Centers..., and the business development staffs of each department and agency of the United States.[43]

P.L. 106-50 reemphasized the SBA's responsibility "to reach out to and include veterans in its programs providing financial and technical assistance."[44] It included veterans as a target group for the SBA's 7(a), 504 Certified Development Company (504/CDC), and Microloan lending programs. It also required the SBA to enter into a memorandum of

---

[41] U.S. Congress, House Committee on Small Business, *Veterans Entrepreneurship and Small Business Development Act of 1999*, report to accompany H.R. 1568, 106th Cong., 1st sess., June 29, 1999, H.Rept. 106-206 (Washington: GPO, 1999), pp. 14-15.

[42] Veteranscorp, "About Us," Oxford, MD at http://www.veteranscorp.org/2012/01/a-new-veteranscorp-org-gets-thechance-to-help-veteran-entrepreneurs-2/.

[43] P.L. 106-50, the Veterans Entrepreneurship and Small Business Development Act of 1999, Section 33. National Veterans Business Development Corporation. Also, see 15 U.S.C. §657c.

[44] U.S. Congress, House Committee on Small Business, *Veterans Entrepreneurship and Small Business Development Act of 1999*, report to accompany H.R. 1568, 106th Cong., 1st sess., June 29, 1999, H.Rept. 106-206 (Washington: GPO, 1999), p. 14.

understanding with SCORE to, among other things, establish "a program to coordinate counseling and training regarding entrepreneurship to veterans through the chapters of SCORE throughout the United States."[45] In addition, it directed the SBA to enter into a memorandum of understanding with small business development centers, the VA, and the National Veterans Business Development Corporation "with respect to entrepreneurial assistance to veterans, including service-disabled veterans."[46] The act specified that the following services were to be provided:

(1) Conducting of studies and research, and the distribution of information generated by such studies and research, on the formation, management, financing, marketing, and operation of small business concerns by veterans.
(2) Provision of training and counseling to veterans concerning the formation, management, financing, marketing, and operation of small business concerns.
(3) Provision of management and technical assistance to the owners and operators of small business concerns regarding international markets, the promotion of exports, and the transfer of technology.
(4) Provision of assistance and information to veterans regarding procurement opportunities with Federal, State, and local agencies, especially such agencies funded in whole or in part with Federal funds.
(5) Establishment of an information clearinghouse to collect and distribute information, including by electronic means, on the assistance programs of Federal, State, and local governments, and of the private sector, including information on office locations, key personnel, telephone numbers, mail and electronic addresses, and contracting and subcontracting opportunities.

---

[45] P.L. 106-50, Section 301. Score Program.
[46] Ibid., Section 302. Entrepreneurial Assistance.

(6) Provision of Internet or other distance learning academic instruction for veterans in business subjects, including accounting, marketing, and business fundamentals.
(7) Compilation of a list of small business concerns owned and controlled by service-disabled veterans that provide products or services that could be procured by the United States and delivery of such list to each department and agency of the United States. Such list shall be delivered in hard copy and electronic form and shall include the name and address of each such small business concern and the products or services that it provides.[47]

The SBA's OVBD was established to address these statutory requirements by promoting "veterans' small business ownership by conducting comprehensive outreach, through program and policy development and implementation, ombudsman support, coordinated agency initiatives, and direct assistance to veterans, service-disabled veterans, reserve and National Guard members, and discharging active duty servicemembers and their families."[48]

As mentioned previously, the OVBD provides, or supports third parties to provide, management and technical assistance training services to more than 100,000 veterans each year. These services are provided

> through funded SBA district office outreach; OVBD-developed and distributed materials; websites; partnering with DOD [Department of Defense], DOL [Department of Labor] and universities; agreements with regional veterans business outreach centers; direct guidance, training and assistance to Agency veteran customers; and through enhancements to intra-agency programs used by the military and veteran communities.[49]

---

[47] Ibid.

[48] SBA, "FY2013 Congressional Budget Justification and FY2011 Annual Performance Report," p. 62, at https://www.sba.gov/sites/default/files/files/FY%202015%20CBJ%20FY%202013%20APR%20FINAL%20508(1).pdf.

[49] SBA, "FY2013 Congressional Budget Justification and FY2011 Annual Performance Report," p. 62, at https://www.sba.gov/sites/default/files/files/1-508%20Compliant%20FY%202013%20CBJ%20FY%202011%20APR(1).pdf.

The expansion of the SBA's veteran outreach efforts has led some Members and organizations to ask if the nation's veterans might be better served if some of the veteran employment and business development programs offered by federal agencies were consolidated. For example, as mentioned previously, DOD, in cooperation with several federal agencies, operates the recently revised Transition Assistance Program, Transition GPS, which provides employment information and training to exiting servicemembers to assist them in transitioning from the military into the civilian labor force. In addition, DOL's Jobs for Veterans State Grants program provides states funding for Disabled Veterans' Outreach Program specialists and Local Veterans' Employment Representatives to provide outreach and assistance to veterans, and their spouses, seeking employment.[50] DOL also administers the Veterans Workforce Investment Program, which provides grants to fund programs operated by eligible state and local government workforce investment boards, state and local government agencies, and private nonprofit organizations to provide various services designed to assist veterans' transitions into the civilian labor force.[51] The DOL-administered Homeless Veterans Reintegration Program provides grants to fund programs operated by eligible state and local government workforce investment boards, state and local government agencies, and private nonprofit organizations that provide various services designed to assist homeless veterans achieve meaningful employment and to aid in the development of a service delivery system to address problems facing homeless veterans.[52]

Advocates of consolidating veteran employment and business development programs argue that eliminating program duplication among federal agencies would result in lower costs and improved services. For example, H.R. 4072, the Consolidating Veteran Employment Services for

---

[50] For information on the Disabled Veterans' Outreach Program and Local Veterans' Employment Representatives Program, see DOL, "Jobs for Veterans State Grants," at http://www.dol.gov/vets/grants/state/jvsg.htm.

[51] For further information and analysis of federal programs outside of the SBA that are designed to assist veterans seeking civilian employment, see CRS Report R42790, *Employment for Veterans: Trends and Programs*, coordinated by Benjamin Collins.

[52] For further information and analysis concerning the Homeless Veterans Reintegration Program, see CRS Report RL34024, *Veterans and Homelessness*, by Libby Perl.

Improved Performance Act of 2012, which was introduced during the 112th Congress and ordered to be reported by the House Committee on Veterans' Affairs on April 27, 2012, would have transferred several veteran employment training programs from the DOL to the VA.[53]

In addition, in 2011, 2012, 2013, 2014, and 2015, the House Committee on Small Business, in its "Views and Estimates" letter to the House Committee on the Budget, recommended that funding for the SBA's VBOCs be either eliminated or transferred to the Department of Veterans Affairs because, as it stated in 2012, "the SBA already provides significant assistance to veterans who are seeking to start or already operate small businesses. The VBOCs duplicate services already available from the SBA, other entrepreneurial development partners and programs available from the Department of Veterans Affairs."[54] In 2014, the House Committee on Small Business also recommended that if additional funds were to be provided to VBOCs, those funds should come from the SBA's Boots to Business initiative.

Advocates of consolidating federal veteran employment and business development programs cite U.S. Government Accountability Office (GAO) reports that have characterized the broader category of federal

---

[53] U.S. House of Representatives, Committee on Veterans' Affairs, "Debunking the Myths: H.R. 4072," at http://veterans.house.gov/4072.

[54] U.S. House of Representatives, Committee on Small Business, "Views and Estimates of the Committee on Small Business on Matters to be set forth in the Concurrent Resolution on the Budget for Fiscal Year 2012," March 17, 2011, at http://smallbusiness.house.gov/uploadedfiles/march_17_views_and_estimates_letter.pdf. Also, see U.S. House of Representatives, Committee on Small Business, "Views and Estimates of the Committee on Small Business on Matters to be set forth in the Concurrent Resolution on the Budget for Fiscal Year 2013," March 7, 2012, at http://smallbusiness.house.gov/uploaded files/views_and_estimates_fy_2013.pdf; U.S. House of Representatives, Committee on Small Business, "Views and Estimates of the Committee on Small Business on Matters to be set forth in the Concurrent Resolution on the Budget for Fiscal Year 2014," February 27, 2013, at http://smallbusiness.house.gov/uploadedfiles/revised_2014_views_and_estimates _document. pdf; U.S. House of Representatives, Committee on Small Business, "Views and Estimates of the Committee on Small Business on Matters to be set forth in the Concurrent Resolution on the Budget for Fiscal Year 2015," March 25, 2014, at http://small business.house.gov/uploadedfiles/3-25-2014_revised_budget_views_and_estimates_fy _2015_v2.pdf; and U.S. House of Representatives, Committee on Small Business, "Views and Estimates of the Committee on Small Business on Matters to be set forth in the Concurrent Resolution on the Budget for Fiscal Year 2016," February 12, 2015, at http://smallbusiness.house.gov/uploadedfiles/2-12-2015_views_and_estimates_docu ment.pdf.

support for entrepreneurs, including veteran entrepreneurs, as fragmented and having overlapping missions. For example, in 2012, GAO identified 53 programs within the SBA and the Departments of Commerce, Housing and Urban Development, and Agriculture designed to support entrepreneurs, including 36 programs that provide entrepreneurs technical assistance, such as business training, counseling, and research and development support. GAO found that "the overlap among these programs raise[s] questions about whether a fragmented system is the most effective way to support entrepreneurs" and suggested agencies should "determine whether there are more efficient ways to continue to serve the unique needs of entrepreneurs, including consolidating programs."[55]

Instead of consolidating programs, some argue that improved communication and cooperation among the federal agencies providing entrepreneur support programs, and among the SBA's management and technical assistance training resource partners, would enhance program efficiencies while preserving the ability of these programs to offer services that match the unique needs of various underserved populations, such as veterans. For example, during the 111th Congress, the House passed H.R. 2352, the Job Creation through Entrepreneurship Act of 2009, on May 20, 2009, by a vote of 406-15. The Senate did not take action on the bill. In its committee report accompanying the bill, the House Committee on Small Business concluded at that time that

> each ED [Entrepreneurial Development] program has a unique mandate and service delivery approach that is customized to its particular clients. However, as a network, the programs have established local connections and resources that benefit entrepreneurs within a region. Enhanced coordination among this network is critical to make the most of scarce resources available for small firms. It can also ensure that best

[55] U.S. Government Accountability Office (GAO), *2012 Annual Report: Opportunities to Reduce Duplication, Overlap and Fragmentation, Achieve Savings, and Enhance Revenue*, GAO-12-342SP, February 28, 2012, p. 55, at http://www.gao.gov/assets/590/588818.pdf. Also see GAO, *Entrepreneurial Assistance: Opportunities Exist to Improve Programs' Collaboration, Data-Tracking, and Performance Management*, GAO-12-819, August 23, 2012, pp. 60-61, at http://www.gao.gov/assets/650/647267.pdf.

practices are shared amongst providers that have similar goals but work within different contexts.[56]

The bill was designed to enhance oversight and coordination of the SBA's management and technical assistance training programs by requiring the SBA to coordinate these programs "with State and local economic development agencies and other federal agencies as appropriate" and to "report annually to Congress, in consultation with other federal departments and agencies as appropriate, on opportunities to foster coordination, limit duplication, and improve program delivery for federal entrepreneurial development activities."[57]

In a related development, as mentioned previously, the Obama Administration formed the Interagency Task Force for Veterans Small Business Development by executive order on April 26, 2010. The SBA's representative chairs the task force, which is composed of senior representatives from seven federal agencies and four representatives from veterans' organizations.[58] One of the task force's goals is to improve "collaboration, integration and focus across federal agencies, key programs (e.g., the Transition Assistance Program), veterans' service organizations, states, and academia."[59]

On November 1, 2011, the task force issued 18 recommendations, including recommendations designed to increase and augment federal entrepreneurial training and technical assistance programs offered to veterans. For example, it recommended the development of a "standardized, national entrepreneurship training program specifically for

---

[56] U.S. Congress, House Committee on Small Business, *Job Creation through Entrepreneurship Act of 2009*, report to accompany H.R. 2352, 111th Cong., 1st sess., May 15, 2009, H.Rept. 111-112 (Washington: GPO, 2009), pp. 17-18.

[57] H.R. 2352, the Job Creation through Entrepreneurship Act of 2009, Section 601. Expanding Entrepreneurship.

[58] The seven federal agencies are the SBA, U.S. General Services Administration, U.S. Office of Management and Budget, and the Departments of Defense, Labor, Treasury, and Veterans Affairs. The four veterans' organizations are Association of State Directors of Veterans Affairs, Student Veterans of America, the American Legion, and VET-Force.

[59] Interagency Task Force on Veterans Small Business Development, "Report to the President: Empowering Veterans through Entrepreneurship," November 1, 2011, p. 6, at https://www.sba.gov/sites/default/files/FY2012-Final%20Veterans%20TF%20Report%20to%20President.pdf.

veterans" that "could utilize expert local instructors, including academics and successful small business owners, to provide training in skills used to create and grow entrepreneurial ventures and small business. The national program could provide engaging training modules and workshops dedicated to the basics of launching a business."[60] The task force also recommended the development of a web portal "that allows veterans to access entrepreneurship resources from across the government."[61] Since then, the task force has met quarterly and its annual reports document its efforts to address the 18 recommendations.[62]

VETERANS' ACCESS TO CAPITAL

The SBA administers several loan guaranty programs, including the 7(a) and the 504/CDC programs, to encourage lenders to provide loans to small businesses "that might not otherwise obtain financing on reasonable terms and conditions."[63]

SBA's 7(a) Loan Guaranty Program

The SBA's 7(a) loan guaranty program is considered the agency's flagship loan guaranty program. Its name is derived from Section 7(a) of the Small Business Act of 1953 (P.L. 83-163, as amended), which authorizes the SBA to provide business loans to American small businesses.

The 7(a) program provides SBA-approved lenders a guaranty of up to 85% of loans of $150,000 or less and up to 75% of loans exceeding

---

[60] Ibid., p. 15.

[61] Ibid., p. 8.

[62] SBA, "Office of Veterans Business Development, Resources: Interagency Task Force on Veterans Small Business Development," at https://www.sba.gov/offices/headquarters/ovbd/resources/14372.

[63] SBA, *Fiscal Year 2010 Congressional Budget Justification*, p. 30, at https://www.sba.gov/sites/default/files/aboutsbaarticle/Congressional_Budget_Justification_2010.pdf. Also see no credit elsewhere clause in P.L. 83-163, the Small Business Act (as amended).

$150,000, up to the program's maximum gross loan amount of $5 million (up to $3.75 million maximum guaranty). In FY2017, the average approved 7(a) loan amount was $407,616.[64]

Table 3. 7(a) Loan Guaranty Program Approvals, FY2010-FY2017 ($ in millions)

FY	total # of 7(a) loans approved	total amount of 7(a) loans approved	# of veteran 7(a) loans approved	total amount of veteran 7(a) loans approved
2017	62,420	$25,447	3,303	$983
2016	64,073	$24,126	3,268	$1,176
2015	63,461	$23,584	3,132	$1,235
2014	52,044	$19,191	2,113	$605
2013	46,395	$17,865	2,261	$616
2012	44,376	$15,153	2,256	$597
2011	53,710	$19,640	3,269	$920
2010	47,000	$12,406	3,201	$615

Sources: U.S. Small Business Administration, "SBA Lending Statistics for Major Programs (as of 9/30/2014)," at http://www.sba.gov/sites/default/files/aboutsbaarticle/WebsiteReport_asof9_30_2014.pdf; and "SBA Lending Statistics for Major Programs (as of 9/30/2017)," at https://www.sba.gov/sites/default/files/aboutsbaarticle/WebsiteReport_asof 20170930.pdf.

Notes: The number of 7(a) loans approved annually is typically 10% to 20% higher than the number of loans disbursed (e.g., a borrower decides not to accept the loan or a change in business ownership). The amount of 7(a) loans approved annually is typically 10% to 15% higher than the amount disbursed.

Proceeds from 7(a) loans may be used to establish a new business or to assist in the operation, acquisition, or expansion of an existing business. Specific uses include to acquire land (by purchase or lease); improve a site (e.g., grading, streets, parking lots, and landscaping); purchase, convert, expand, or renovate one or more existing buildings; construct one or more new buildings; acquire (by purchase or lease) and install fixed assets; purchase inventory, supplies, and raw materials; finance working capital; and refinance certain outstanding debts. The 7(a) program's loan maturity for working capital, machinery, and equipment (not to exceed the life of the equipment) is typically 5 years to 10 years, and the loan maturity for

---

[64] SBA, "SBA Lending Statistics for Major Programs (as of 9/30/2017)," at https://www.sba.gov/sites/default/files/aboutsbaarticle/WebsiteReport_asof_20170930.pdf.

real estate is up to 25 years. Interest rates are negotiated between the borrower and lender but are subject to maximum rates.[65]

As shown in Table 3, the number and amount of veteran 7(a) loan approvals have generally increased since FY2012. In FY2017, the SBA approved 62,430 7(a) loans totaling $25.4 billion, including 3,303 loans to veterans (5.3%) totaling $982.8 million (3.9%). In FY2017, the average approved veteran 7(a) loan amount was $297,536.[66]

SBA's 504/CDC Loan Guaranty Program

The SBA's 504/CDC loan guaranty program is administered through nonprofit certified development companies (CDCs). It provides long-term fixed rate financing for major fixed assets, such as land, buildings, equipment, and machinery. Of the total project costs, a third-party lender must provide at least 50% of the financing, the CDC provides up to 40% of the financing through a 100% SBA-guaranteed debenture, and the applicant provides at least 10% of the financing. The 504/CDC program's name is derived from Section 504 of the Small Business Investment Act of 1958 (P.L. 85-699, as amended), which provides the most recent authorization for the sale of 504/CDC debentures.[67] In FY2017, the average approved 504/CDC loan amount was $806,324.[68]

As shown in Table 4, in recent years, the number and amount of veteran 504/CDC loan approvals peaked in FY2012, declined in FY2013 and FY2014, increased in FY2015 and FY2016, and declined somewhat in FY2017. In FY2017, the SBA approved 6,218 504/CDC loans totaling $5.01 billion, including 229 loans to veterans (3.7%) totaling $164.2

[65] For further information and analysis concerning the SBA's 7(a) loan guaranty program, see CRS Report R41146, *Small Business Administration 7(a) Loan Guaranty Program*, by Robert Jay Dilger.

[66] SBA, "SBA Lending Statistics for Major Programs (as of 9/30/2017)," at https://www.sba.gov/sites/default/files/aboutsbaarticle/WebsiteReport_asof_20170930.pdf.

[67] For further information and analysis concerning the SBA's 504 Certified Development Company (504/CDC) loan guaranty program, see CRS Report R41184, *Small Business Administration 504/CDC Loan Guaranty Program*, by Robert Jay Dilger.

[68] SBA, "SBA Lending Statistics for Major Programs (as of 9/30/2017)," at https://www.sba.gov/sites/default/files/aboutsbaarticle/WebsiteReport_asof_20170930.pdf.

million (3.3%). In FY2017, the average approved veteran 504/CDC loan amount was $716,908.[69]

Table 4. 504/CDC Loan Guaranty Program Approvals, FY2010-FY2017 ($ in millions)

FY	Total # of 504/CDC loans approved	Total amount of 504/CDC loans approved	# of veteran 504/CDC loans approved	Total amount of veteran 504/CDC loans approved
2017	6,218	$5,014	229	$164
2016	5,938	$4,740	270	$185
2015	5,787	$4,298	264	$169
2014	5,885	$4,199	259	$164
2013	7,708	$5,227	382	$223
2012	9,471	$6,712	472	$319
2011	7,983	$4,845	411	$248
2010	7,833	$4,433	367	$185

Sources: U.S. Small Business Administration, "SBA Lending Statistics for Major Programs (as of 9/30/2014)," at http://www.sba.gov/sites/default/files/aboutsbaarticle/WebsiteReport_asof 9_30_2014.pdf; and "SBA Lending Statistics for Major Programs (as of 9/30/2017)," at https://www. sba.gov/sites/default/files/aboutsbaarticle/WebsiteReport_asof_20170930.pdf.

Notes: Based on previous experience, the number of 504/CDC loans approved is typically about 4% to 5% higher than the actual number of loans disbursed (e.g., some borrowers decide not to accept the loan or there is a change in ownership); and the amount of debentures (loans) approved is typically 10% to 12% higher than the amount of debentures disbursed.

SBA's 7(a) Loan Guaranty Subprograms and Fee Waivers

The SBA administers several 7(a) loan guaranty subprograms that offer streamlined and expedited loan procedures to encourage lenders to provide loans to specific groups of borrowers identified by the SBA as having difficulty accessing capital. In the past, the Patriot Express program (2007-2013) encouraged lenders to provide loans to veterans and their

---

[69] Ibid.

spouses. It provided loans of up to $500,000 (with a guaranty of up to 85% of loans of $150,000 or less and up to 75% of loans exceeding $150,000).[70]

The SBA considered the Patriot Express program a success, but some veterans' organizations expressed concern that many veterans, especially during and immediately following the Great Recession (December 2007 to June 2009), experienced difficulty finding lenders willing to provide them Patriot Express loans.[71] In addition, GAO reported in September 2013 that with the exception of loans approved in 2007, Patriot Express loans defaulted at a higher rate than regular 7(a) loans and loans made under the SBAExpress program (a 7(a) loan guaranty subprogram offering streamlined borrower application and lender approval procedures).[72] Over its history, the Patriot Express program disbursed 9,414 loans totaling more than $791 million.[73]

On January 1, 2014, the SBA implemented a new, streamlined application process for 7(a) loans of $350,000 or less. As part of an overall

---

[70] Eligible businesses were required to be owned and controlled (51% or more) by one or more of the following groups: veteran, active duty military participating in the military's Transition Assistance Program, reservist or National Guard member or a spouse of any of these groups, a widowed spouse of a servicemember who died while in service, or a widowed spouse of a veteran who died of a service-connected disability. See SBA, "SOP 50 10 5(E): Lender and Development Company Loan Programs," (effective June 1, 2012), pp. 83, 127, at https://www.sba.gov/sites/default/files/SOP%2050%2010%205(E)%20(5-16-2012)%20 clean.pdf. The program's interest rates were negotiable with the lender, subject to the same maximum rate limitations as the 7(a) program, which vary depending upon the size and maturity of the loan. It also had the same fees as the 7(a) program, which also varies depending on the size and maturity of the loan.

[71] U.S. Congress, Senate Committee on Small Business and Entrepreneurship, *Assessing Federal Small Business Assistance Programs for Veterans and Reservists*, hearing, 110th Cong., 1st sess., January 31, 2007, S.Hrg. 110-209 (Washington: GPO, 2007), p. 32; U.S. Congress, House Committee on Veterans' Affairs, Subcommittee on Economic Opportunity, *Status of Veterans Small Business*, hearing, 111th Cong., 2nd sess., April 29, 2010, House Committee on Veterans' Affairs Serial No. 111-74 (Washington: GPO, 2010), pp. 17, 75; SBA, "Popular SBA Patriot Express Loan Initiative Renewed for Three More Years," December 10, 2010, at https://www.sba.gov/content/popular-sba-patriotexpress-loan-initiative-renewed-three-more-years; and U.S. Congress, House Committee on Veterans' Affairs, Subcommittee on Economic Opportunity, *Status of Veterans Small Business*, hearing, 111th Cong., 2nd sess., April 29, 2010, House Committee on Veterans' Affairs Serial No. 111-74 (Washington: GPO, 2010), p. 17.

[72] GAO, *Patriot Express: SBA Should Evaluate the Program and Enhance Eligibility Controls*, GA)-13-727, September 13, 2013, pp. i, 10, 16-20, 25-30, 46-49, at http://www.gao.gov/assets/660/657793.pdf.

[73] SBA, Office of Congressional and Legislative Affairs, "Correspondence with the authors," February 21, 2014.

effort to streamline and simplify its loan application process, the SBA also eliminated several 7(a) subprograms, including the Patriot Express program. In anticipation of ending the Patriot Express program, the SBA announced on November 8, 2013, that it would waive the up-front, one-time loan guaranty fee for loans to a veteran or veteran's spouse under the SBAExpress program from January 1, 2014, through the end of FY2014 (called the Veterans Advantage Program).[74]

The SBA announced that this fee waiver was part "of SBA's broader efforts to make sure that veterans have the tools they need to start and grow a business."[75] The Obama Administration continued this fee waiver for veterans through the end of FY2015.

During the 113th Congress, S. 2143, the Veterans Entrepreneurship Act, would have authorized and made the Veterans Advantage Program's fee waiver permanent. P.L. 113-235, the Consolidated and Further Continuing Appropriations Act, 2015, provided statutory authorization for the fee waiver for FY2015.

During the 114th Congress, P.L. 114-38, the Veterans Entrepreneurship Act of 2015, authorized and made the SBA's practice of waiving the SBAExpress loan program's one time, up-front guaranty fee for veterans

---

[74] The SBAExpress program's fees are the same as the 7(a) loan program's fees. SBAExpress loans of $150,000 or less approved in FY2014 do not have an up-front, one-time loan guaranty fee, and these loans do not have an annual, ongoing loan servicing fee. SBAExpress loans of $150,001 to the SBAExpress limit of $350,000, with a maturity of one year or less, have a 0.25% up-front, one-time loan guaranty fee and a 0.52% annual, ongoing loan servicing fee. SBAExpress loans of $150,001 to the SBAExpress limit of $350,000, with a maturity over one year have a 3.0% upfront, one-time loan guaranty fee and a 0.52% annual, ongoing loan servicing fee. To qualify for a waiver of the 3.0% up-front, one-time loan guaranty fee, the business must be 51% or more owned and controlled by an individual or individuals in one or more of the following groups: veterans (other than dishonorably discharged); service-disabled veterans; active duty military servicemembers participating in the military's Transition Assistance Program (TAP); reservists and National Guard members; current spouse of any veteran, active duty servicemember, or any reservist or National Guard member; or widowed spouse of a servicemember who died while in service or of a service-connected disability. See SBA, "SBA Announces New Measures to Help Get Small Business Loans Into the Hands of Veterans," November 8, 2013, at https://www.sba.gov/content/sba-announces-new-measures-help-get-small-business-loans-handsveterans; and SBA, "Procedural Notice: SBA Veterans Advantage," December 18, 2013, at https://www.sba.gov/sites/ default/files/lender_notices/5000-1299_0.pdf.

[75] SBA, "SBA Announces New Measures to Help Get Small Business Loans Into the Hands of Veterans," November 8, 2013, at https://www.sba.gov/content/sba-announces-new-measures-help-get-small-business-loans-hands-veterans.

(and their spouse) permanent beginning on or after October 1, 2015, except during any upcoming fiscal year for which the President's budget, submitted to Congress, includes a cost for the 7(a) program, in its entirety, that is above zero.[76]

The SBAExpress program is designed to increase the availability of credit to small businesses by permitting lenders to use their existing documentation and procedures in return for receiving a reduced SBA guaranty on loans.[77] It provides a 50% loan guaranty on loan amounts up to $350,000. In FY2017, the SBA approved 29,450 SBAExpress loans (47.2% of total 7(a) program loan approvals) totaling $2.11 billion (8.3% of total 7(a) program amount approvals).[78]

In FY2014, the SBA also waived the up-front, one-time loan guaranty fee and the annual, ongoing servicing fee for all 7(a) loans of $150,000 or less (including veteran loans). The SBA continued both of these fee waivers through the end of FY2016. In FY2017, the SBA reinstated the annual ongoing servicing fee for all 7(a) loans, and retained the waiver of the up-front, one-time loan guaranty fee for all 7(a) loans of $150,000 or less. In FY2018, the SBA is waiving the up-front, one-time loan guaranty fee for all 7(a) loans of $125,000 or less.

In FY2015 and FY2016, the SBA also waived 50% of the up-front, one-time loan guaranty fee on all non-SBAExpress 7(a) loans to veterans exceeding $150,000. In FY2017, the SBA waived 50% of the up-front, one-time loan guaranty fee on all non-SBAExpress 7(a) loans to veterans of $150,001 to $500,000.[79] In FY2018, the SBA is waiving 50% of the up-

---

[76] U.S. Congress, House Committee on Small Business, Veterans Entrepreneurship Act of 2015, report to accompany H.R. 2499, 114th Cong., 1st sess., June 25, 2015, H.Rept. 114-187 (Washington: GPO, 2015), p. 9. The act also increased the 7(a) program's FY2015 authorization limit to $23.5 billion from $18.75 billion.

[77] SBA, "The SBA Express Pilot Program: Inspection Report," June 1998, p. 3.

[78] SBA, "SBA Lending Statistics for Major Programs (as of 9/30/2017)," at https://www.sba.gov/sites/default/files/aboutsbaarticle/WebsiteReport_asof_20170930.pdf.

[79] SBA, "SBA Information Notice: SBA Veterans Advantage – Renewal and Expansion of Fee Relief," September 19, 2014, at https://www.sba.gov/sites/default/files/lender_notices/5000-1319.pdf; SBA, "SBA Information Notice: SBA Veterans Advantage – Renewal and Expansion of Fee Relief," September 30, 2015, at https://www.sba.gov/sites/default/files/lender_notices/5000-1354.pdf; and SBA, "SBA Information Notice: Fees for 7(a) Loans Made to Veteran Owned Small Businesses, Effective October 1, 2016," September 28, 2016, at https://www.sba.gov/sites/default/files/lender_notices/5000-1390.pdf.

front, one-time loan guaranty fee on all non-SBAExpress 7(a) loans to veterans of $150,001 to $350,000.[80]

Congressional Issues: Access

As mentioned previously, the SBA has indicated in both testimony at congressional hearings and in press releases that it viewed the Patriot Express program and its own overall effort to enhance veterans' access to capital as a success.[81] For example, when the SBA announced its veterans' fee waiver for the SBAExpress program, it also announced that its lending to veteran-owned small businesses had nearly doubled since 2009 and that "in FY2013, SBA supported $1.86 billion in loans for 3,094 veteran-owned small businesses."[82]

Congressional testimony provided by various veteran service organizations provides a somewhat different perspective. The SBA's self-evaluation of its success in assisting veterans access capital has focused primarily on the agency's efforts to streamline the loan application approval process (e.g., minimizing paperwork requirements and reducing the time necessary for the SBA to review and approve applications submitted by local lenders) and aggregate lending amounts (e.g., the number and amount of loans approved). In contrast, veteran service organizations focus primarily on program outcomes, especially the likelihood of a veteran being approved for a SBA loan by a local lender. For example, a representative of the American Legion testified at a congressional hearing in 2010 that, at that time, being turned down for a SBA Patriot Express loan by a private lender "is probably the largest, most

---

[80] SBA, "SBA Information Notice: Fees for 7(a) Loans Made to Veteran Owned Small Businesses Effective October 1, 2017," at https://www.sba.gov/sites/default/files/files/Notice_5000-1955_Veteran_Fees_FY18_1.pdf.

[81] U.S. Congress, House Committee on Veterans' Affairs, Subcommittee on Economic Opportunity, *Status of Veterans Small Business*, hearing, 111th Cong., 2nd sess., April 29, 2010, House Committee on Veterans' Affairs Serial No. 111 74 (Washington: GPO, 2010), p. 75.

[82] SBA, "SBA Announces New Measures to Help Get Small Business Loans Into the Hands of Veterans," November 8, 2013, at https://www.sba.gov/content/sba-announces-new-measures-help-get-small-business-loans-hands-veterans.

frequent complaint that we receive from our business owners."[83] At that same congressional hearing, a representative of the Vietnam Veterans of America testified in response to that statement that "I would have to concur ... in talking with some of the veterans with regard to the Patriot Express Loan, they are having difficulties also to acquire that capital. The rationale seems to be ... the banks in general seem to be tightening the credit, their lending practices, so that is ... what we are hearing."[84] More recently, GAO reported in 2013 that "selected loan recipients, lenders, and veteran service organizations said that a low awareness of the Patriot Express program among the military community was among the most frequently cited challenges."[85]

No empirical assessments of veterans' experiences with either the SBA's Patriot Express or SBAExpress loan programs exist that would be useful for determining the relative ease or difficulty for veteran-owned small business owners of accessing capital through the SBA's loan programs. Since 2010, many lenders report that they have eased their credit standards, at least somewhat, for small business loans, suggesting the experiences of veterans seeking a SBA loan guaranty today may be improved compared with their experiences in 2010. However, GAO found in 2013 that many veterans were not fully aware of the SBA's Patriot Express program and that "over half of the Patriot Express loan recipients, six of the eight lenders, and two veteran service organizations ... said that [the] SBA could do more to increase outreach to veteran entrepreneurs and better market the program to the military community."[86] GAO reported that low awareness of the SBA's Patriot Express program and the SBA's participating lenders were a continuing challenge for the SBA.[87]

---

[83] U.S. Congress, House Committee on Veterans' Affairs, Subcommittee on Economic Opportunity, *Status of Veterans Small Business*, hearing, 111th Cong., 2nd sess., April 29, 2010, House Committee on Veterans' Affairs Serial No. 111 74 (Washington: GPO, 2010), p. 17.

[84] Ibid.

[85] GAO, *Patriot Express: SBA Should Evaluate the Program and Enhance Eligibility Controls*, GA)-13-727, September 13, 2013, p. 33, at http://www.gao.gov/assets/660/657793.pdf.

[86] Ibid.

[87] Ibid.

One option to provide additional information concerning veterans' experiences with the SBA's lenders would be to survey veterans who have received a SBA guaranteed loan. The survey could include questions concerning these veterans' views of the programs, including the application process. However, obtaining a comprehensive list of veterans to survey who have been turned down for a SBA guaranteed loan by a private lender would be difficult given privacy concerns.

In a related development concerning veterans' access to capital, legislation was introduced during the 114th Congress (S. 1870, the Veterans Entrepreneurial Transition Act of 2015, and its House companion bill, H.R. 3248) to authorize a three-year pilot program, administered by the SBA, to provide grants to no more than 250 GI-Bill benefit-eligible veterans to start or acquire a qualifying business. The grant amount would have been calculated according to a formula related to the unused portion of the recipient's GI-Bill benefits. Recipients would have been required to complete specified training and meet other program requirements, such as having an approved business plan. S. 1870 was ordered to be reported with an amendment in the nature of a substitute by the Senate Committee on Small Business and Entrepreneurship on July 29, 2015.

In addition, H.R. 5698, the Strengthening Technical Assistance, Resources, and Training to Unleash the Potential of Veterans Act of 2016 (STARTUP Vets Act of 2016), and its companion bill in the Senate, S. 2273, would have authorized the SBA to provide up to $1.5 million in grants annually "from amounts made available to the Office of Veterans Business Development" to organizations to create and operate business incubators and accelerators that provide technical assistance and training to veterans (including their spouse and dependents) to enable them "to effectively transfer relevant skills to launch and accelerate small business concerns owned and controlled by covered individuals; and to create an avenue for high-performing covered individuals to meet and collaborate on business ideas."[88]

---

[88] H.R. 5698, Section 3. Incubator and accelerator grant program.

During the 115th Congress, S. 1056, the Veteran Small Business Export Promotion Act, and H.R. 2835. To amend the Small Business Act, would permanently "waive the guarantee fee for loans of not more than $150,000 provided to veterans and spouses of veterans under the [SBA's] Export Working Capital, International Trade, and Export Express programs."

FEDERAL CONTRACTING GOALS FOR SERVICE-DISABLED VETERAN-OWNED SMALL BUSINESSES

Since 1978, federal agency heads have been required to establish federal procurement contracting goals, in consultation with the SBA, "that realistically reflect the potential of small business concerns" to participate in federal procurement. Each agency is required, at the conclusion of each fiscal year, to report its progress in meeting the goals to the SBA.[89] The SBA negotiates the goals with each federal agency and establishes a *small business eligible* baseline for evaluating the agency's performance.

The small business eligible baseline excludes certain contracts that the SBA has determined do not realistically reflect the potential for small business participation in federal procurement, such as contracts awarded to mandatory and directed sources, awarded and performed overseas, funded predominately from agency-generated sources, not covered by Federal Acquisition Regulations, and not reported in the Federal Procurement Data System (e.g., contracts or government procurement card purchases valued less than $3,000).[90] These exclusions typically account for 18% to 20% of all federal prime contracts each year.

The SBA then evaluates the agencies' performance against their negotiated goals annually, using data from the Federal Procurement Data System–Next Generation, managed by the U.S. General Services

---

[89] P.L. 95-507, a bill to amend the Small Business Act and the Small Business Investment Act of 1958.

[90] See U.S. General Services Administration, Federal Procurement Data System—Next Generation, "Small Business Goaling Report: Fiscal Year 2013," at https://www.fpds.gov/downloads/top_requests/FPDSNG_SB_Goaling_FY_2013.pdf.

Administration, to generate the small business eligible baseline. This information is compiled into the official Small Business Goaling Report, which the SBA releases annually.

Over the years, federal government-wide procurement contracting goals have been established for small businesses generally (P.L. 100-656, the Business Opportunity Development Reform Act of 1988, and P.L. 105-135, the HUBZone Act of 1997—Title VI of the Small Business Reauthorization Act of 1997); small businesses owned and controlled by socially and economically disadvantaged individuals (P.L. 100-656); women (P.L. 103-355, the Federal Acquisition Streamlining Act of 1994); small businesses located within a Historically Underutilized Business Zone, or HUBZone (P.L. 105-135); and small businesses owned and controlled by a service-disabled veteran (P.L. 106-50, the Veterans Entrepreneurship and Small Business Development Act of 1999).

The current federal small business contracting goals are

- at least 23% of the total value of all small business eligible prime contract awards to small businesses for each fiscal year;
- 5% of the total value of all small business eligible prime contract awards and subcontract awards to small disadvantaged businesses for each fiscal year;
- 5% of the total value of all small business eligible prime contract awards and subcontract awards to women-owned small businesses;
- 3% of the total value of all small business eligible prime contract awards and subcontract awards to HUBZone small businesses; and
- 3% of the total value of all small business eligible prime contract awards and subcontract awards to service-disabled veteran-owned small businesses.[91]

There are no punitive consequences for not meeting the small business procurement goals. However, the SBA's Small Business Goaling Report is distributed widely, receives media attention, and heightens public

---

[91] 15 U.S.C. §644(g)(1)-(2).

awareness of the issue of small business contracting. For example, agency performance as reported in the SBA's report is often cited by Members during their questioning of federal agency witnesses in congressional hearings.

As shown in Table 5, the *FY2016 Small Business Goaling Report*, using data in the Federal Procurement Data System, indicates that federal agencies met the federal contracting goal for small businesses generally, small disadvantaged businesses, and service-disabled veteran-owned small businesses in FY2016.

Federal agencies awarded 24.34% of the value of their small business eligible contracts ($410.7 billion) to small businesses ($100.0 billion), 9.53% to small disadvantaged businesses ($39.1 billion), 4.79% to women-owned small businesses ($19.7 billion), 1.67% to HUBZone small businesses ($6.9 billion), and 3.98% to service-disabled veteran-owned small businesses ($16.3 billion).[92]

The percentage of total reported federal contracts (without exclusions) awarded to those small businesses in FY2016 is also provided in the table for comparative purposes.

In a related development, on November 17, 2015, the House passed H.R. 1694, the Fairness to Veterans for Infrastructure Investment Act of 2015. The bill would have revised the requirement that 10% of the award of contracts for federal-aid highway, federal public transportation, and highway safety research and development programs be set-aside for small businesses owned and controlled by socially and economically disadvantaged individuals. The bill would have required the set-aside to include veteran-owned small businesses.

In another related development, the U.S. Supreme Court's decision in *Kingdomware Technologies, Inc. v. United States* (decided on June 16, 2016) requiring the VA to grant VOSBs certain preferences when awarding procurement contracts could result in the VA awarding additional contracts to VOSBs.

---

[92] U.S. General Services Administration, Federal Procurement Data System—Next Generation, "Small Business Goaling Report: Fiscal Year 2016," at https://www.fpds.gov/downloads/top_requests/FPDSNG_SB_Goaling_FY_2016.pdf.

Table 5. Federal Contracting Goals and Percentage of FY2016 Federal Contract Dollars Awarded to Small Businesses, by Type (in percentages)

Business Type	Federal Goal	FY2016 Federal Contracts (small business eligible)	FY2016 Federal Contracts (all reported contracts)
Small Businesses	23.0	24.34	22.27
Small Disadvantaged Businesses	5.0	9.53	8.61
Women-Owned Small Businesses	5.0	4.79	4.23
HUBZone Small Businesses	3.0	1.67	1.50
Service-Disabled Veteran-Owned Small Businesses	3.0	3.98	3.73

Sources: U.S. Small Business Administration, "Statutory Guidelines," at https://www.sba.gov/content/statutoryguidelines-0 (federal goals); U.S. General Services Administration, Federal Procurement Data System—Next Generation, "Small Business Goaling Report: Fiscal Year 2016," at https://www.fpds.gov/downloads/top_requests/FPDSNG_SB_Goaling_FY_2015.pdf; and U.S. General Services Administration, Federal Procurement Data System—Next Generation, at https://www.fpds.gov/fpdsng/ (contract dollars).

Notes: The Federal Procurement Data System (FPDS) is a dynamic system with records updated daily. The Small Business Goaling Report for FY2016 reports that small business eligible contracts, as of May 16, 2017, totaled $410.7 billion and that $99.9 billion was awarded to small businesses, $39.1 billion to small disadvantaged businesses, $19.7 billion to women-owned small businesses, $6.8 billion to SBA-certified HUBZone small businesses, and $16.3 billion to service-disabled veteran-owned small businesses. The Small Business Goaling Report for FY2016 does not indicate the total amount of federal contracts reported in the FPDS on May 16, 2017. The percentages provided in the column for all reported contracts in FY2016 were calculated using FPDS data as reported on May 24, 2017: $473.7 billion in total contracts, $105.5 billion awarded to small businesses, $40.8 billion to small disadvantaged businesses, $20.3 billion to women-owned small businesses, $7.1 billion to HUBZone small businesses, and $17.7 billion to service-disabled veteran-owned small businesses.

In addition, the prevention of fraud in federal small business contracting programs, and in the SBA's loan programs as well, has been a priority for both Congress and the SBA for many years, primarily because reports of fraud in these programs emerge with some regularity.[93] Of

[93] For example, see GAO, *Small Business Administration: Undercover Tests Show HUBZone Program Remains Vulnerable to Fraud and Abuse*, GAO-10-920T, July 28, 2010, at http://www.gao.gov/assets/130/125130.pdf; GAO, *8(a) Program: Fourteen Ineligible Firms Received $325 Million in Sole-Source and Set-Aside Contracts*, GAO-10-425, March 30, 2010, at http://www.gao.gov/assets/310/302472.pdf; GAO, *Service-Disabled Veteran-*

particular interest to veterans, GAO has found that "the lack of an effective government-wide fraud-prevention program" has left the service-disabled veteran-owned small business program "vulnerable to fraud and abuse."[94]

Under the Small Business Act, a small business owned and controlled by a service-disabled veteran can qualify for a federal government procurement set-aside (a procurement in which only certain businesses may compete) or a sole-source award (awards proposed or made after soliciting and negotiating with only one source) if the small business is at least 51% unconditionally and directly owned and controlled by one or more service-disabled veteran.[95] A veteran is defined as a person who has served "in the active military, naval, or air service, and who was discharged or released under conditions other than dishonorable."[96] A disability is service related when it "was incurred or aggravated ... in [the] line of duty in the active military, naval, or air service."[97]

Federal agencies may set aside procurements for service-disabled veteran-owned small businesses only if the contracting officer reasonably expects that offers will be received from at least two responsible small businesses and the award will be made at a fair market price (commonly known as the "rule of two" because of the focus on there being at least two small businesses involved).[98]

Federal agencies may award sole contracts to service-disabled veteran-owned small businesses when (1) the contracting officer does not reasonably expect that two or more service-disabled veteran-owned small businesses will submit offers; (2) the anticipated award will not exceed $4.0 million ($6.5 million for manufacturing contracts); and (3) the award

---

Owned Small Business Program: Case Studies Show Fraud and Abuse Allowed Ineligible Firms to Obtain Millions of Dollars in Contracts, GAO-10-108, October 23, 2009, at http://www.gao.gov/products/GAO-10-108; and GAO, *Service-Disabled Veteran-Owned Small Business Program: Vulnerability to Fraud and Abuse Remains*, GAO-12-697, August 1, 2012, at http://www.gao.gov/assets/600/593238.pdf.

[94] GAO, *Service-Disabled Veteran-Owned Small Business Program: Preliminary Information on Actions Taken by Agencies to Address Fraud and Abuse and Remaining Vulnerabilities*, GAO-11-589T, July 28, 2011, p. 3, at http://www.gao.gov/products/GAO-11-589T.

[95] 15 U.S.C. §632(q)(1) & (4); P.L. 108-183, the Veterans Benefits Act of 2003; and P.L. 109-461, the Veterans Benefits, Health Care, and Information Technology Act of 2006.

[96] 38 U.S.C. §101(2).

[97] 38 U.S.C. §101(16).

[98] 15 U.S.C. §657f(b).

can be made at a fair and reasonable price.[99] Otherwise, sole-source awards may only be made to service-disabled veteran-owned small businesses under other authority, such as the Competition in Contracting Act.[100] Service-disabled veteran-owned small businesses are not eligible for price evaluation preferences in unrestricted competitions.

The VA is statutorily required to establish annual goals for the awarding of VA contracts to both service-disabled veteran-owned small businesses and small businesses owned by other veterans.[101] The VA is authorized to use "other than competitive procedures" in meeting these goals. For example, it may award any contract whose value is below the simplified acquisition threshold (generally $150,000) to a veteran-owned business on a sole-source basis, and it may also make sole-source awards of contracts whose value (including options) is between $150,000 and $5 million, provided that certain conditions are met. When these conditions are not met, the VA is generally required to set aside the contract for service-disabled or other veteran-owned small businesses.[102]

Service-disabled veteran-owned small businesses can generally self-certify as to their eligibility for contracting preferences available under the Small Business Act.[103] However, in an effort to address fraud in VA contracting, veteran-owned and service-disabled veteran-owned small businesses must be listed in the VA's VetBiz database and have their

---

[99] 15 U.S.C. §657f(a)(1)-(3) (statutory requirements); and 48 C.F.R. §19.1406(a) (increasing the price thresholds).

[100] 10 U.S.C. §2304(c)(1)-(7) (procurements of defense agencies); and 41 U.S.C. §3304(a)(1)-(7) (procurements of civilian agencies). *See also* 48 C.F.R. §§6.302-1 to 6.302-7; and CRS Report R40516, *Competition in Federal Contracting: Legal Overview*, by Kate M. Manuel.

[101] P.L. 109-461 and P.L. 110-389, the Veterans' Benefits Improvements Act of 2008. In FY2015, the Department of Veterans Affairs' small business procurement goals were 32.0% for small businesses generally, 12.0% for veteran-owned small businesses, 10.0% for service-disabled veteran-owned small businesses, 5.0% for small disadvantaged businesses (including Section 8(a)), 5.0% for women-owned small businesses, and 3.0% for Historically Underutilized Business Zone (HUBZone) small businesses. See The Department of Veterans Affairs, "VA Small Business Program Goals," at http://www.va.gov/OSDBU/library/socioeconomic_procurement_goals.asp.

[102] For further information and analysis of federal contracting legal authorities generally and affecting the Department of Veterans Affairs, see CRS Report R42391, *Legal Authorities Governing Federal Contracting and Subcontracting with Small Businesses*, by Kate M. Manuel and Erika K. Lunder.

[103] 13 C.F.R. §125.15.

eligibility verified by the VA to be eligible for preferences in certain VA contracts.[104]

Firms that fraudulently misrepresent their size or status have long been subject to civil and criminal penalties under Section 16 of the Small Business Act; SBA regulations implementing Section 16; and other provisions of law, such as the False Claims Act, Fraud and False Statements Act, Program Fraud Civil Remedies Act, and Contract Disputes Act.[105]

Several bills were introduced during the 112th Congress to address fraud in small business contracting programs in various ways. Of particular interest to veterans, S. 3572, the Restoring Tax and Regulatory Certainty to Small Businesses Act of 2012, and S. 633, the Small Business Contracting Fraud Prevention Act of 2011, would have, among other changes, amended Section 16 of the Small Business Act to expressly include service-disabled veteran-owned small businesses among the types of small businesses subject to penalties for fraud under that section.[106] The bills would also have required service-disabled veteran-owned small businesses to register in the VA's VetBiz database, or any successor database, and have their status verified by the VA to be eligible for contracting preferences for service-disabled veteran-owned small businesses under the Small Business Act.

---

104 38 U.S.C. §8127(a)(1)(A). P.L. 109-461 requires the Secretary of Veterans Affairs to "establish a goal for each fiscal year for participation in Department contracts (including subcontracts)" by veteran-owned small businesses. The Secretary is also required to establish a separate goal for the participation of service-disabled veteran-owned small businesses in agency contracts and subcontracts. 38 U.S.C. §8127(a)(1)(A). However, the latter goal can be no less than the government-wide goal for the percentage of contract and subcontract dollars awarded to service-disabled veteran-owned small businesses given in Section 15(g)(1) of the Small Business Act (currently 3%), while the former goal is within the Secretary's discretion. *See* 38 U.S.C. §8127(a)(2)-(3).

105 See 15 U.S.C. §645; and 13 C.F.R. §125.29.

106 Currently, Section 36 of the Small Business Act, which governs set-asides and sole-source awards for service-disabled veteran-owned small businesses, provides that "[r]ules similar to the rules of paragraphs (5) and (6) of Section 637(m) of this title shall apply for purposes of this section." Section 8(m) governs set-asides for women-owned small businesses and itself provides that such businesses are subject to penalties for fraud under Section 16. Thus, an argument could potentially be made that service-disabled veteran-owned small businesses are currently subject to penalties under Section 16 even if they are not expressly included there. See CRS Report R43573, *Federal Contracting and Subcontracting with Small Businesses: Legislation in the 113th Congress*, by Kate M. Manuel.

In addition, during the 113th Congress, S. 2334, the Improving Opportunities for Service-Disabled Veteran-Owned Small Businesses Act of 2013, and its companion bill in the House, H.R. 2882, and H.R. 4435, the Howard P. "Buck" McKeon National Defense Authorization Act for Fiscal Year 2015, which was passed by the House on May 22, 2014, included a provision that would have authorized the transfer of the VetBiz database's administration and the verification of service-disabled veteran owned small businesses from the VA to the SBA.

Advocates of requiring service-disabled veteran-owned small businesses to register in the VetBiz database and have their status verified by the VA (or the SBA) to be eligible for contracting preferences under the Small Business Act argue that doing so would reduce fraud.[107] As then-Senator Snowe stated on the Senate floor when she introduced S. 633, "Our legislation attempts to remedy the spate of illegitimate firms siphoning away contracts from the rightful businesses trying to compete within the SBA's contracting programs."[108]

Others worry that requiring service-disabled veteran-owned small businesses to register in the VetBiz database and have their status verified by the VA (or the SBA) to be eligible for contracting preferences under the Small Business Act may add to the paperwork burdens of small businesses. They seek alternative ways to address the need to reduce fraud in federal small business procurement programs that do not increase the paperwork requirements of small businesses.[109] Still others note that the effectiveness of any change to prevent fraud in veteran-owned and service-disabled veteran-owned small business procurement programs largely depends upon how the change is implemented. For example, in July 2011, the VA's Office of Inspector General concluded that the VA's implementation of its

---

[107] See 13 C.F.R. §§125.9-125.13.

[108] Senator Olympia Snowe, "Statements on Introduced Bills and Joint Resolutions," remarks in the Senate, *Congressional Record*, vol. 157, part no. 41 (March 17, 2011), p. S1843.

[109] U.S. Congress, House Committee on Oversight and Government Reform, Subcommittee on Technology, Information Policy, Intergovernmental Relations and Procurement Reform, *Jobs for Wounded Warriors: Increasing Access to Contracts for Service Disabled Veterans*, 112th Cong., 2nd sess., February 7, 2012, Serial No. 112-143 (Washington: GPO, 2012), pp. 86-90.

veteran-owned and service-disabled veteran-owned small business procurement fraud prevention programs needed improvement:

> We project that VA awarded ineligible businesses at least 1,400 VOSB [Veteran Owned Small Business] and SDVOSB [Service-Disabled Veteran Owned Small Business] contracts valued at $500 million annually and that it will award about $2.5 billion in VOSB and SDVOSB contracts to ineligible businesses over the next 5 years if it does not strengthen oversight and verification procedures. VA and the Office of Small and Disadvantaged Business Utilization (OSDBU) need to improve contracting officer oversight, document reviews, completion of site visits for "high-risk" businesses, and the accuracy of VetBiz Vendor Information Pages information.[110]

THE MILITARY RESERVIST ECONOMIC INJURY DISASTER LOAN PROGRAM

P.L. 106-50, the Veterans Entrepreneurship and Small Business Development Act of 1999, signed into law on August 17, 1999, authorized the SBA's Military Reservist Economic Injury Disaster Loan (MREIDL) program. The SBA published the final rule establishing the program in the *Federal Register* on July 25, 2001, with an effective date of August 24, 2001.[111]

The Senate Committee on Small Business provided, in its committee report on the Veterans Entrepreneurship and Small Business Development Act of 1999, the following reasons for supporting the authorization of the MREIDL Program:

---

[110] U.S. Department of Veterans Affairs, Office of Inspector General, "Audit of Veteran-Owned and Service-Disabled Veteran-Owned Small Business Programs," July 25, 2011, p. i, at http://www.va.gov/oig/52/reports/2011/VAOIG-10 02436-234.pdf.

[111] SBA, "Military Reservist Economic Injury Disaster Loans," 66 *Federal Register* 38528-38531, July 25, 2001.

> During and after the Persian Gulf War in the early 1990's, the Committee heard from reservists whose businesses were harmed, severely crippled, or even lost, by their absence. Problems faced by reservists called to active duty and their small businesses were of a varied nature and included cash-flow problems, difficulties with training an appropriate alternate manager on very short notice to run the business during the period of service, lost clientele upon return, and on occasion, bankruptcy. These hardships can occur during a period of national emergency or during a period of contingency operation when troops are deployed overseas.
>
> To help such reservists and their small businesses, the Committee seeks to provide credit and management assistance to small businesses when an essential employee (i.e., an owner, manager or vital member of the business' staff) is a reservist called to active duty. The Committee believes that financial assistance in the form of loans, loan deferrals and managerial guidance are effective ways to minimize the adverse financial demands of the call to active duty. They not only ameliorate financial difficulties but also strengthen small businesses.[112]

The House Committee on Small Business also supported the program's authorization, indicating in its committee report that the program

> will also fulfill a long unmet need to assist our military reservists who are small business owners. Often these individuals, called to service at short notice, come back from fighting to protect our freedoms only to find their businesses in shambles. H.R. 1568 will establish loan deferrals, technical and managerial assistance, and loan programs for these citizen soldiers so that while they risk their lives they need not risk their livelihoods.[113]

As mentioned previously, the SBA provides direct loans for owners of businesses of all sizes, homeowners, and renters to assist their recovery from natural disasters. The SBA's MREIDL program provides disaster

---

[112] U.S. Congress, Senate Committee on Small Business, *Veterans Entrepreneurship and Small Business Development Act of 1999*, report to accompany H.R. 1568, 106th Cong., 1st sess., August 4, 1999, S.Rept. 106-136 (Washington: GPO, 1999), p. 4.

[113] Ibid., p. 15.

assistance in the form of direct loans of up to $2 million to help small business owners who are not able to obtain credit elsewhere to (1) meet ordinary and necessary operating expenses that they could have met but are not able to meet; or (2) enable them to market, produce, or provide products or services ordinarily marketed, produced, or provided by the business that cannot be done because an essential employee has been called up to active duty in his or her role as a military reservist or member of the National Guard due to a period of military conflict.[114] Under specified circumstances, the SBA may waive the $2 million limit (e.g., the small business is in immediate danger of going out of business, is a major source of employment, employs 10% or more of the workforce within the commuting area in which the business is located).[115]

P.L. 106-50 defines an essential employee as "an individual who is employed by a small business concern and whose managerial or technical expertise is critical to the successful day-to-day operations of that small business concern."[116] The act defines a military conflict as (1) a period of war declared by Congress; or (2) a period of national emergency declared by Congress or the President; or (3) a period of contingency operation. A contingency operation is designated by the Secretary of Defense as an operation in which our military may become involved in military actions, operations, or hostilities (peacekeeping operations).[117]

The SBA is authorized to make such disaster loans either directly or in cooperation with banks or other lending institutions through agreements to participate on an immediate or deferred basis. The loan term may be up to a maximum of 30 years and is determined by the SBA in accordance with

---

[114] SBA, "Disaster Assistance Program: SOP 50-30-7," May 13, 2011, p. 48, at https://www.sba.gov/sites/default/files/ sops/SOP%2050%2030%207.pdf; and 13 C.F.R. §123.508. For further information and analysis concerning the SBA's disaster assistance loan program, see CRS Report R41309, *The SBA Disaster Loan Program: Overview and Possible Issues for Congress*, by Bruce R. Lindsay.

[115] 13 C.F.R. §123.507.

[116] P.L. 106-50, the Veterans Entrepreneurship and Small Business Development Act of 1999, Section 402. Assistance To Active Duty Military Reservists; and 15 U.S.C. §636(b). The SBA's Military Reservist Economic Injury Disaster Loan Program applies to economic injury suffered or likely to be suffered as the result of a period of military conflict occurring or ending on or after March 24, 1999.

[117] P.L. 106-50, Section 402 and 15 U.S.C. §636(c).

the borrower's ability to repay the loan. The loan's interest rate is the SBA's published interest rate for an Economic Injury Disaster Loan at the time the application for assistance is approved by the SBA. Economic Injury Disaster Loan interest rates may not exceed 4%.

The SBA is not required by law to require collateral on disaster loans. However, the SBA has established collateral requirements for disaster loans based on "a balance between protection of the Agency's interest as a creditor and as a provider of disaster assistance."[118] The SBA generally does not require collateral to secure a MREIDL loan of $50,000 or less. Larger loan amounts require collateral, but the SBA will not decline a request for a MREIDL loan for a lack of collateral if the SBA is reasonably certain the borrower can repay the loan.[119]

The SBA disbursed one MREIDL loan in FY2014, none in FY2015, three in FY2016, and three in FY2017. Since the MREIDL's inception through December 31, 2017, the SBA has disbursed 352 MREIDL loans amounting to $32.97 million. Of these 352 loans, 85 loans (24.2% of the total number of MREIDL loans disbursed), amounting to $7.8 million (23.8% of the total amount of MREIDL loans disbursed), have been charged off (a declaration that the debt is unlikely to be collected) by the SBA.[120] Because the MREIDL program is relatively small and noncontroversial, this chapter does not present a discussion of the congressional issues affecting the program.

CONCLUSION

Congress has demonstrated a continuing interest in federal programs designed to assist veterans transition from military to civilian life. For

---

[118] SBA, "Disaster Assistance Program: SOP 50-30-7," May 13, 2011, p. 152, at https://www.sba.gov/sites/default/ files/sops/SOP%2050%2030%207.pdf.

[119] 13 C.F.R. §123.513.

[120] SBA, Office of Congressional and Legislative Affairs, "Correspondence with the authors," January 13, 2017 and January 10, 2018. In FY2011, the SBA disbursed 10 MREIDL loans amounting to $1.15 million. In FY2012, the SBA disbursed seven MREIDL loans amounting to $834,300. In FY2013, the SBA disbursed three MREIDL loans amounting to $121,200.

example, the SBA's veteran business development programs, loan guaranty programs, and federal procurement programs for small businesses generally, including service-disabled veteran-owned small businesses, have all been subject to congressional hearings during the past several Congresses. Also, as has been discussed, several bills have been introduced in recent Congresses to address the SBA's management of these programs and fraud.

Given the many factors that influence business success, measuring the effectiveness of the SBA's veteran assistance programs, especially the programs' effect on veteran job retention and creation, is both complicated and challenging. For example, it is difficult to determine with any degree of precision or certainty the extent to which any changes in the success of a small business result primarily from that business's participation in the SBA's programs or from changes in the broader economy. That task is made even more challenging by the absence of performance outcome measures that could serve as a guide. In most instances, the SBA uses program performance measures that focus on indicators that are primarily output related, such as the number and amount of loans approved for veteran-owned small businesses and the number and amount of federal contracts awarded to service-disabled veteran-owned small businesses.

Both GAO and the SBA's Office of Inspector General have recommended that the SBA adopt more outcome-related performance measures for the SBA's loan guaranty programs, such as tracking the number of borrowers that remain in business after receiving a SBA guaranteed loan to measure the extent to which the SBA contributed to their ability to stay in business.[121] Other performance-oriented measures that Congress might also consider include requiring the SBA to survey veterans who participate in its business development programs or who have received a SBA guaranteed loan. This survey could provide information related to the difficulty the veterans experienced in obtaining a

---

[121] GAO, *Small Business Administration: 7(a) Loan Program Needs Additional Performance Measures*, GAO-08-226T, November 1, 2007, p. 2, http://www.gao.gov/new.items/d08226t.pdf; and SBA, Office of the Inspector General, *SBA's Administration of the Microloan Program under the Recovery Act*, December 28, 2009, pp. 6, 7, https://www.sba.gov/content/rom-10-10-sbas-administration-microloan-program-under-recovery-act.

loan from the private sector, their experiences with the SBA's loan application process, and the role the SBA loan had in creating or retaining jobs. The SBA could also survey service-disabled veteran-owned small businesses that were awarded a federal contract to determine the extent to which the SBA was instrumental in their receiving the award and the extent to which the award contributed to their ability to create jobs or expand their scope of operations.

ACKNOWLEDGMENTS

The authors would like to express their appreciation to CRS legislative attorney Erika Lunder for assisting with this chapter's section on Congressional Issues: Contracting Fraud.

In: Business Trends in the 21st Century ISBN: 978-1-53614-260-0
Editor: C. O. Clemente Escamilla

Chapter 2

SMALL BUSINESS SIZE STANDARDS: A HISTORICAL ANALYSIS OF CONTEMPORARY ISSUES (UPDATED)*

Robert Jay Dilger

ABSTRACT

Small business size standards are of congressional interest because the standards determine eligibility for receiving Small Business Administration (SBA) assistance as well as federal contracting and tax preferences. Although there is bipartisan agreement that the nation's small businesses play an important role in the American economy, there are differences of opinion concerning how to define them. The Small Business Act of 1953 (P.L. 83-163, as amended) authorized the SBA to establish size standards for determining eligibility for federal small business assistance. The SBA currently uses two types of size standards to determine SBA program eligibility: industry-specific size standards and alternative size standards based on the applicant's maximum tangible net worth and average net income after federal taxes.

* This is an edited, reformatted and augmented version of a Congressional Research Service report, R40860, dated April 17, 2018.

The SBA's industry-specific size standards determine program eligibility for firms in 1,037 industrial classifications in 19 sub-industry activities described in the 2017 North American Industry Classification System (NAICS). The size standards are based on one of four measures: (1) number of employees, (2) average annual receipts in the previous three years, (3) average asset size as reported in the firm's four quarterly financial statements for the preceding year, or (4) a combination of number of employees and barrel per day refining capacity. Overall, the SBA currently classifies about 97% of all employer firms as small. These firms represent about 30% of industry receipts.

The SBA has always based its size standards on economic analysis of each industry's overall competitiveness and the competitiveness of firms within each industry. However, in the absence of precise statutory guidance and consensus on how to define small, the SBA's size standards have often been challenged, typically by industry representatives seeking to increase the number of firms eligible for assistance and by Members concerned that the size standards may not adequately target assistance to firms that they consider to be truly small.

During the 111th Congress, P.L. 111-240, the Small Business Jobs Act of 2010

- authorized the SBA to establish an alternative size standard using maximum tangible net worth and average net income after federal taxes for both the 7(a) and 504/CDC loan guaranty programs;
- established, until the SBA acted, an interim alternative size standard for the 7(a) and 504/CDC programs of not more than $15 million in tangible net worth and not more than $5 million in average net income after federal taxes (excluding any carry-over losses) for the two full fiscal years before the date of the application; and
- required the SBA to conduct a detailed review of not less than one-third of the SBA's industry size standards every 18 months beginning on the new law's date of enactment (September 27, 2010) and ensure that each size standard is reviewed at least once every five years.

This chapter provides a historical examination of the SBA's size standards and assesses competing views concerning how to define a small business. It also discusses

- P.L. 112-239, the National Defense Authorization Act for Fiscal Year 2013, which requires the SBA to make available a justification when establishing or approving a size standard that the size standard is appropriate for each individual industry classification. It addresses the SBA's recent practice of combining size standards within industrial groups as a means to reduce the complexity of its size standards and to provide greater consistency for industrial classifications that have similar economic characteristics.

- P.L. 114-328, the National Defense Authorization Act for Fiscal Year 2017, which authorizes the SBA to establish different size standards for agricultural enterprises using existing methods and appeal processes. Previously, the small business size standard for agricultural enterprises was set in statute as having annual receipts not in excess of $750,000.
- Legislation introduced during the 112th Congress (H.R. 585, the Small Business Size Standard Flexibility Act of 2011), 113th Congress (H.R. 2542, the Regulatory Flexibility Improvements Act of 2013, and included in H.R. 4, the Jobs for America Act), 114th Congress (H.R. 527, the Small Business Regulatory Flexibility Improvements Act of 2015, and its Senate companion bill, S. 1536), and 115th Congress (H.R. 33, the Small Business Regulatory Flexibility Improvements Act of 2017, and its Senate companion bill, S. 584, and included in H.R. 5, the Regulatory Accountability Act of 2017) to authorize the SBA's Office of Chief Counsel for Advocacy to approve or disapprove a size standard requested by a federal agency for purposes other than the Small Business Act or the Small Business Investment Act of 1958. The SBA's Administrator currently has that authority.

WHAT IS A SMALL BUSINESS?

There is bipartisan agreement that small businesses play an important role in the American economy.[1] However, there are differences of opinion concerning how to define them. This issue is of congressional interest

[1] Senate Democratic Policy Committee, "Senate Democrats Are Committed to America's Small Businesses," Washington, DC: Senate Democratic Policy Committee, May 18, 2009, at http://sbc.senate.gov/ DPC_small_biz_doc.pdf; Senate Republican Policy Committee, "Taxing Success: President Obama's Tax Increases on Small Businesses are Bad for Job Creation," Washington, DC: Senate Republican Policy Committee, March 17, 2009, at http://rpc.senate.gov/public/_files/031709TaxingSuccess.pdf; and President Barack Obama, "Remarks by the President to Small Business Owners, Community Lenders and Members of Congress," press release, Office of the Press Secretary, March 16, 2009, at http://www.whitehouse.gov/the_press_office/Remarks-by-the-President-to-smallbusiness-owners/.

because the definition used determines business eligibility for Small Business Administration (SBA) assistance as well as federal contracting and tax preferences.

The Small Business Act of 1953 (P.L. 83-163, as amended) authorized the SBA and justified the agency's existence on the grounds that small businesses are essential to the maintenance of the free enterprise system.[2] In economic terms, the congressional intent was to use the SBA to deter monopoly and oligarchy formation within all industries and the market failures they cause by eliminating competition in the marketplace.

The Small Business Act of 1953 provides the SBA authority to establish size standards for determining eligibility for federal small business assistance. The SBA currently uses two types of size standards to determine SBA program eligibility: (1) industry-specific size standards and (2) alternative size standards based on the applicant's maximum tangible net worth and average net income after federal taxes. The SBA's industry-specific size standards are also used to determine eligibility for federal small business contracting purposes.

The SBA's industry-specific size standards determine program eligibility for firms in 1,037 industrial classifications (hereinafter industries) in 19 sub-industry activities described in the 2017 North American Industry Classification System (NAICS). Given its mandate to promote competition in the marketplace, the SBA has based its size standards on an economic analysis of each industry's overall competitiveness and the competitiveness of firms within the industry.[3] The size standards are based on four measures: (1) number of employees (504 industries), (2) average annual receipts in the previous three years (527 industries), (3) average asset size as reported in the firm's four quarterly financial statements for the preceding year (5 industries), or (4) a combination of number of employees and barrel per day refining capacity (1 industry). Overall, the SBA currently classifies about 97% of all

---

[2] P.L. 83-163, the Small Business Act of 1953, §202.

[3] U.S. Small Business Administration (SBA), Office of Government Contracting and Business Development, "SBA Size Standards Methodology," April 2009, p. 1, at http://www.sba.gov/sites/default/files/size_standards_methodology.pdf.

employer firms as small.[4] These firms represent about 30% of industry receipts.

As will be discussed, the SBA began a comprehensive size standards review in 2008. At that time, the SBA used 41 different size standards: 7 employee based size standards, 31 receipts based size standards (based on average annual receipts over the previous three years), 1 asset based size standard, 1 megawatt hours size standard (based on electrical output over the preceding fiscal year), and 1 size standard based on a combination of the number of employees and barrel per day refining capacity. The SBA also had 11 other size standards for its financial and assistance programs.

From April 2009 through February 2016, the SBA reduced the number of size standards that can be applied when establishing new, or reviewing existing, size standards to eight receipts based size standards and eight employee based size standards. The SBA argued that reducing the number of receipts based size standards from 31 to 8 would simplify the management and use of size standards and provide "greater consistency in size standards among industries that are similar in their economic characteristics."[5]

Because SBA size standards remain in force until after they are reviewed, the number of SBA size standards did not immediately drop from 41 to 16 in 2009. Instead, the number of size standards began to decline gradually as new size standard final rules were issued.

On February 26, 2016, the SBA added a new employee based size standard (no more than 1,250 employees) and reinstated the use of another (no more than 1,500 employees) in its final rule for size standards in the Manufacturing sector.[6] As a result, the SBA is now limiting the number of

---

[4] SBA, "SBA's Size Standards Analysis: An Overview on Methodology and Comprehensive Size Standards Review," power point presentation, Khem R. Sharma, SBA Office of Size Standards, July 13, 2011, p. 4, at http://www.actgov.org/sigcom/SIGs/SIGs/SBSIG/Documents/2011%20-%20Documents%20and%20Presentations/Size%20Stds%20Presentation_SIG%20Meeting.pdf.

[5] SBA, Office of Government Contracting and Business Development, "SBA Size Standards Methodology," April 2009, p. 22, at http://www.sba.gov/sites/default/files/size_standards_methodology.pdf.

[6] SBA, "Small Business Size Standards for Manufacturing," 79 *Federal Register* 54150, September 10, 2014; SBA, "Small Business Size Standards for Manufacturing," 80 *Federal Register* 78044, December 15, 2015; and SBA, "Small Business Size Standards for

size standards that can be applied when establishing new, or reviewing existing, size standards to 8 receipts based size standards and 10 employee based size standards.

The SBA currently has 27 SBA industry size standards in effect (16 receipts based size standards, 9 employee based sized standards, 1 asset based size standard, and 1 size standard based on a combination of the number of employees and barrel per day refining capacity).[7] That number typically declines when new size standard final rules are issued.

In the absence of precise statutory guidance and consensus on how to define small, the SBA's size standards have often been challenged, typically by industry representatives seeking to increase the number of firms eligible for assistance. The size standards have also been challenged by Members of Congress concerned that the size standards may not adequately target federal assistance to firms that they consider to be truly small.

During the 111th Congress, P.L. 111-240, the Small Business Jobs Act of 2010

- authorized the SBA to establish an alternative size standard using maximum tangible net worth and average net income after federal taxes for both the 7(a) and 504/CDC loan guaranty programs;
- established, until the SBA acted, an interim alternative size standard for the 7(a) and 504/CDC programs of not more than $15

Manufacturing," 81 *Federal Register* 4469-4492, January 26, 2016. The final rule, issued on January 26, 2016, was effective as of February 26, 2016. It increased the number of manufacturing industries with a size standard of no more than 1,500 employees from 3 to 26.

[7] Since February 26, 2016, the SBA's receipts based size standards have been no more than $0.75 million, $5.5 million, $7.5 million, $11.0 million, $15.0 million, $18.0 million, $19.0 million, $20.5 million, $25.0 million, $27.5 million, $29.5 million, $32.0 million, $32.5 million, $36.5 million, $37.5 million, and $38.5 million in average annual receipts over the most recently completed three fiscal years or average annual receipts on a pro rata basis if the firm has been in business for less than three years. The employee based size standards have been no more than 100 employees, 150 employees, 200 employees, 250 employees, 500 employees, 750 employees, 1,000 employees, 1,250 employees, and 1,500 employees. The assets based size standard has been $550 million as reported by the institution's four quarterly financial statements for the preceding year. The combined size standard has been no more than 1,500 employees or no more than 200,000 barrels per calendar day total Operable Atmospheric Crude Oil Distillation capacity.

million in tangible net worth and not more than $5 million in average net income after federal taxes (excluding any carry-over losses) for the two full fiscal years before the date of the application;[8] and

- required the SBA to conduct a detailed review of not less than one-third of the SBA's industry size standards every 18 months beginning on the new law's date of enactment (September 27, 2010) and ensure that each size standard is reviewed at least once every five years.[9]

This chapter provides a historical examination of the SBA's size standards and assesses competing views concerning how to define a small business. It also discusses

- P.L. 112-239, the National Defense Authorization Act for Fiscal Year 2013, which requires the SBA to make available a justification when establishing or approving a size standard that the size standard is appropriate for each individual industry classification. It addresses the SBA's recent practice of combining

---

[8] On December 20, 2010, the SBA announced that it planned to issue a notice of proposed rulemaking concerning the new alternative size standard in February 2011. It did not do so. On January 8, 2013, the SBA announced that it would issue an interim final rule, to be effective when published, establishing an alternative size standard for the 7(a) and 504/CDC programs by October 2013. See SBA, "Small Business Jobs Act: Small Business Size Standards; Alternative Size Standard for 7(a) and 504 Business Loan Programs," 75 *Federal Register* 79868, December 20, 2010 and SBA, "Small Business Jobs Act: Small Business Size Standards; Alternative Size Standard for 7(a) and 504 Business Loan Programs," 78 *Federal Register* 1638, January 8, 2013. The SBA also indicated in its notice of proposed rulemaking on January 8, 2013, that "the amendments will increase the current alternative standard for applicants for 504 loans." On December 15, 2015, the SBA announced that it would issue a notice of proposed rulemaking concerning the new alternative size standard by November 2016. See SBA, "Small Business Size Standards; Alternative Size Standard for 7(a), 504, and Disaster Loan Programs," 80 *Federal Register* 78045, December 15, 2015.

[9] For congressional intent concerning the need for updated size standards, see S. 2989, the Small Business Contracting Revitalization Act of 2010; and U.S. Congress, Senate Committee on Small Business and Entrepreneurship, *Small Business Contracting Revitalization Act of 2010*, report to accompany S. 2989, 111th Cong., 2nd sess., September 29, 2010, S.Rept. 111-343 (Washington: GPO, 2010), p. 9 ("...The Committee has heard testimony that the current size standards are in dire need of a comprehensive update").

size standards within industrial groups to reduce the complexity of its size standards and to provide greater consistency for industrial classifications that have similar economic characteristics.[10]

- P.L. 114-328, the National Defense Authorization Act for Fiscal Year 2017, which authorizes the SBA to establish different size standards for agricultural enterprises using existing methods and appeal processes. Previously, the small business size standard for agricultural enterprises was set in statute as having annual receipts not in excess of $750,000.
- Legislation introduced during the 112th Congress (H.R. 585, the Small Business Size Standard Flexibility Act of 2011), 113th Congress (H.R. 2542, the Regulatory Flexibility Improvements Act of 2013, and included in H.R. 4, the Jobs for America Act), 114th Congress (H.R. 527, the Small Business Regulatory Flexibility Improvements Act of 2015, and its Senate companion bill, S. 1536), and 115th Congress (H.R. 33, the Small Business Regulatory Flexibility Improvements Act of 2017, and its Senate companion bill, S. 584, and included in H.R. 5, the Regulatory Accountability Act of 2017) to authorize the SBA's Office of Chief Counsel for Advocacy to approve or disapprove a size standard requested by a federal agency for purposes other than the Small Business Act or the Small Business Investment Act of 1958. The SBA's Administrator currently has that authority.

How Big Is Small?

In 2015, there were an estimated 30.2 million businesses in the United States, including about 5.9 million employer firms and 24.3 million nonemployer firms.[11] Nonemployer firms have no paid employees, annual

---

[10] SBA, "Small Business Size Standards: Professional, Scientific and Technical Services," 76 *Federal Register* 14327, March 16, 2011.

[11] U.S. Census Bureau, "Statistics of U.S. Businesses: U.S. & States, totals," at https://www.census.gov/data/tables/2015/econ/susb/2015-susb-annual.html; and U.S. Census Bureau,

business receipts of $1,000 or more ($1 or more in the construction industries), and are subject to federal income tax.[12] Most nonemployers are self-employed individuals operating very small unincorporated businesses, which may or may not be the owner's principal source of income. These firms are excluded from most business statistics.[13]

Table 1. Number of Employer Firms, Employer Firm Employment, and Employer Firm Annual Payroll, by Employer Firm Employment Size, 2015

Number of Employees	Number of Employer Firms	Cumulative Percentage of Total Number of Employer Firms	Employment	Cumulative Percentage of Employer Firm Total Employment	Employer Firm Annual Payroll ($1,000)	Cumulative Percentage of Employer Firm Total Annual Payroll
0-4[a]	3,643,737	61.8%	5,877,075	4.7%	$263,152,063	4.2%
5-9	1,004,555	78.8%	6,614,340	10.1%	$243,719,141	8.1%
10-19	617,390	89.2%	8,297,864	16.8%	$321,846,938	13.3%
20-99	526,106	98.2%	20,645,466	33.4%	$876,330,967	27.3%
100-499	89,479	99.7%	17,503,402	47.5%	$846,259,493	40.8%
500-999	9,684	99.8%	6,678,648	52.9%	$341,872,334	46.3%
1,000-1,999	4,726	99.9%	6,593,071	58.2%	$359,261,033	52.0%
2,000-4,999	3,004	99.9%	9,248,278	65.6%	$541,744,215	60.6%
5,000+	2,050	100.0%	42,627,803	100.0%	$2,459,302,068	100.0%
Total	5,900,731		124,085,947		$6,253,488,252	

Source: U.S. Census Bureau, "Statistics of U.S. Businesses: U.S. & States, totals," at https://www.census.gov/data/tables/2015/econ/susb/2015-susb-annual.html; and U.S. Census Bureau, "Statistics of U.S. Businesses: U.S., NAICS sectors, large employment sizes," at https://www.census.gov/data/tables/2015/econ/susb/2015-susb-annual.html.

[a] Employment is measured in March, thus some employer firms (start-ups after March, closures before March, and seasonal firms) will have zero employment and some annual payroll.

"Nonemployer Statistics," at https://www.census.gov/programs-surveys/nonemployer-statistics/data/tables.html. There were an estimated 24.3 million nonemployer firms in 2015.

[12] U.S. Census Bureau, "Nonemployer Statistics: About this Program," at https://www.census.gov/programssurveys/nonemployer-statistics/about.html.

[13] Ibid. Nonemployer firms account for less than 4% of business annual sales or receipts.

As Table 1 indicates, in 2015 (the latest available data) there were 5,900,731 employer firms in the United States employing 124,085,947 people and providing total payroll of $6.25 trillion.

Most employer firms (61.8%) had 4 or fewer employees, 78.8% had fewer than 10 employees, 89.2% had fewer than 20 employees, 98.2% had fewer than 100 employees, and 99.7% had fewer than 500 employees in 2015. The table also provides data concerning other economic factors that might be used to define a small business: an employer firm's number of employees as a share (cumulative percentage) of the total number of employer firms, as a share of employer firm total employment, and as a share of employer firm total annual payroll.

As will be discussed, the SBA has traditionally applied economic factors to specific industries, not to cumulative statistics for all employer firms, to determine which firms are small businesses. Nonetheless, the data in Table 1 illustrate how the selection of economic factors used to define small business affects the definition's outcome. For example, for illustrative purposes only, if the mid-point (50%) for these three economic factors was used to define what is a small business, three different employee firm sizes would be used to designate firms as small:

- Businesses would be required to have no more than 4 employees to be defined as small if the definition for small used the mid-point (50%) share of the total number of employer firms (employer firms with no more than four employees accounted for 61.8% of the total number of employer firms in 2015).
- Businesses would be required to have no more than 999 employees to be defined as small if the definition for small used the mid-point (50%) share of employer firm total employment (employer firms with no more than 999 employees accounted for 52.9% of employer firm total employment in 2015).
- Businesses would be required to have no more than 1,999 employees to be defined as small if the definition for small used the mid-point (50%) share of employer firm total annual payroll

(employer firms with no more than 1,999 employees accounted for 52.0% of employer firm total annual payroll in 2015).

Other economic factors that might be used to define a small business include the value of the employer firm's assets or its market share, expressed as a firm's sales revenue from that market divided by the total sales revenue available in that market or as a firm's unit sales volume in that market divided by the total volume of units sold in that market.

WHO MAKES THE CALL?

The Small Business Act of 1953 (P.L. 83-163, as amended) authorized the SBA to establish size standards for determining eligibility for small business assistance. Sixty years have passed since the SBA established its initial small business size standards on January 1, 1957.[14] Yet, decisions made then concerning the rationale and criteria used to define small businesses established precedents that continue to shape current policy. Moreover, as mentioned previously, since its beginnings the SBA has based its size standards on economic analysis of each industry's overall competitiveness and the competitiveness of firms within each industry. However, in the absence of precise statutory guidance and consensus on how to define small, the SBA's size standards have often been challenged, typically by industry representatives seeking to increase the number of firms eligible for assistance and by Members of Congress concerned that the size standards do not adequately target the SBA's assistance to firms that they consider to be truly small.

Over the years, the SBA typically reviewed its size standards piecemeal, reviewing specific industries when the SBA determined that an industry's market conditions had changed or the SBA was asked to undertake a review by an industry claiming that its market conditions had changed. On five occasions, in 1980, 1982, 1992, 2004, and 2008, the SBA

---

[14] SBA, "Part 103 - Small Business Size Standards," 21 *Federal Register* 9709-9714, December 7, 1956.

proposed a comprehensive revision of its size standards. The SBA did not fully implement any of these proposals, but the arguments presented, both for and against the proposals, provide a context for understanding the SBA's current size standards, and the rationale and criteria that have been presented to retain and replace them.

As mentioned previously, P.L. 111-240 requires the SBA to conduct a detailed review of not less than one-third of the SBA's industry size standards during the 18-month period beginning on the date of enactment (September 27, 2010) and during every 18-month period thereafter.[15] The act also requires the SBA to review each size standard at least once every five years. The SBA completed its first five-year review of all SBA industry size standards in 2016.[16] As a result of its five-year review, the SBA estimates that more than 72,000 small businesses gained SBA eligibility.[17]

Early Definitions of Small Business Vary in Approach and Criteria

There is no uniform or accepted definition for a small business. Instead, several criteria are used to determine eligibility for small business spending and tax programs.[18] This was also the case when Congress considered establishing the SBA during the early 1950s. For example, in 1952, the House Select Committee on Small Business reviewed federal

---

[15] P.L. 111-240, the Small Business Act of 2010, §1344. Updated Size Standards.

[16] SBA, "A Report on the First Five-Year Comprehensive Review of Small Business Size Standards Under The Small Business Jobs Act of 2010," April 2017, at https://www.sba.gov/document/support--comprehensive-review-size-standards.

[17] Ibid., p. 34.

[18] According to one source, the Internal Revenue Code contains at least 24 different definitions of a small business. See Douglas K. Barney, Chris Bjornson, and Steve Wells, "Just How Small Is Your Business?," *The National Public Accountant*, August 2003, pp. 4-6, at http://findarticles.com/p/articles/mi_m4325/is_2003_August/ai_n25073718/, cited in CRS Report RL32254, *Small Business Tax Benefits: Current Law and Main Arguments For and Against Them*, by Gary Guenther.

statutes, executive branch directives, and the academic literature to serve as a guide for determining how to define small businesses.

The Select Committee began its review by asserting that the need to define the concept of small business was based on a general consensus that assisting small business was necessary to enhance economic competition, combat monopoly formation, inhibit the concentration of economic power, and maintain "the integrity of independent enterprise."[19] It noted that the definition of small businesses in federal statutes reflected this consensus by taking into consideration the firm's size relative to other firms in its field and "matters of independence and nondominance."[20] For example, the War Mobilization and Reconversion Act of 1944 defined a small business as either "employing 250 wage earners or less" or having "sales volumes, quantities of materials consumed, capital investments, or any other criteria which are reasonably attributable to small plants rather than medium- or large-sized plants."[21] The Selective Service Act of 1948 classified a business as small for military procurement purposes if "(1) its position in the trade or industry of which it is a part is not dominant, (2) the number of its employees does not exceed 500, and (3) it is independently owned and operated."[22]

The Select Committee also found that, for data-gathering purposes, the executive branch defined small businesses in relative, as opposed to absolute, terms within specific industries. For example, the Bureau of Labor Statistics "defined small business in terms of an average for each industry based on the volume of employment or sales. All firms which fall below this average are deemed to be small."[23] The U.S. Census Bureau

---

[19] U.S. Congress, House Select Committee on Small Business, *Review of Small Business: 82nd Congress*, final report pursuant to H.Res. 33, A Resolution Creating a Select Committee to Conduct a Study and Investigation of the Problems of Small Business, 82nd Cong., 2nd sess., December 31, 1952 (Washington: GPO, 1952), pp. 5, 13, 14, 78, and 136.

[20] Ibid., p. 3.

[21] Ibid., p. 2.

[22] Ibid.; and U.S. Congress, Conference Committee, *Selective Service Act of 1948*, conference report no. 2438, 80th Cong., 2nd sess., June 19, 1948 (Washington: GPO, 1948), p. 24.

[23] U.S. Congress, House Select Committee on Small Business, *Review of Small Business: 82nd Congress*, final report pursuant to H.Res. 33, A Resolution Creating a Select Committee to Conduct a Study and Investigation of the Problems of Small Business, 82nd Cong., 2nd sess., December 31, 1952 (Washington: GPO, 1952), p. 3.

also used different criteria for different industries. For example, manufacturing firms were classified as small if they had fewer than 100 employees, wholesalers were considered small if they had annual sales below $200,000, and retailers were considered small if they had annual sales below $50,000. According the Census Bureau, in 1952, small businesses accounted for "roughly 92 percent of all business establishments, 45 percent of all employees, and 34 percent of all dollar value of all sales."[24]

The Select Committee also noted that in 1951, the National Production Authority's Office of Small Business proposed defining all manufacturing firms with fewer than 50 employees as small and any with more than 2,500 employees as large. Manufacturers employing between these numbers of employees would be considered large or small depending on the general structure of the industry to which they belonged. The larger the percentage of total output produced by large firms, the larger the number of employees a firm could have to be considered small. Using this definition, most manufacturing firms with fewer than 50 employees would be classified as small, but others, such as an aircraft manufacturer, could have as many as 2,500 employees and still be considered small.[25]

For procurement purposes, the Select Committee found that executive branch agencies defined small businesses in absolute, as opposed to relative, terms, using 500 employees as the dividing line between large and small firms. Federal agencies defended the so-called 500 employee rule on the grounds that it "had the advantage of easy administration" across federal agencies.[26]

In reviewing the academic literature, the Select Committee reported that Abraham Kaplan's *Small Business: Its Place and Problems* defined small businesses as those with no more than $1 million in annual sales, $100,000 in total assets, and no more than 250 employees. Applying this definition would have classified about 95% of all business concerns as

---

[24] Ibid.

[25] Ibid., p. 4.

[26] U.S. Congress, House Select Committee on Small Business, Subcommittee No. 2, *Definition of "Small Business" Within Meaning of the Small Business Act of 1953, as Amended*, hearing on H.Res. 114, 84th Cong., 2nd sess., July 5, 1956 (Washington: GPO, 1956), p. 19.

small, and would have accounted for about half of all nonagricultural employees.[27]

Based on its review of federal statutes, executive branch directives, and the academic literature, the Select Committee decided that it would not attempt "to formulate a rigid definition of small business" because "the concept of small business must remain flexible and adaptable to the peculiar needs of each instance in which a definition may be required."[28] However, it concluded that the definition of *small* should be a relative one, as opposed to an absolute one, that took into consideration variations among economic sectors:

> This committee is also convinced that whatever limits may be established to the category of small business, they must vary from industry to industry according to the general industrial pattern of each. Public policy may demand similar treatment for a firm of 2,500 employees in one industry as it does for a firm of 50 employees in another industry. Each may be faced with the same basic problems of economic survival.[29]

The Small Business Act of 1953's Definition of Small Provides Room for Interpretation

Reflecting the view that formulating a rigid definition of small business was impractical, the Small Business Act of 1953 provided leeway in defining small businesses. It defined a small firm as "one that is independently owned and operated and which is not dominant in its field of

[27] U.S. Congress, House Select Committee on Small Business, *Review of Small Business: 82nd Congress*, final report pursuant to H. Res. 33, A Resolution Creating a Select Committee to Conduct a Study and Investigation of the Problems of Small Business, 82nd Cong., 2nd sess., December 31, 1952 (Washington: GPO, 1952), p. 4. See Abraham David Hannath Kaplan, *Small Business: Its Place and Problems* (NY: McGraw-Hill Book Co., 1948), pp. 21, 22.

[28] U.S. Congress, House Select Committee on Small Business, *Review of Small Business: 82nd Congress*, final report pursuant to H.Res. 33, A Resolution Creating a Select Committee to Conduct a Study and Investigation of the Problems of Small Business, 82nd Cong., 2nd sess., December 31, 1952 (Washington: GPO, 1952), p. 4.

[29] Ibid., p. 5.

operation."[30] The SBA was authorized to establish and subsequently alter size standards for determining eligibility for federal programs to assist small business, some of which are administered by the SBA.[31] The act specifies that the size standards "may utilize number of employees, dollar volume of business, net worth, net income, a combination thereof, or other appropriate factors."[32] It also notes that the concept of small is to be defined in a relative sense, varying from industry to industry to the extent necessary to reflect "differing characteristics" among industries.[33]

The House Committee on Banking and Currency's report accompanying H.R. 5141, the Small Business Act of 1953, issued on May 28, 1953, provided the committee's rationale for not providing a detailed definition of small:

> It would be impractical to include in the act a detailed definition of small business because of the variation between business groups. It is for this reason that the act authorizes the Administration to determine within any industry the concerns which are to be designated small-business concerns for the purposes of the act.[34]

The chapter did not provide specific guidance concerning what the committee might consider to be small, but it did indicate that data on industry employment, as of March 31, 1948, "reveals that on the basis of employment, small business truly is small in size. Of the approximately 4

---

[30] 15 U.S.C. §632(a)(1).

[31] Initially, the SBA size standards applied only to its own programs. Other federal agencies used the SBA size standards for procurement purposes on a voluntary basis. The Regulatory Flexibility Act of 1980 directed federal agencies to use SBA size standards or establish their own definitions after conferring directly with the SBA's Bureau (now Office) for Advocacy. U.S. Congress, Senate Committee on Small Business, *Small Business Administration's Size Standards*, hearing, 97th Cong., 1st sess., May 5, 1981 (Washington: GPO, 1981), p. 18. Also, see 5 U.S.C. §601(3).

[32] 15 U.S.C. §632(a)(2).

[33] 15 U.S.C. §632(a)(3).

[34] U.S. Congress, House Committee on Banking and Currency, *Small Business Act of 1953*, report to accompany H.R. 5141, 83rd Cong., 1st sess., May 28, 1953, H.Rept. 83-494 (Washington: GPO, 1953), p. 3.

million business concerns, 87.4% had fewer than 8 employees and 95.2% of the total number of concerns, employed fewer than 20 people."[35]

Industry Challenges the SBA's Initial Size Standards, Claiming They Are Too Restrictive

Initially, the SBA created two sets of size standards, one for federal procurement preferences and another for the SBA's loan and management training services. At the request of federal agencies, the SBA adopted the then-prevailing small business size standard used by federal agencies for procurement, which was no more than 500 employees. The SBA retained the right to make exceptions to the no more than 500 employee procurement size standard if the SBA determined that a firm having more than 500 employees was not dominant in its industry.

For the SBA's loan and management training services, the SBA's staff reviewed economic data provided by the Census Bureau to arrive at what Wendell Barnes, SBA's Administrator, described at a congressional hearing in 1956 as "a fairly accurate conclusion as to what comprises small business in each industry."[36] Jules Abels, SBA's economic advisor to the Administrator, explained at that congressional hearing how the SBA's staff determined what constituted a small business:

> There are various techniques for the demarcation lines, but in a study of almost any industry, you will find a large cluster of small concerns around a certain figure.... On the other hand, above a certain dividing line you will find relatively few and as you map out a picture of an industry it appears that a dividing line at a certain point is fair.[37]

---

[35] Ibid., p. 4.

[36] U.S. Congress, House Select Committee on Small Business, Subcommittee No. 2, *Definition of "Small Business" Within Meaning of the Small Business Act of 1953, as Amended*, hearing on H. Res. 114, 84th Cong., 2nd sess., July 5, 1956 (Washington: GPO, 1956), p. 24.

[37] Ibid., p. 39.

On January 5, 1956, the SBA published a notice of proposed rulemaking in the *Federal Register* announcing its first proposed small business size standards.[38] During the public comment period, representatives of several industries argued that the proposed standards were too restrictive and excluded too many firms. In response, Mr. Abels testified that the SBA decided to adjust its figures to make them "a little bit more liberal because there was some feeling on the part of certain industries that they were too tight and that they excluded too many firms."[39] The SBA published its final rule concerning its small business size standards on December 7, 1956, and they became effective on January 1, 1957.[40]

The SBA decided to use number of employees as the sole criterion for determining if manufacturing firms were small and annual sales or annual receipts as the sole criterion for all other industries. Mr. Abels explained at the congressional hearing the SBA's rationale for using number of employees for classifying manufacturing firms as small and annual sales or annual receipts for all other firms:

> in the absence of automation which would give one firm in an industry a great advantage over another, roughly speaking if the firms were mechanized to the same extent, a firm with 400 employees would have an output which would be twice as large as the output of a firm with 200 employees.... However when you depart from the manufacturing field and go into, say, a distributive field or trade, it then becomes necessary to discard the number of employees, because it is a matter of judicial notice, that one man for example in the distributive trades can sell as much as 100 men can sell. One small construction firm possibly can do a lot more business than one with a lot more employees. A service trade again has its volume geared to something other than the number of employees. So I think that one can say with reasonable certainty that it is

---

[38] SBA, "Small Business Size Standards," 21 *Federal Register* 79-80, January 5, 1956.

[39] U.S. Congress, House Select Committee on Small Business, Subcommittee No. 2, *Definition of "Small Business" Within Meaning of the Small Business Act of 1953, as Amended*, hearing on H. Res. 114, 84th Cong., 2nd sess., July 5, 1956 (Washington: GPO, 1956), p. 40.

[40] SBA, "Part 103 - Small Business Size Standards," 21 *Federal Register* 9709-9714, December 7, 1956.

only within the manufacturing field that the employee standard is the uniform yardstick, but that other than manufacturing the dollar volume is the appropriate yardstick.[41]

The SBA's initial size standards defined most manufacturing firms employing no more than 250 employees as small. In addition, the SBA considered manufacturing firms in some industries (e.g., metalworking and small arms) as small if they employed no more than 500 employees, and in some others (e.g., sugar refining and tractors) as small if they employed no more than 1,000 employees. To be considered small, wholesalers were required to have annual sales volume of $5 million or less; construction firms had to have average annual receipts of $5 million or less over the preceding three years; trucking and warehousing firms had to have annual receipts of $2 million or less; taxicab companies and most firms in the service trades had to have annual receipts of $1 million or less; and most retail firms had to have annual sales of $1 million or less.[42]

Mr. Abels testified that the SBA experienced "continual" protests of its size standards by firms denied financial or support assistance because they were not considered small. He also testified that in each case, the SBA denied the protest and determined, in his words, that the standard was "valid and accurate."[43]

GAO and Several Members of Congress Challenge the SBA's Size Standards, Claiming They Are Too Broad

In 1977, the U.S. General Accounting Office (GAO, now the U.S. Government Accountability Office) was asked by the Senate Select

[41] Ibid., p. 41.

[42] Ibid., p. 3. In the retail sector, department and variety stores, grocery stores with fresh meats, and new and used automobile stores were considered small if they had annual sales volume of $2 million or less. In the service trades sector, hotels and power industry firms were considered small if they had annual receipts of $2 million or less.

[43] Ibid., p. 40.

Committee on Small Business to review the SBA's size standards. At that time, most of the SBA's size standards remained at their original 1957 levels, other than a one-time upward adjustment for inflation in 1975 for industries using annual sales and receipts to restore eligibility to firms that may have lost small-business status due solely to the effect of inflation.[44]

GAO's report, issued in 1978, found that the SBA's size standards "are often high and often are not justified by economic rationale."[45] Specifically, GAO reported that

> many size standards may not direct assistance to the target group described in SBA regulations as businesses "struggling to become or remain competitive" because the loan and procurement size standards for most industries were established 15 or more years ago and have not been periodically reviewed; SBA records do not indicate how most standards were developed; and the standards often define as small a very high percentage of the firms in the industries to which they apply.[46]

GAO recommended that the SBA reexamine its size standards "by collecting data on the size of bidders on set-aside and unrestricted contracts, determining the size of businesses which need set-aside protection because they cannot otherwise obtain Federal contracts" and then consider reducing its size standards or "establishing a two-tiered system for set-aside contracts, under which certain procurements would be

---

[44] U.S. Congress, House Committee on Small Business, Subcommittee on General Oversight and Minority Enterprise, *Size Standards for Small Business*, hearing, 96th Cong., 1st sess., July 10, 1979 (Washington: GPO, 1979), p. 3. GAO reported that adjustments to the size standards had been made to "only 81 of the 534 industries covered by the special standards" from January 1, 1968 through April 25, 1978. The upward inflation adjustments for industries using annual sales or receipts ranged from 10.3% to 92.9% depending on the date when the standards were adopted. See SBA, "Small Business Size Standards," 40 *Federal Register* 24210-24215, June 5, 1975, and SBA, "Small Business Size Standards Regulation," 40 *Federal Register* 32824-32826, August 5, 1975.

[45] Ibid., p. 3. Also, see U.S. Government Accountability Office (GAO), *What Is A Small Business? The Small Business Administration Needs To Reexamine Its Answer*, CED-78-149, August 9, 1978, at http://www.gao.gov/assets/130/ 123644.pdf.

[46] Ibid.

available for bidding only to the smaller firms and others would be opened for bidding to all businesses considered small under present standards."[47]

Citing the GAO report, several Members objected to the SBA's size standards at a House Committee on Small Business oversight hearing conducted on July 10, 1979. Representative John J. LaFalce, chair of the House Committee on Small Business Subcommittee on General Oversight and Minority Enterprise, stated that "what we have faced from 1953 to the present is virtually nothing other than acquiescence to the demands of the special interest groups. That is how the size standards have been set."[48] Representative Tim Lee Carter, the subcommittee's ranking minority member, stated that "it seems to me that we may be fast growing into just a regular bank forum not just to small business but to all business."[49] At that time, approximately 99% of all firms with employees were classified by the SBA as a small business.[50]

Roger Rosenberger, SBA's associate administrator for policy, planning and budgeting, testified at the hearing that the SBA would undertake a comprehensive economic analysis of industry data to determine if its size standards should be changed. However, he also defended the validity of the SBA's size standards, arguing that the task of setting size standards was a complicated and difficult one because of "how market structure and size distribution of firms vary from industry to industry."[51] He testified that some industries are dominated by a few large firms, some are comprised almost entirely of small businesses, and others "can be referred to as a mixed industry."[52] He argued that each market structure presents unique challenges for defining small businesses within that industry group. For example, he argued that it was debatable whether the SBA should provide

---

[47] Ibid., p. 20.

[48] U.S. Congress, House Committee on Small Business, Subcommittee on General Oversight and Minority Enterprise, *Size Standards for Small Business*, hearing, 96th Cong., 1st sess., July 10, 1979 (Washington: GPO, 1979), p. 9.

[49] Ibid., p. 6.

[50] U.S. Congress, Senate Committee on Small Business, *Small Business Administration's Size Standards*, hearing, 97th Cong., 1st sess., May 5, 1981 (Washington: GPO, 1981), p. 14.

[51] U.S. Congress, House Committee on Small Business, Subcommittee on General Oversight and Minority Enterprise, *Size Standards for Small Business*, hearing, 96th Cong., 1st sess., July 10, 1979 (Washington: GPO, 1979), p. 17.

[52] Ibid.

any assistance to any of the businesses within industries where "smaller firms are flourishing."[53]

SBA Proposes More Restrictive Size Standards Based on Industry Competitiveness

On March 10, 1980, the SBA issued a notice of proposed rulemaking designed to "reduce administrative complexity" by replacing its two sets of size standards, one for procurement preferences and another for its loan and consultative support services, with a single set of size standards for both purposes.[54] The SBA also proposed to use a single factor, the firm's number of employees, for definitional purposes for nearly all industries instead of using the firm's number of employees for some industries, the firm's assets for others, and the firm's annual gross receipts for still others. The SBA argued that

> when size standards are denominated in dollars, i.e., annual revenues, its ability to help the small business sector is undermined by inflation. Using employment, as opposed to dollar sales, will provide greater stability for SBA and its clients; will remove inter-industry distortions generated by differential inflation rates; and reduce the need for SBA to make frequent revisions in the size standards merely to reflect price increases.[55]

In setting its proposed new size standards for each industry (ranging from no more than 15 to no more than 2,500 employees), the SBA first placed each industry into one of three groups: concentrated (characterized by a highly unequal distribution of sales among the firms in the industry), competitive (characterized by a more equal distribution of sales in the

---

[53] Ibid., p. 28.

[54] U.S. Congress, House Committee on Small Business, *Small Business Size Standards*, hearing, 96th Cong., 2nd sess., March 13, 1980 (Washington: GPO, 1980), p. III.

[55] Ibid., p. 50.

industry), or mixed (industries that do not meet the criteria of competitive or concentrated industries).[56]

The SBA determined that there were 160 concentrated industries, 317 competitive industries, and 249 mixed industries.[57] The SBA argued that establishing a size standard for the 160 concentrated industries was a "straight-forward task—simply identify and exclude those few firms which account for a disproportionately large share of the industry's sales."[58] For competitive industries, the SBA argued that the size standard should be set "relatively low, so as to support entry and moderate growth."[59] The SBA argued that mixed industries require "relatively high size standards ... to reinforce competition and offset the pressures to increase the degree of concentration in these industries."[60]

The proposed new SBA size standards would have had the net effect of reducing the number of firms classified as small by about 225,000.[61] In percentage terms, the number of firms classified as small would have been reduced from about 99% of all employer firms to 96%.[62]

Over 86% of the more than 1,500 public comments received by the SBA concerning its proposed new size standards criticized it. Most of the criticism was from firms that would no longer be considered small under the new size standards.[63] In addition, several federal agencies indicated that the proposed size standards in the services and construction industries were set too low, reducing the number of small firms eligible to compete for procurement contracts below levels they deemed necessary to ensure adequate competition to prevent agency costs from rising.

On October 21, 1980, Congress required the SBA to take additional time to consider the consequences of the proposed changes to the size standards by adopting the Small Business Export Expansion Act of 1980

---

[56] Ibid., p. 48.

[57] U.S. Congress, House Committee on Small Business, *Small Business Size Standards*, hearing, 96th Cong., 2nd sess., March 13, 1980 (Washington: GPO, 1980), p. 48.

[58] Ibid., p. 49.

[59] Ibid.

[60] Ibid.

[61] U.S. Congress, Senate Committee on Small Business, *Small Business Administration's Size Standards*, hearing, 97th Cong., 1st sess., May 5, 1981 (Washington: GPO, 1981), p. 11.

[62] Ibid., p. 25.

[63] Ibid., pp. 4, 10, 16.

(P.L. 96-481). It prohibited "the SBA from promulgating any final rule or regulation relating to small business size standards until March 31, 1981."[64] In the meantime, the Reagan Administration entered office, and, as is customary when there is a change in Administration, replaced the SBA's senior leadership.

The SBA's new Administrator, Michael Cardenas, was sympathetic to the concerns of federal agencies that the proposed size standards in the services and construction industries were set too low to meet those agencies' procurement needs. As a result, he indicated that the SBA would modify its size standards proposal by (1) increasing the proposed size standards for 51 industries, mostly in the services and construction industries; (2) lowering the proposed size standards in 157 manufacturing industries (typically from no more than 2,500 employees to no more than 500 employees) to prevent one or more of the largest producers in those industries from being classified as small; and (3) increasing the SBA's proposed lowest size standard from no more than 15 employees to no more than 25 employees (affecting 93 service and trade industries).[65] The net effect of these changes would have restored eligibility for approximately 60,000 of the 225,000 firms expected to lose eligibility under the previous Administration's proposal.[66]

The SBA subsequently met with various trade organizations and federal agency procurement officials to discuss the proposal. As these consultations took place, the SBA experienced another turnover in its senior leadership.

The SBA, headed by the new appointee, James C. Sanders, issued a notice of proposed rulemaking concerning its size standards on May 3, 1982.[67] The proposal differed from its March 10, 1980, predecessor in three ways:

---

[64] Ibid., p. 5; and P.L. 96-481, the Small Business Export Expansion Act of 1980.

[65] U.S. Congress, Senate Committee on Small Business, *Small Business Administration's Size Standards*, hearing, 97th Cong., 1st sess., May 5, 1981 (Washington: GPO, 1981), p. 12.

[66] Ibid., p. 11.

[67] SBA, "Small Business Size Standards; Size Standards Revisions," 47 *Federal Register* 18992-19011, May 3, 1982.

> First, the range of size standards was narrowed to a range of 25 employees to 500 employees. This reflected a widespread view that 15 employees was too low a cutoff while 2,500 employees was too high. Second, SBA proposed a 500-employee ceiling, focusing on smaller firms. Third, SBA responded to sentiments within many procurement-sensitive industries that the proposed size standards in some cases were too low to accommodate the average procurement currently being performed by small business. Therefore, SBA proposed higher size standards in a number of procurement-sensitive industries, while maintaining the 500-employee cap.[68]

The SBA received over 500 comments on the proposed rule, with about 72% of those comments opposing the rule.[69]

Taking those comments into consideration, the SBA reexamined its size standards once again, and, after a year of further consultation with various trade organizations and federal agency procurement officials, issued another notice of proposed rulemaking on May 6, 1983.[70] The 1983 proposal (1) replaced the use of two sets of size standards, one for procurement and another for the SBA's loan and consultative support services, with a single set for all programs; (2) retained most of the size standards that were expressed in terms of average annual sales or receipts; (3) adjusted those size standards for inflation (an upward adjustment of 81%); (4) retained most of the size standards for manufacturing; and (5) made relatively minor changes to the size standards in other industries, with a continued emphasis on a 500-employee ceiling for most industries.

---

[68] U.S. Congress, House Committee on Small Business, Subcommittee on SBA and SBIC Authority, Minority Enterprise and General Small Business Problems, *Size Standards*, hearing, 98th Cong., 1st sess., October 20, 1983 (Washington: GPO, 1983), p. 17. Congress created the Small Business Investment Company (SBIC) program in 1958 to provide small businesses enhanced access to equity capital, long-term loans, and consultative management assistance.

[69] U.S. Congress, House Committee on Small Business, Subcommittee on SBA and SBIC Authority, Minority Enterprise and General Small Business Problems, *H.R. 1178· Small Business Size Standards*, hearing, 99th Cong., 1st sess., July 30, 1985 (Washington: GPO, 1985), p. 198.

[70] SBA, "Small Business Size Standards; Revision," 48 *Federal Register* 20560-20590, May 6, 1983.

The SBA received 630 comments on the proposed rule, with almost 70% supporting it.[71]

SBA Administrator Sanders characterized the SBA's revised size standard proposal as "a fine-tuning of current standards which has the basic support of both the private sector and the Federal agencies that use the basic size standards to achieve their set-aside procurement goals."[72] He also added that "since almost no size standard is proposed to decrease, and most will in fact increase, very few firms will lose their small business status. We estimate that about 39,000 firms will gain small business status."[73] He testified that in percentage terms, in 1983, 97.9% of the nation's 5.2 million firms with employees were classified by the SBA as small. Under the SBA's proposal, 98.6% of all firms with employees would be classified as small.[74] The final rule was published in the *Federal Register* on February 9, 1984.[75]

Representative Parren J. Mitchell, chair of the House Committee on Small Business, expressed disappointment in the SBA's final rule, stating at a congressional oversight hearing on July 30, 1985, that "the government and the business community are still victimized by that same ad hoc, sporadic system that the SBA promised to fix some six years ago."[76] He introduced legislation (H.R. 1178, a bill to amend the Small Business Act) that would have required the SBA to adjust its size standard for an industrial classification downward by at least 20% if small business' share of that market equaled or exceeded 60%, and at least 40% of the market share was achieved through the receipt of federal procurement contracts. The bill also mandated a minimum 10% increase in the SBA's

---

[71] U.S. Congress, House Committee on Small Business, Subcommittee on SBA and SBIC Authority, Minority Enterprise and General Small Business Problems, *Size Standards*, hearing, 98th Cong., 1st sess., October 20, 1983 (Washington: GPO, 1983), p. 18.

[72] Ibid.

[73] Ibid.

[74] Ibid.

[75] SBA, "Small Business Size Standards; Revision," 49 *Federal Register* 5024-5048, February 9, 1984.

[76] U.S. Congress, House Committee on Small Business, Subcommittee on SBA and SBIC Authority, Minority Enterprise and General Small Business Problems, *H.R. 1178: Small Business Size Standards*, hearing, 99th Cong., 1st sess., July 30, 1985 (Washington: GPO, 1985), p. 4.

size standard for an industrial classification if small business' share of that market was less than 20% and less than 10% of the market share was achieved through the receipt of federal procurement contracts.[77] The bill was opposed by various trade associations, the SBA, and federal agency procurement officials, and was not reported out of committee.[78]

SBA Proposes to Streamline Its Size Standards

On December 31, 1992, the SBA issued a notice of proposed rulemaking "to streamline its size standards" by reducing the number of fixed size standard levels from 30 to 9.[79] The nine proposed size standards were no more than 100, 500, 750, 1,000, or 1,500 employees; and no more than $5 million, $10 million, $18 million, or $24 million in annual receipts. The annual receipts levels reflected an upward adjustment of 43% for inflation. The SBA argued that the proposed changes would make the size standards more user-friendly for small business owners and restore eligibility to nearly 20,000 firms that were no longer considered small solely because of the effects of inflation. The proposed rule was later withdrawn as a courtesy to allow the incoming Clinton Administration time to review it.[80] The SBA ultimately decided not to pursue this approach because it felt that converting "receipts based size standards in effect at that time to one of four proposed receipts levels created a number of unacceptable anomalies."[81]

Over the subsequent decade, the SBA reviewed the size standards for some industries on a piecemeal basis and, in 1994, adjusted for inflation its size standards based on firm's annual sales or receipts (an upward

---

[77] Ibid., pp. 237-250.

[78] Ibid., pp. 6, 8, 53, 153, 181, 244, 245, 261.

[79] SBA, "Small Business Size Standards: Fixed Size Standard Levels," 57 *Federal Register* 62515, December 31, 1992.

[80] U.S. Congress, House Committee on Small Business, Subcommittee on Minority Enterprise, Finance, and Urban Development, *SBA's Efforts to Streamline Size Standards*, hearing, 103rd Cong., 1st sess., May 25, 1993 (Washington: GPO, 1993), pp. 5, 6.

[81] SBA, "Small Business Size Standards: Restructuring of Size Standards," 69 *Federal Register* 13130, March 19, 2004.

adjustment of 48.2%). The SBA estimated that the adjustment would restore eligibility to approximately 20,000 firms that lost small-business status due solely to the effects of inflation.[82]

In 2002, the SBA adjusted for inflation its annual sales and receipts based size standards for the fourth time (an upward adjustment of 15.8%). The SBA estimated that the adjustment would restore eligibility to approximately 8,760 firms that lost small-business status due solely to the effects of inflation. The rule also included a provision that the SBA would assess the impact of inflation on its annual sales- and receipts based size standards at least once every five years.[83] Then, on March 19, 2004, the SBA, once again, issued a notice of proposed rulemaking to streamline its size standards.[84]

The proposed rule would have established size standards based on the firm's number of employees for all industries, avoiding the need to adjust for inflation size standards based on sales or receipts.[85] At that time, the SBA size standards consisted of 37 different size levels: 30 based on annual sales or receipts, 5 on the number of employees (both full- and part-time), 1 on financial assets, and 1 on generating capacity. Under the proposed rule, the SBA would use 10 size standards, 5 new employee size standards (adding no more than 50, 150, 200, 300, and 400 employees), and the existing 5 employee size standards (no more than 100, 500, 750, 1,000, and 1,500 employees).[86]

The proposed rule would not have changed any of the size standards that were already based on number of employees. The SBA argued that the use of a single size standard would "help to simplify size standards" and "tends to be a more stable measure of business size" than other measures.[87] It added that the proposed rule would change 514 size standards and that,

---

[82] SBA, "Small Business Size Standards: Inflation Adjusted Size Standards," 59 *Federal Register* 16513-16538, April 7, 1994.

[83] SBA, "Small Business Size Standards: Inflation Adjustment to Size Standards," 67 *Federal Register* 65285-65290, October 24, 2002.

[84] SBA, "Small Business Size Standards: Restructuring of Size Standards," 69 *Federal Register* 13129-13164, March 19, 2004.

[85] Ibid.

[86] Ibid., p. 13130.

[87] Ibid., pp. 13131-13132.

after the proposed conversion to the use of number of employees, of the "approximately 4.4 million businesses in the industries with revised size standards, 35,200 businesses could gain and 34,100 could lose small business eligibility, with the net effect of 1,100 additional businesses defined as small."[88]

The SBA received more than 4,500 comments on the proposed rule, with a majority (51%) supporting the rule, but with "a large number of comments opposing various aspects of SBA's approach to simplifying size standards."[89] In addition, the chairs of the House Committee on Small Business and Senate Committee on Small Business and Entrepreneurship opposed the proposed rule, largely because they were concerned about potential job losses resulting from more than 34,000 small businesses losing program eligibility.[90] The SBA withdrew the proposed rule on July 1, 2004.

In 2005, the SBA adjusted for inflation size standards based on firms' annual sales or receipts (an upward adjustment of 8.7%). The SBA estimated that the adjustment restored eligibility to approximately 12,000 firms that lost small-business status due solely to the effects of inflation. In 2008, the SBA made another adjustment for inflation to its annual sales and receipts based standards (another upward adjustment of 8.7%). The SBA estimated that the adjustment restored eligibility for approximately 10,400 firms that lost small-business status due solely to the effects of inflation.[91]

---

[88] Ibid., p. 13138.

[89] SBA, "Small Business Size Standards: Selected Size Standards Issues," 69 *Federal Register* 70197, December 3, 2004; and SBA, "Small Business Size Standards: Selected Size Standards Issues," 70 *Federal Register* 2976, January 19, 2005.

[90] Rep. Donald A. Manzullo and Rep. Nydia M. Velázquez, "Small Business Size Standards; Restructuring of Size Standards," 69 *Federal Register* 13,130 (March 19, 2004); Letter to Gary M. Jackson, SBA Assistant Administrator for Size Standards, July 8, 2004; and U.S. Newswire, "Snowe Hails SBA's Withdrawal of New Size Standards Proposal; Decision Spares Small Firms Costly Disruptions," July 1, 2004, p. 1, at http://proquest.umi.com/pqdweb?did=657675071&sid=1&Fmt=3&clientId=45714&RQT=309&VName=PQD.

[91] SBA, "Small Business Size Standards, Inflation Adjustment to Size Standards; Business Loan Program; Disaster Assistance Loan Program," 70 *Federal Register* 72577, December 6, 2005; and SBA, "Small Business Size Standards: Inflation Adjustment to Size Standards; Business Loan Program, and Disaster Assistance Loan Program," 73 *Federal Register* 41237-41254, July 18, 2008.

BA Adopts a More Incremental, Targeted Approach

In June 2008, the SBA announced that it would undertake a comprehensive, two-year review of its size standards, proceeding one industrial sector at a time, starting with Retail Trade (NAICS Sector 44-45), Accommodations and Food Services (NAICS Sector 72), and Other Services (NAICS Sector 81).[92] The SBA argued that it was concerned that "not all of its size standards may now adequately define small businesses in the U.S. economy, which has seen industry consolidations, technological advances, emerging new industries, shifting societal preferences, and other significant industrial changes."[93] It added that its reliance on an ad hoc approach "scrutinizing the limited number of specific industries during a year, while worthwhile, leaves unexamined many deserving industries for updating and may create over time a set of illogical size standards."[94]

The SBA announced that it would begin its analysis of its size standards by assuming that "$6.5 million [now $7.5 million] is an appropriate size standard for those industries with receipts size standards and 500 employees for those industries with employee size standards."[95] It would then analyze the following industry characteristics: "average firm size; average asset size (a proxy for startup costs); competition, as measured by the market share of the four largest firms in the industry; and, the distribution of market share by firm size—that is, are firms in the industry generally very small firms, or dominated by very large firms."[96] Then, before making its final determination on the size standard, it would "examine the participation of small businesses in federal contracting and SBA's guaranteed loan program at the current size standard level.

---

[92] SBA, "Small Business Size Standards: Public Meetings on a Comprehensive Review of Small Business Size Standards," 73 *Federal Register* 30440-30442, May 27, 2008. Other Services (NAICS Sector 81) include repair and maintenance, personal and laundry services, and religious, grantmaking, civic, professional, and similar organizations.

[93] SBA, "Small Business Size Standards: Public Meetings on a Comprehensive Review of Small Business Size Standards," 73 *Federal Register* 30441, May 27, 2008.

[94] Ibid.

[95] SBA, "Size Standards Comprehensive Review," June 3, 2008.

[96] Ibid.

Depending on the level of small business participation, additional consideration may be given to the level of the current size standard and the analysis of industry factors."[97]

The SBA later announced that it planned to issue a notice of proposed rulemaking concerning size standards for Retail Trade (NAICS Sector 44-45), Accommodations and Food Services (NAICS Sector 72), and Other Services (NAICS Sector 81) in January 2009.[98] The SBA issued the notices for those industries on October 21, 2009.[99]

In April 2009, the SBA announced that was simplifying the administration and use of its size standards by reducing the number of receipts based size standards it used when establishing a new size standard or reviewing an existing size standard:

> For many years, SBA has been concerned about the complexity of determining small business status caused by a large number of varying receipts based size standards (see 69 FR 13130 (March 4, 2004) and 57 FR 62515 (December 31, 1992)). At the start of current comprehensive size standards review, there were 31 different levels of receipts based size standards. They ranged from $0.75 million to $35.5 million, and many of them applied to one or only a few industries. The SBA believes that to have so many different size standards with small variations among them is unnecessary and difficult to justify analytically. To simplify managing and using size standards, SBA proposes that there be fewer size standard levels. This will produce more common size standards for businesses operating in related industries. This will also result in greater consistency among the size standards for industries that have similar economic characteristics.

---

97 Ibid.

98 SBA, "Small Business Administration Semiannual Regulatory Agenda," 73 *Federal Register* 71449, 71450, November 24, 2008.

99 SBA, "Small Business Size Standards: Retail Trade," 74 *Federal Register* 53924-53940, October 21, 2009; SBA, "Small Business Size Standards: Accommodation and Food Services Industries," 74 *Federal Register* 53913-53924, October 21, 2009; and SBA, "Small Business Size Standards: Other Services Industries," 74 *Federal Register* 53941 53954, October 21, 2009.

> Under the current comprehensive size standards review, SBA is proposing to establish eight "fixed-level" receipts based size standards: $5.0 million, $7.0 million, $10.0 million, $14.0 million, $19.0 million, $25.5 million, $30.0 million, and $35.5 million. These levels are established by taking into consideration the minimum, maximum and the most commonly used current receipts based size standards.[100]

These eight receipts-based size standards were increased to $5.5 million, $7.5 million, $11.0 million, $15.0 million, $20.5 million, $27.5 million, $32.5 million, and $38.5 million in 2014 to account for inflation.[101]

The SBA also announced in 2009 that it would use eight employee based size standards when establishing a new size standard or reviewing an existing size standard: no more than 50, 100, 150, 200, 250, 500, 750, and 1,000 employees.[102] At that time, the SBA had seven employee based size standards: no more than 50, 100, 150, 500, 750, 1,000, and 1,500 employees. The SBA stopped using the no more than 1,500 employee size standard when establishing a new or reviewing an existing size standard, noting that only three manufacturing industries had a no more than 1,500 employee size standard at that time.[103]

The SBA also announced that "to simplify size standards further" it "may propose a common size standard for closely related industries."[104] The SBA argued

> although the size standard analysis may support a separate size standard for each industry, SBA believes that establishing different size standards for closely related industries may not always be appropriate. For example, in cases where many of the same businesses operate in the

---

100 SBA, "Small Business Size Standards Methodology," April 2009, pp. 21, 22, at http://www.sba.gov/sites/default/ files/size_standards_methodology.pdf.

101 SBA, "Small Business Size Standards: Inflation Adjustment to Monetary Size Standards," 79 *Federal Register* 33647-33669, June 12, 2014; and SBA, "Small Business Size Standards: Inflation Adjustment to Monetary Based Size Standards," 81 *Federal Register* 3949-3956, January 25, 2016.

102 SBA, "Small Business Size Standards Methodology," April 2009, p. 23, at http://www.sba.gov/sites/default/files/ size_standards_methodology.pdf.

103 Ibid.

104 Ibid., pp. 22-23.

same multiple industries, a common size standard for those industries might better reflect the Federal marketplace. This might also make size standards among related industries more consistent than separate size standards for each of those industries.[105]

Table 2. Industry Size Standards Being Applied during the SBA's Ongoing Review of Its Small Business Size Standards

Receipts Based Levels	**Employee Based Levels**
No more than $5.5 million	No more than 50 employees
No more than $7.5 million (anchor)	No more than 100 employees (wholesale trade anchor)
No more than $11.0 million	No more than 150 employees
No more than $15.0 million	No more than 200 employees
No more than $20.5 million	No more than 250 employees
No more than $27.5 million	No more than 500 employees (manufacturing anchor)
No more than $32.5 million	No more than 750 employees
No more than $38.5 million	No more than 1,000 employees
	No more than 1,250 employees
	No more than 1,500 employees

Source: U.S. Small Business Administration, "Small Business Size Standards Methodology," April 2009, pp. 21-23, at http://www.sba.gov/sites/default/files/size_standards_methodology.pdf; U.S. Small Business Administration, "Small Business Size Standards: Inflation Adjustment to Monetary Size Standards," 79 *Federal Register* 33647 33669, June 12, 2014; U.S. Small Business Administration, "Small Business Size Standards: Inflation Adjustment to Monetary Based Size Standards," 81 *Federal Register* 3949-3956, January 25, 2016; and U.S. Small Business Administration, "Small Business Size Standards for Manufacturing," 81 *Federal Register* 4469-4492, January 26, 2016.

Notes: The SBA currently has 27 SBA industry size standards in effect: 16 receipts based size standards, 9 employee based sized standards (no firms currently have the no more than 50 employees size standard), 1 asset based size standard, and 1 size standard based on a combination of the number of employees and barrel per day refining capacity).

As mentioned previously, effective February 26, 2016, the SBA added a new employee based size standard (no more than 1,250 employees) and reinstated the use of another (no more than 1,500 employees) when establishing a new, or revising an existing, size standard.[106]

---

[105] Ibid., p. 23.

[106] SBA, "Small Business Size Standards for Manufacturing," 79 *Federal Register* 54150, September 10, 2014; SBA, "Small Business Size Standards for Manufacturing," 80 *Federal Register* 78044, December 15, 2015; and SBA, "Small Business Size Standards for

Table 2 shows the 8 receipts based size standards and 10 employee based size standards that the SBA applies when establishing a new, or revising an existing, size standard.

The SBA issued the final rules for size standards for the Retail Trade (NAICS Sector 44-45), Accommodations and Food Services (NAICS Sector 72), and Other Services (NAICS Sector 81) industries in the *Federal Register* on October 6, 2010, with an effective date of November 5, 2010.[107] The SBA increased size standards for 46 of the 76 industries in Retail Trade (NAICS Sector 44-45), 5 of the 15 industries in Accommodations and Food Services (NAICS Sector 72), and 18 of the 47 industries in Other Services (NAICS Sector 81).[108]

The SBA's analysis supported a decrease to the size standards for 23 industries in Retail Trade (NAICS Sector 44-45), 7 industries in Accommodations and Food Services (NAICS Sector 72), and 20 industries in Other Services (NAICS Sector 81). However, the SBA retained those size standards because "proposing to lower small business size standards would be inconsistent with its on-going effort to promote small business assistance under the Recovery Act."[109] The SBA has continued the practice of retaining size standards when the SBA's economic analysis supports a

---

Manufacturing," 81 *Federal Register* 4469-4492, January 26, 2016. On September 10, 2014, the SBA announced its intention to eliminate its no more than 150 employee based size standard in its proposed rule for industries with employee based size standards not part of the manufacturing, wholesale trade, and retail trade industries. However, the SBA decided to retain the no more than 150 employee-size standard in the size standard final rule for those industries, which was issued on January 26, 2016. See SBA, "Small Business Size Standards: Industries With Employee Based Size Standards Not Part of Manufacturing, Wholesale Trade, or Retail Trade," 79 *Federal Register* 53647, September 10, 2014; and SBA, "Small Business Size Standards: Industries With Employee Based Size Standards Not Part of Manufacturing, Wholesale Trade, or Retail Trade," 81 *Federal Register* 4436-4469, January 26, 2016.

[107] SBA, "Small Business Size Standards: Retail Trade," 75 *Federal Register* 61597-61604, October 6, 2010; SBA, "Small Business Size Standards: Accommodations and Food Service Industries," 75 *Federal Register* 61604-61609, October 6, 2010; and SBA, "Small Business Size Standards: Other Services," 75 *Federal Register* 61591-61596, October 6, 2010. The final rule for the retail trade industries also converted the measure of size for new car dealers from annual receipts to number of employees.

[108] Ibid.

[109] SBA, "Small Business Size Standards: Retail Trade," 75 *Federal Register* 61598, October 6, 2010; SBA, "Small Business Size Standards: Accommodations and Food Service Industries," 75 *Federal Register* 61605, October 6, 2010; and SBA, "Small Business Size Standards: Other Services," 75 *Federal Register* 61592, October 6, 2010.

decrease because "lowering small business size standards is not in the best interest of small businesses in the current economic environment" and would "run counter to what SBA and the federal government are doing to help small businesses and create jobs."[110] The SBA's only exception to this practice is if lowering the size standard is necessary to exclude dominant firms from becoming eligible for SBA assistance.

Congress Requires Periodic Size Standard Reviews

As mentioned previously, P.L. 111-240 requires the SBA to conduct a detailed review of not less than one-third of the SBA's industry size standards during the 18-month period beginning on the date of enactment (September 27, 2010) and during every 18-month period thereafter.[111]

The act directs the SBA to "make appropriate adjustments to the size standards" to reflect market conditions, and to report to the House Committee on Small Business and the Senate Committee on Small Business and Entrepreneurship and make publicly available "not later than 30 days" after the completion of each review information regarding the factors evaluated as part of each review, the criteria used for any revised size standard, and why the SBA did, or did not, adjust each size standard that was reviewed. The act also requires the SBA to ensure that each industry size standard is reviewed at least once every five years.[112]

On July 7, 2011, the SBA announced that its "comprehensive review of all small business size standards" would begin with the following six industries:

---

[110] SBA, "Small Business Size Standards: Agriculture, Forestry, Fishing, and Hunting," 77 *Federal Register* 55763, September 11, 2012.

[111] P.L. 111-240, the Small Business Act of 2010, §1344. Updated Size Standards.

[112] Ibid.

- Educational Services (final rule was issued on September 24, 2012);
- Health Care and Social Assistance Services (final rule was issued on September 24, 2012);
- Real Estate Rental and Leasing (final rule was issued on September 24, 2012);
- Administrative and Support, Waste Management and Remediation Services (final rule was issued on December 6, 2012);
- Information (final rule was issued on December 6, 2012); and
- Utilities (final rule was issued on December 23, 2013).[113]

The SBA subsequently completed size standard reviews for all industries in January 2016 (listed by when the final rule was issued) and is currently beginning its second five-year cycle of reviews for all of its size standards:

- Professional, Scientific and Technical Services (final rule was issued on February 24, 2012);
- Transportation and Warehousing (final rule was issued on February 24, 2012);
- Agriculture, Forestry, Fishing and Hunting (final rule was issued on June 20, 2013);
- Arts, Entertainment, and Recreation (final rule was issued on June 20, 2013);
- Finance and Insurance (final rule was issued on June 20, 2013);
- Management of Companies (final rule was issued on June 20, 2013);
- Support Activities for Mining (final rule was issued on June 20, 2013);
- Construction (final rule was issued on December 23, 2013);
- Wholesale Trade (final rule was issued on January 25, 2016);

---

[113] SBA, "Semiannual Regulatory Agenda," 76 *Federal Register* 40140-40142, July 7, 2011.

- Industries with Employee Based Size Standards not Part of Manufacturing, Wholesale Trade, or Retail Trade (final rule was issued on January 26, 2016); and
- Manufacturing (final rule was issued on January 26, 2016).

A summary of the final rules issued for each industry is provided in Table A-1.

In addition, effective October 1, 2017, the SBA amended its small business size standards to incorporate the U.S. Office of Management and Budget's (OMB's) 2017 NAICS designations. NAICS 2017 created 21 new industries by reclassifying, combining, or splitting 29 existing industries designated under NAICS 2012. The SBA's size standards for the industries affected by OMB's revisions increased size standards for six NAICS 2012 industries and part of another, decreased size standards for two others, changed the size standards measure from average annual receipts to number of employees for another, and resulted in no change for 20 industries and parts of another.[114]

SBA's Definitions for Small Business

The SBA, relying on statutory language, defines a small business as a concern that is organized for profit; has a place of business in the United States; operates primarily within the United States or makes a significant contribution to the economy through payment of taxes or use of American products, materials, or labor; is independently owned and operated; and is not dominant in its field on a national basis. The business may be a sole proprietorship, partnership, corporation, or any other legal form.[115]

---

[114] SBA, "Small Business Size Standards; Adoption of 2017 North American Industry Classification System for Size Standards," 82 *Federal Register* 18253, April 18, 2017; and SBA, "Small Business Size Standards; Adoption of 2017 North American Industry Classification System for Size Standards," 82 *Federal Register* 44886-44895, September 27, 2017.

[115] 13 C.F.R. §121.105. Affiliations between businesses, or relationships allowing one party control or the power of control over another, generally count in size determinations.

The SBA uses two measures to determine if a business is small: industry specific size standards or a combination of the business's net worth and net income. For example, the SBA's Small Business Investment Company (SBIC) program allows businesses to qualify as small if they meet the SBA's size standard for the industry in which the applicant is primarily engaged, or an alternative net worth and net income based size standard which has been established for the SBIC program. The SBIC's alternative size standard is currently set as a maximum net worth of not more than $19.5 million and average after-tax net income for the preceding two years of not more than $6.5 million.[116] All of the company's subsidiaries, parent companies, and affiliates are considered in determining if it meets the size standard. The SBA decided to apply the net worth and net income measures to the SBIC program "because investment companies evaluate businesses using these measures to decide whether or not to make an investment in them."[117]

Businesses participating in the SBA's 504/Certified Development Company (504/CDC) loan guaranty program are to be deemed small if they did not have a tangible net worth in excess of $8.5 million and did not have an average net income in excess of $3 million after taxes for the preceding two years.[118] As discussed below, P.L. 111-240 increased these threshold amounts on an interim basis to not more than $15 million in tangible net worth and not more than $5 million in average net income after federal taxes for the two full fiscal years before the date of the

---

Businesses can thus be determined to be other than small because of their involvement in joint ventures, subcontracting arrangements, or franchise or license agreements, among other things, provided that their personnel numbers or income, plus those of their affiliate(s), are over the pertinent size threshold. 13 C.F.R. §121.103. For further analysis, see CRS Report R44844, *SBA's "8(a) Program": Overview, History, and Current Issues*, by Robert Jay Dilger.

116 13 C.F.R. §107.700; 13 C.F.R. §107.710; 13 C.F.R. §301(c)(2); and 13 C.F.R. §301(c)(1).

117 SBA, Office of Government Contracting and Business Development, "SBA Size Standards Methodology," April 2009, p. 8, at http://www.sba.gov/sites/default/files/size_standards_methodology.pdf.

118 SBA, "SOP 50 10 5(C): Lender and Development Company Loan Programs," (effective October 1, 2010), p. 266, at http://www.sba.gov/sites/default/files/serv_sops_50105c_loan_0.pdf; and SBA, "SOP 50 10 5(E): Lender and Development Company Loan Programs," (effective June 1, 2012), p. 92, at http://www.sba.gov/sites/default/files/SOP%2050%2010%205(E)%20(6-27-2013)%20change%20of%20ownership%20eff%20date%207-1-13%20clean.pdf.

application. All of the company's subsidiaries, parent companies, and affiliates are considered in determining if it meets the size standard. Also, before May 5, 2009, businesses participating in the SBA's 7(a) loan guaranty program, including its express programs, were deemed small if they met the SBA's size standards for firms in the industries described in NAICS.[119]

Alternative Size Standards

Using authority provided under P.L. 111-5, the American Recovery and Reinvestment Act of 2009, the SBA temporarily applied the 504/CDC program's size standards as an alternative for 7(a) loans approved from May 5, 2009, through September 30, 2010.[120] Firms applying for a 7(a) loan during that time period qualified as small using either the SBA's industry size standards or the 504/CDC program's size standard. The provision's intent was to enhance the ability of small businesses to access the capital necessary to create and retain jobs during the economic recovery.

P.L. 111-240 made the use of alternative size standards for the 7(a) program permanent. The act directs the SBA to establish an alternative size standard for both the 7(a) and 504/CDC programs that uses maximum tangible net worth and average net income as an alternative to the use of industry standards. The act also establishes, until the date on which the alternative size standard is established, an interim alternative size standard for the 7(a) and 504/CDC programs of not more than $15 million in tangible net worth and not more than $5 million in average net income after federal taxes (excluding any carry-over losses) for the two full fiscal years before the date of the application.[121]

---

[119] 13 C.F.R. §121.201.

[120] SBA, "Small Business Size Standards; Temporary Alternative Size Standards for 7(a) Business Loan Program," 74 *Federal Register* 20577, May 5, 2009.

[121] P.L. 111-240, the Small Business Act of 2010, §1116. Alternative Size Standards. S. 3103, the Small Business Job Creation Act of 2010, introduced by then-Senator Olympia Snowe on March 10, 2010, and referred to the Senate Committee on Finance, and S. 2869, the Small

Industry Size Standards

The SBA Administrator has the authority to establish and modify size standards for particular industries. Overall, the SBA currently classifies about 97% of all employer firms as small.[122] These firms account for about 30% of industry receipts.

The SBA generally "prefers to use average annual receipts as a size measure because it measures the value of output of a business and can be easily verified by business tax returns and financial records."[123] However, historically, the SBA has used the number of employees to determine if manufacturing and mining companies are small. As a starting point, the SBA

> presumes $7.0 million [now $7.5 million] as an appropriate size standard for the services, retail trade, construction, and other industries with receipts based size standards; 500 employees for the manufacturing, mining and other industries with employee based size standards; and 100 employees for the wholesale trade industries. These three levels, referred to as "anchor size standards," are not minimum size standards, but rather benchmarks or starting points. To the extent an industry displays "differing

---

Business Job Creation and Access to Capital Act of 2009, introduced by Senator Mary Landrieu on December 10, 2009, and reported favorably by the Senate Committee on Small Business and Entrepreneurship, would have authorized the SBA to establish an alternative size standard for the SBA's 7(a) and 504/CDC loan programs. Both bills would have used maximum tangible net worth of not more than $15 million and average net income after federal taxes of not more than $5 million for the two full fiscal years before the date of the application as an alternative to the use of the SBA's industry size standards. Senator Snowe stated on the Senate floor, on December 10, 2009, that the proposed alternative size standard in S. 2869 would "help more small businesses meet the SBA's requirements to access SBA-backed loans." Senator Olympia Snowe, "Statements on Introduced Bills and Joint Resolutions," remarks in the Senate, *Congressional Record*, daily edition, vol. 155, no. 185 (December 10, 2009), p. S12913.

122 SBA, "SBA's Size Standards Analysis: An Overview on Methodology and Comprehensive Size Standards Review," power point presentation, Khem R. Sharma, SBA Office of Size Standards, July 13, 2011, p. 4, at http://www.actgov.org/sigcom/SIGs/SIGs/SBSIG/Documents/2011%20-%20Documents%20and%20Presentations/Size%20Stds%20Presentation_SIG%20Meeting.pdf.

123 SBA, Office of Government Contracting and Business Development, "SBA Size Standards Methodology," April 2009, p. 8, at http://www.sba.gov/sites/default/files/size_standards_methodology.pdf.

industry characteristics," a size standard higher, or in some cases lower, than an anchor size standard is supportable.[124]

Before a proposed change to the size standards can take effect, the SBA's Office of Size Standards (OSS) undertakes an analysis of the change's likely impact on the affected industry, focusing on the industry's overall degree of competition and the competitiveness of the firms within the industry. The analysis includes an assessment of the following five industry factors: average firm size, degree of competition within the industry, start-up costs and entry barriers, distribution of firms by size, and small business share in federal contracts.[125] The SBA also considers several other secondary factors "as they are relevant to the industries and the interests of small businesses, including technological change, competition among industries, industry growth trends, and impacts on SBA programs."[126]

Any changes to size standards must follow the rulemaking procedures of the Administrative Procedure Act. A proposed rule changing a size standard is first published in the *Federal Register*, allowing for public comment. It must include documentation establishing that a significant problem exists that requires a revision of the size standard, plus an economic analysis of the change. Comments from the public, plus any other new information, are reviewed and evaluated before a final rule is promulgated establishing a new size standard.

The SBA currently uses employment size to determine eligibility for 504 of 1,037 industries (48.6%), including all 360 manufacturing industries, 24 mining industries, and 71 wholesale trade industries. As of October 1, 2017,

---

[124] Ibid., p. 1. The SBA established 500 employees as its anchor size standard for manufacturing industries at the SBA's inception in 1953. Shortly thereafter, the SBA established a receipts based anchor size standard of $1 million in average annual receipts for nonmanufacturing industries. The receipts based anchor size standard has been adjusted periodically for inflation.

[125] 13 C.F.R. §121.102.

[126] SBA, Office of Government Contracting and Business Development, "SBA Size Standards Methodology," April 2009, p. 1, at http://www.sba.gov/sites/default/files/size_standards_methodology.pdf.

- 98 manufacturing industries have an upper limit of 500 employees (27.2%); 91 have an upper limit of 750 employees (25.2%); 89 have an upper limit of 1,000 employees (24.7%); 56 have an upper limit of 1,250 employees (15.6%); and 26 have an upper limit of 1,500 employees (7.2%).[127]
- three of the 24 mining industries have an upper limit of 250 employees (12.5%), seven have an upper limit of 500 employees (29.2%), seven have an upper limit of 750 employees (29.2%), two have an upper limit of 1,000 employees (8.3%), three have an upper limit of 1,250 employees (12.5%), and two have an upper limit of 1,500 employees (8.3%).[128]
- 25 of the 71 wholesale trades industries have an upper limit of 100 employees (35.2%), 16 have an upper limit of 150 employees (22.5%), 21 have an upper limit of 200 employees (29.6%), and 9 have an upper limit of 250 employees (12.7%).[129]

The SBA currently has nine employee based industry size standards in effect (no more than 100, 150, 200, 250, 500, 750, 1,000, 1,250, and 1,500 employees).

The SBA uses average annual receipts over the three most recently completed fiscal years to determine program eligibility for most other industries (527 of 1,037 industries, or 50.8%).[130] The SBA also uses average asset size as reported in the firm's four quarterly financial statements for the preceding year to determine eligibility for five finance

---

[127] SBA, "Small Business Size Standards for Manufacturing," 81 *Federal Register* 4469-4492, January 26, 2016.

[128] SBA, "Table of Small Business Size Standards," at http://www.sba.gov/content/table-small-business-size-standards.

[129] SBA, "Small Business Size Standards: Employee Based Size Standards in Wholesale Trade and Retail Trade," 81 *Federal Register* 3941-3949, January 25, 2016. Until February 26, 2016 (and since 1986) all industries in the Wholesale Trade Sector had an upper limit of 100 employees. See SBA, "Table of Small Business Size Standards," July 14, 2014, at http://www.sba.gov/content/table-small-business-size-standards. Also, for procurement purposes, the SBA's size standard is no more than 500 employees for all industries in both the Retail Trade and Wholesale Trade Sectors.

[130] The annual receipts of a concern which has been in business for fewer than three complete fiscal years is determined by dividing the total receipts for the period the concern has been in business by the number of weeks in business, multiplied by 52. See 13 C.F.R. §121.104.

industries, and a combination of number of employees and barrel per day refining capacity for petroleum refineries.[131]

The SBA currently has 16 receipts based industry size standards in effect.[132] In some instances, there is considerable variation in the size standards used within each industrial sector. For example, the SBA uses 11 different size standards to determine eligibility for 66 industries in the retail trade sector. In general

- most administrative and support service industries have an upper limit of either $15.0 million or $20.5 million in average annual sales or receipts;
- most agricultural industries have an upper limit of $0.75 million in average annual sales or receipts;[133]
- most construction of buildings and civil engineering construction industries have an upper limit of $36.5 million in average annual sales or receipts, and most construction specialty trade contractors have an upper limit of $15.0 million in average annual sales or receipts;
- most educational services industries have an upper limit of either $7.5 million or $11.0 million in average annual sales or receipts;
- most health care industries have an upper limit of either $7.5 million or $15.0 million in average annual sales or receipts;
- most social assistance industries have an upper limit of $11.0 million in average annual sales or receipts;

---

131 SBA, "Table of Small Business Size Standards," July 14, 2014, at http://www.sba.gov/content/table-small-businesssize-standards.

132 The receipts based size standards in use as of April 21, 2016 were no more than: $0.75 million, $5.5 million, $7.5 million, $11.0 million, $15.0 million, $18.0 million, $19.0 million, $20.5 million, $25.0 million, $27.5 million, $29.5 million, $32.0 million, $32.5 million, $36.5 million, $37.5 million, and $38.5 million.

133 P.L. 99-272, the Consolidated Omnibus Budget Reconciliation Act of 1985 (Title XVIII, Section 18016) inserted a requirement that notwithstanding any other provision of law, an agricultural enterprise shall be deemed to be a small business concern if it, including its affiliates, has annual receipts not in excess of $500,000. P.L. 106-554, the Consolidated Appropriations Act, 2001 (Title VIII, Section 806(b)), substituted "$750,000" for "$500,000."

- there is considerable variation within the professional, scientific, and technical service industries, ranging from an upper limit of $7.5 million in average annual sales or receipts to $38.5 million;
- there is considerable variation within the transportation and warehousing industrial sector, ranging from an upper limit of $7.5 million in average annual sales or receipts to $38.5 million for 43 industries and from an upper limit of 500 employees to 1,500 employees for 15 industries); and
- most finance and insurance industries have an upper limit of $38.5 million in average annual sales or receipts.

The SBA also applies a $550 million average asset limit (as reported in the firm's four quarterly financial statements for the preceding year) to determine eligibility in five finance industries: commercial banks, saving institutions, credit unions, other depository credit intermediation, and credit card issuing.[134]

As mentioned previously, the SBA is currently using eight receipts based size standards when establishing new or reviewing existing size standards. The SBA has argued that reducing the number of receipts based size standards will simplify the management and use of size standards and provide "greater consistency in size standards among industries that are similar in their economic characteristics."[135]

The SBA's decision to reduce the number of receipts based size standards and to use a common size standard for closely related industries when establishing or approving industry size standards raised the possibility of establishing or approving a size standard that may not be directly supported by its economic assessment of that industrial classification. For example, in the final rule issued for Professional, Technical, and Scientific Services (Sector 54), on February 10, 2012, the SBA argued that "it should continue to maintain similar or comparable size

---

[134] SBA, "Table of Small Business Size Standards," at http://www.sba.gov/content/table-small-business-size-standards.

[135] SBA, Office of Government Contracting and Business Development, "SBA Size Standards Methodology," April 2009, p. 22, at http://www.sba.gov/sites/default/files/size_standards_methodology.pdf.

standards among the surveying and mapping industries and the architectural and engineering service industries."[136] As a result

> although the industry data point to a size standard higher than $14 million for NAICS 541360 and lower than $14 million for NAICS 541370, SBA believes a common size standard of $14 million is more appropriate than establishing two very different size standards for the two very similar types of industries, because (1) it represents a significant increase to the current size standard, as the commenters desired and (2) it maintains the historical common size standard between mapping and surveying services and architecture and engineering services.[137]

H.R. 3987, the Small Business Protection Act of 2012, introduced on February 8, 2012, and ordered to be reported by the House Committee on Small Business on March 21, 2012, addressed the SBA's practice of combining size standards within industrial groups to promote greater consistency for industries that have similar economic characteristics.

The bill would have authorized the SBA's Administrator to "establish or approve a single size standard for a grouping of four digit North American Industrial Classification codes only if the Administrator makes publicly available, not later than the date on which such size standard is established or approved, a justification demonstrating that such size standard is appropriate for each individual industry classification included in the grouping."[138] The bill would have required the SBA's Administrator

> to provide a detailed description of the industry for which the new size standard is proposed; an analysis of the competitive environment for that industry; the approach the Administrator used to develop the proposed standard including the source of all data used to develop the proposed rulemaking; and the anticipated effect of the proposed rulemaking on the industry, including the number of concerns not

[136] SBA, "Small Business Size Standards: Professional, Technical, and Scientific Services," 77 *Federal Register* 7498, February 10, 2012.

[137] Ibid.

[138] H.R. 3987, the Small Business Protection Act of 2012, Section 2, Small Business Concern Size Standards.

currently considered small that would be considered small under the proposed rulemaking and the number of concerns currently considered small that would be deemed other than small under the proposed rulemaking.[139]

P.L. 112-239, the National Defense Authorization Act for Fiscal Year 2013, which became law on January 2, 2013, included these provisions. The Senate's version of the bill did not include these provisions, but the conference report accompanying the bill (H.R. 4310), which was agreed to by the House on December 20, 2012, and by the Senate on December 21, 2012, included them.

Other Federal Agency Size Standards

Many federal statutes provide special considerations for small businesses. For example, small businesses are provided preferences through set-asides and sole source awards in federal contracting and pay lower fees to apply for patents and trademarks.[140] In most instances, businesses are required to meet the SBA's size standards to be considered a small business. However, in some cases, the underlying statute defines the eligibility criteria for defining a small business. In other cases, the statute authorizes the implementing agency to make those determinations.

Under current law, a federal agency that decides that it would like to exercise its authority to establish its own size standard through the federal rulemaking process is required to, among other things, (1) undertake an

---

[139] Ibid.

[140] The federal government has a goal of awarding at least 23% of all small business eligible federal government procurement contracts to small businesses, including 5% for small disadvantaged businesses, 5% for women-owned small businesses, 3% for small businesses owned by service-disabled veterans, and 3% for small businesses located in a HUBZone. See U.S. General Services Administration, Federal Procurement Data System – Next Generation, "Small Business Goaling Reports," at https://www.fpds.gov/fpdsng_cms/index.php/en/reports. For further information and analysis concerning federal contracting preferences for small businesses see CRS Report R41268, *Small Business Administration HUBZone Program*, by Robert Jay Dilger.

initial regulatory flexibility analysis to determine the potential impact of the proposed rule on small businesses, (2) transmit a copy of the initial regulatory flexibility analysis to the SBA's Chief Counsel for Advocacy for comment, and (3) publish the agency's response to any comments filed by the SBA's Chief Counsel for Advocacy in response to the proposed rule and a detailed statement of any change made to the proposed rule in the final rule as a result of those comments.[141] In addition, the federal agency must provide public notice of the proposed rule and an opportunity for the public to comment on the proposed rule, typically through the publication of an advanced notice of proposed rulemaking in the *Federal Register* and notification of interested small businesses and related organizations.[142] Also, prior to issuing the final rule, the federal agency must have the approval of the SBA's Administrator.[143] Under current practice, the SBA's Administrator, through the SBA's Office of Size Standards, consults with the SBA's Office of Advocacy prior to making a final decision concerning such requests.[144] The Office of Advocacy is an independent office within the SBA.

---

[141] 5 U.S.C. 601; 5 U.S.C. 603; and 5 U.S.C. 604. The SBA last published a list of size standards set by agencies other than the SBA in 1995. See SBA, "Small Business Size Standards," 60 *Federal Register* 57988-57991, November 24, 1995. For a related example (establishing a size standard for Regulatory Flexibility Act compliance), see U.S. Department of Commerce, National Oceanic and Atmospheric Administration, "Establish a Single Small Business Size Standard for Commercial Fishing Business," 80 *Federal Register* 81194-80872, December 29, 2015.

[142] 15 U.S.C. 632.

[143] Ibid. The SBA reports "that there have been approximately 25 requests by other agencies under the authority of amended §3 of the Small Business Act since the date of amendment in 1992." See U.S. Congress, House Committee on Small Business, *Small Business Size Standard Flexibility Act of 2011*, report to accompany H.R. 585, 112th Cong., 2nd sess., November 16, 2011, H.Rept. 112-288 (Washington: GPO, 2011), p. 7.

[144] Rep. Sam Graves, "Full Committee Hearing, Lifting the Weight of Regulations: Growing Jobs By Reducing Regulatory Burdens (III. H.R. 585—Small Business Size Standard Flexibility Act of 2011)," letter to House Committee on Small Business, June 8, 2011, p. 44, at http://smbiz.house.gov/UploadedFiles/6-15_Memo.pdf; U.S. Congressional Budget Office, "Congressional Budget Office Cost Estimate: H.R. 585—Small Business Size Standard Flexibility Act of 2011," p. 2, at http://www.cbo.gov/ftpdocs/124xx/doc12449/hr585.pdf; and U.S. Congress, House Committee on Small Business, *Small Business Size Standard Flexibility Act of 2011*, report to accompany H.R. 585, 112th Cong., 2nd sess., November 16, 2011, H.Rept. 112-288 (Washington: GPO, 2011), pp. 6-8. Also, see 13 C.F.R §121.901-903.

During the 112th Congress, H.R. 585, the Small Business Size Standard Flexibility Act of 2011, was reported by the House Committee on Small Business on November 16, 2011, by a vote of 13 to 8. The bill would have retained the SBA's Administrator's authority to approve or disapprove size standards for programs under the Small Business Act of 1953 (as amended) and the Small Business Investment Act of 1958 (as amended). The Office of Chief Counsel for Advocacy would have assumed the SBA Administrator's authority to approve or disapprove size standards for purposes of any other act.[145]

Similar legislative provisions have been introduced during the 113th Congress (H.R. 2542, the Regulatory Flexibility Improvements Act of 2013, and included in H.R. 4, the Jobs for America Act), 114th Congress (H.R. 527, the Small Business Regulatory Flexibility Improvements Act of 2015, and its Senate companion bill, S. 1536), and 115th Congress (H.R. 33, the Small Business Regulatory Flexibility Improvements Act of 2017, and its Senate companion bill, S. 584, and included in H.R. 5, the Regulatory Accountability Act of 2017).

Advocates of splitting the SBA Administrator's small business size standards' authority between the Office of Chief Counsel for Advocacy and the SBA's Administrator have argued that

> Should an agency wish to draft a regulation that adopts a size standard different from the one already adopted by the Administrator in regulations implementing the Small Business Act, the agency must obtain approval of the Administrator. However, that requires the Administrator to have a complete understanding of the regulatory regime of that other act—knowledge usually outside the expertise of the SBA. However, the Office of the Chief Counsel for Advocacy, an independent office within the SBA, represents the interests of small businesses in rulemaking

---

[145] U.S. Congressional Budget Office, "Congressional Budget Office Cost Estimate: H.R. 585—Small Business Size Standard Flexibility Act of 2011," p. 2, at http://www.cbo.gov/ftpdocs/124xx/doc12449/hr585.pdf; and H.Rept. 112 288, the Business Size Standard Flexibility Act of 2011. CBO has estimated that the Office of Advocacy would ultimately need 10 additional staff positions to implement its new authority; and that the bill would cost $6 million over the 2012-2016 period.

proceedings (as part of its responsibility to monitor agency compliance with the Regulatory Flexibility Act, 5 U.S.C. 601-12, (RFA)) does have such expertise. Therefore, it is logical to transfer the limited function on determining size standards of small businesses for purposes other than the Small Business Act and Small Business Investment Act of 1958 to the Office of the Chief Counsel for Advocacy...

the Administrator is not the proper official to determine size standards for purposes of other agencies' regulatory activities. The Administrator is not fluent with the vast array of federal regulatory programs, is not in constant communication with small entities that might be affected by another federal agency's regulatory regime, and does not have the analytical expertise to assess the regulatory impact of a particular size standard on small entities. Furthermore, the Administrator's standards are: very inclusive, not developed to comport with other agencies' regulatory regimes, and lack sufficient granularity to examine the impact of a proposed rule on a spectrum of small businesses.[146]

Opponents have argued that

When an agency is seeking to use a size standard other than those approved by the SBA, the agency may consult with the Office of Advocacy. Such consultation is sensible, as the Office of Advocacy has significant knowledge of the regulatory environment outside of the canon of SBA law. However, the SBA's Office of Size Standards, with its historical involvement, expertise, and staff resources in this area, remains the appropriate entity to approve such size standards....

While the legislation permits the SBA to continue to approve size standards for its enabling statutes, it removes SBA's authority to do so for other statutes. The result would be to create a duplicate size standard authority in both the SBA and the Office of Advocacy. Both the SBA and the Office of Advocacy would have personnel who would analyze and

---

[146] U.S. Congress, House Committee on Small Business, *Small Business Size Standard Flexibility Act of 2011*, report to accompany H.R. 585, 112th Cong., 2nd sess., November 16, 2011, H.Rept. 112-288 (Washington: GPO, 2011), p. 6.

> evaluate size standards. Through the bifurcation of these responsibilities, taxpayers would effectively be forgoing the economies of scale that are currently enjoyed by the operation of a single Office of Size Standards in the SBA....
>
> Having two such entities that have the same mission is not a transfer of function, but an inefficient and duplicative reorganization.... Instead of having one central office, there will now be two—further muddling small businesses' relationship with the federal government.[147]

Other Recent Legislation

Two bills were introduced during the 114th Congress (H.R. 3714, the Small Agriculture Producer Size Standards Improvements Act of 2015, and H.R. 4341, the Defending America's Small Contractors Act of 2016) to authorize the SBA to establish size standards for agricultural enterprises not later than 18 months after the date of enactment. The size standard for agricultural enterprises was, at that time, set in statute as having annual receipts not in excess of $750,000.[148] H.R. 4341, among other provisions, would have also limited an industry category to a greater extent than provided under the North American Industry Classification codes for small business procurement purposes if further segmentation of the industry category is warranted.[149]

H.R. 4341 was introduced on January 7, 2016, and ordered to be reported with amendment by the House Committee on Small Business on

147 Ibid., p. 14.

148 P.L. 99-272, the Consolidated Omnibus Budget Reconciliation Act of 1985, established the size standard for agricultural enterprises as annual receipts not in excess of $500,000. P.L. 106-554, the Consolidated Appropriations Act, 2001, increased the size standard for agricultural enterprises to annual receipts not in excess of $750,000.

149 The bill would authorize the SBA Administrator to limit an industry category due to special capital equipment needs, special labor requirements, special geographic requirements (with specified limitations), or to recognize a new industry. See H.R. 4341, the Defending America's Small Contractors Act of 2016, Sec. 101. Plain Language Rewrite of Requirements for Small Business Procurements.

January 13, 2016. H.R. 3714 was introduced on October 8, 2015, considered by the House under suspension of the rules on April 19, 2016, and agreed to by voice vote.

P.L. 114-328, the National Defense Authorization Act for Fiscal Year 2017, includes a provision which authorizes the SBA to establish different size standards for agricultural enterprises using existing methods and appeal processes.

CONGRESSIONAL POLICY OPTIONS

Historically, the SBA has relied on economic analysis of market conditions within each industry to define eligibility for small business assistance. On several occasions in its history, the SBA attempted to revise its small business size standards in a comprehensive manner. However, because (1) the Small Business Act provides leeway in how the SBA is to define small business; (2) there is no consensus on the economic factors that should be used in defining small business; (3) federal agencies have generally opposed size standards that might adversely affect their pool of available small business contractors; and (4) the SBA's initial size standards provided program eligibility to nearly all businesses, the SBA's efforts to undertake a comprehensive reassessment of its size standards met with resistance. Firms that might lose eligibility objected. Federal agencies also objected. As a result, in each instance, the SBA's comprehensive revisions were not fully implemented.

The SBA's congressionally mandated requirement to conduct a detailed review of at least one-third of the SBA's industry size standards every 18 months was imposed by P.L. 111-240, the Small Business Jobs Act of 2010, to prevent small business size standards from becoming outdated.[150] More frequent reviews of the size standards were expected to increase their accuracy and, generally speaking, result in (1) increased numbers of small businesses found to be eligible for SBA assistance and (2) an increase in the number and amount of federal contracts awarded to small businesses (primarily by preventing large businesses from being misclassified as small and by increasing the number of small businesses eligible to compete for federal contracts).[151]

As expected, the SBA's economic analyses during the recent five-year review cycle often supported an increase in the size standards for many industries. However, the SBA's economic analyses also occasionally supported a decrease in the size standards for some industries. The SBA has opted to increase their size standards when their economic analyses indicate that an increase is warranted, make no changes when their economic analyses indicate that no change is necessary, and, in most instances, make no changes when their economic analyses indicate that a decrease is warranted.

Despite the SBA's decision to, in most instances, make no changes when their economic analyses indicate that a decrease is warranted, it could be argued that the increased frequency of the reviews has generally prevented the SBA's size standards from becoming outdated. This, in turn, has, at least to a certain extent, improved the accuracy of the size standards (as measured by the extent to which the size standard is in alignment with the SBA's economic analyses).

---

[150] See U.S. Congress, Senate Committee on Small Business and Entrepreneurship, *Small Business Contracting Revitalization Act of 2010*, report to accompany S. 2989, 111th Cong., 2nd sess., September 29, 2010, S.Rept. 111-343 (Washington: GPO, 2010), p. 9. ...The Committee has heard testimony that the current size standards are in dire need of a comprehensive update.

[151] See Sen. Mary Landrieu, "Statements on Introduced Bills and Joint Resolutions: S. 2989 A bill to improve the Small Business Act, and for other purposes," remarks in the Senate, *Congressional Record*, vol. 156, part 17 (February 4, 2010), p. S487 "...The Committee has heard from a number of small businesses about large businesses parading as small businesses. It is imperative that small business contracts go to small businesses. Small businesses may be losing billions of dollars in opportunities because of size standard loopholes."

In a related matter, the SBA continues to adjust its receipts based size standards for inflation at least once every five years, or more frequently if inflationary circumstances warrant, to prevent firms from losing their small business eligibility solely due to the effects of inflation. The most recent adjustment for inflation took place on July 14, 2014.[152] Prior to that, the last adjustment for inflation took place in 2008.[153] The SBA also continues to review size standards within specific industries whenever it determines that market conditions within that industry have changed.

Congress has several options related to the SBA's ongoing review of its size standards. For example, as part of its oversight of the SBA, Congress can wait for the agency to issue its proposed rule before providing input or establish a dialogue with the agency, either at the staff level or with Members involved directly, prior to the issuance of its proposed rule. Historically, Congress has tended to wait for the SBA to issue proposed rules concerning its size standards before providing input, essentially deferring to the agency's expertise in the technical and methodological issues involved in determining where to draw the line between small and large firms. Congress has then tended to respond to the SBA's proposed rules concerning its size standards after taking into consideration current economic conditions and input received from the SBA and affected industries.

Waiting for the SBA to issue its proposed rule concerning its size standards before providing congressional input has both advantages and disadvantages. It provides the advantage of insulating the proposed rule from charges that it is influenced by political factors. It also has the advantage of respecting the separation of powers and responsibilities of the executive and legislative branches. However, it has the disadvantage of heightening the prospects for miscommunication, false expectations, and

---

[152] SBA, "Small Business Size Standards: Inflation Adjustment to Monetary Size Standards," 79 *Federal Register* 33647-33669, June 12, 2014; and SBA, "Small Business Size Standards: Inflation Adjustment to Monetary Based Size Standards," 81 *Federal Register* 3949-3956, January 25, 2016.

[153] SBA, "Small Business Size Standards: Inflation Adjustment to Size Standards, Business Loan Programs, and Disaster Assistance Program," 73 *Federal Register* 41237-41254, July 18, 2008.

wasted effort, as evidenced by past proposed rules concerning the SBA's size standards that were either rejected outright, or withdrawn, after facing congressional opposition.

Another policy option that has not received much congressional attention in recent years, but which Congress may choose to address, is the targeting of the SBA's resources. When the SBA reviews its size standards, it focuses on the competitive nature of the industry under review, with the goal of removing eligibility of firms that are considered large, or dominant, in that industry. There has been relatively little discussion of the costs and benefits of undertaking those reviews with the goal of targeting SBA resources to small businesses that are struggling to remain competitive. GAO recommended this approach in 1978 and Roger Rosenberger, then SBA's associate administrator for policy, planning, and budgeting, testified at a congressional hearing in 1979 that it was debatable whether the SBA should provide any assistance to any of the businesses within industries where "smaller firms are flourishing."[154]

Revising the SBA's size standards using this more targeted approach would likely reduce the number of firms eligible for assistance. It would also present the possibility of increasing available benefits to eligible small firms in those industries deemed "mixed" or "concentrated" by the SBA without necessarily increasing overall program costs. Perhaps because previous proposals that would result in a reduction in the number of firms eligible for assistance have met with resistance, this alternative approach to determining program eligibility has not received serious consideration in recent years. Nonetheless, it remains an option available to Congress should it decide to change current policy.

---

[154] U.S. Congress, House Committee on Small Business, Subcommittee on General Oversight and Minority Enterprise, *Size Standards for Small Business*, hearing, 96th Cong., 1st sess., July 10, 1979 (Washington: GPO, 1979), p. 28.

APPENDIX. SBA SIZE STANDARD REVIEWS, 2011-2016

Table A-1. Status of SBA Size Standard Reviews, By Issue Date, 2011-2016

NAICS Sectors	Notice of Intent to Review the Standard	Notice of Proposed Rulemaking	Recommended Change	Final Rule	Final Change
Professional, Scientific and Technical Services (NAICS Sector 54)	75 *Federal Register* 21893, 21894, Apr. 26, 2010	76 *Federal Register* 14323-14341, Mar. 16, 2011	Would increase size standards for 35 industries and 1 sub-industry	77 *Federal Register* 7488-7515, Feb. 10, 2012 (effective Mar. 12, 2012)	Increased size standards for 34 industries and 3 sub-industries[a]
Transportation and Warehousing (NAICS Sector 48-49)	75 *Federal Register* 21894, Apr. 26, 2010	76 *Federal Register* 27935-27952, May 13, 2011	Would increase size standards for 22 industries	77 *Federal Register* 10943-10950, Feb. 24, 2012 (effective Mar. 26, 2012)	Increased size standards for 22 industries
Educational Services (NAICS Sector 61)	76 *Federal Register* 40140-40142, July 7, 2011	76 *Federal Register* 70667-70680, Nov. 15, 2011	Would increase size standards for nine industries	77 *Federal Register* 58739-58747, Sept. 24, 2012 (effective Oct. 24, 2012)	Increased size standards for 9 industries
Health Care and Social Assistance Services (NAICS Sector 62)	76 *Federal Register* 40140-40142, July 7, 2011	77 *Federal Register* 11001-11017, Feb. 24, 2012	Would increase size standards for 28 industries	77 *Federal Register* 58755-58761, Sept. 24, 2012 (effective Oct. 24, 2012)	Increased size standards for 28 industries
Real Estate, Rental and Leasing (NAICS Sector 53)	76 *Federal Register* 40140-40142, July 7, 2011	76 *Federal Register* 70680-70694, Nov. 15, 2011	Would increase size standards for 20 industries and 1 sub-industry	77 *Federal Register* 58747-58755, Sept. 24, 2012 (effective Oct. 24, 2012)	Increased size standards for 21 industries and 1 sub-industry
Administrative and Support, Waste Management and Remediation Services (NAICS Sector 56)	76 *Federal Register* 40140-40142, July 7, 2011	76 *Federal Register* 63510-63525, Oct. 12, 2011	Would increase size standards for 37 industries	77 *Federal Register* 72691-72702, Dec. 6, 2012 (effective Jan. 7, 2013)	Increased size standards for 37 industries

Table A-1. (Continued)

NAICS Sectors	Notice of Intent to Review the Standard	Notice of Proposed Rulemaking	Recommended Change	Final Rule	Final Change
Information (NAICS Sector 51)	76 *Federal Register* 40140-40142, July 7, 2011	76 *Federal Register* 63216-63229, Oct. 12, 2011	Would increase size standards for 15 industries	77 *Federal Register* 72702-72709, Dec. 6, 2012 (effective Jan. 7, 2013)	Increased size standards for 15 industries
Agriculture, Forestry, Fishing and Hunting (NAICS Sector 11)	NA	77 *Federal Register* 55755-55768, Sept. 11, 2012	Would increase size standards for 11 industries	78 *Federal Register* 37398-37404, June 20, 2013 (effective July 22, 2013)	Increased size standards for 11 industries
Arts, Entertainment, and Recreation (NAICS Sector 71)	77 *Federal Register* 8024, Feb. 13, 2012	77 *Federal Register* 42211-42225, July 18, 2012	Would increase size standards for 17 industries	78 *Federal Register* 37417-37422, June 20, 2013 (effective July 22, 2013)	Increased size standards for 17 industries
Finance and Insurance (NAICS Sector 52)	NA	77 *Federal Register* 55737-55755, Sept. 11, 2012	Would increase size standards for 37 industries and change the measure of size from total assets to annual receipts for 1 industry	78 *Federal Register* 37409-37417, June 20, 2013 (effective July 22, 2013)	Increased size standards for 36 industries, and changed the measure of size from total assets to annual receipts for 1 industry
Management of Companies (NAICS Sector 55)	NA	77 *Federal Register* 55737-55755, Sept. 11, 2012	Would increase size standards for 2 industries	78 *Federal Register* 37409-37417, June 20, 2013 (effective July 22, 2013)	Increased size standards for 2 industries
Support Activities for Mining (within NAICS Sector 21)	NA	77 *Federal Register* 72766, Dec. 6, 2012	Would increase size standards for 3 industries	78 *Federal Register* 37404-37408, June 20, 2013 (effective July 22, 2013)	Increased size standards for 3 industries

NAICS Sectors	**Notice of Intent to Review the Standard**	**Notice of Proposed Rulemaking**	**Recommended Change**	**Final Rule**	**Final Change**
Construction (NAICS Sector 23)	77 *Federal Register* 8024, Feb. 13, 2012	77 *Federal Register* 42197-42211, July 18, 2012	Would increase size standards for 1 industry and 1 sub-industry	78 *Federal Register* 77334-77343, Dec. 23, 2013 (effective Jan. 22, 2014)	Increased size standards for 1 industry and 1 sub-industry
Utilities(NAICS Sector 22)	76 *Federal Register* 40140-40142, July 7, 2011	77 *Federal Register* 42441-42454, July 19, 2012	Would increase size standards for 3 industries and convert 6 industries from no more than 4 million megawatt hours in electric output in the preceding fiscal year to no more than 500 employees	78 *Federal Register* 77343-77351, Dec. 23, 2013 (effective Jan. 22, 2014)	Increased size standards for 3 industries and converted 10 industries from no more than 4 million megawatt hours in electric output in the preceding fiscal year to number of employees(varying by industry)
Wholesale Trade (NAICS Sector 42) and Retail Trade (two industries with employee based size standards within NAICS Sector 44-45)	78 *Federal Register* 1639, Jan. 8, 2013	79 *Federal Register* 28631-28647, May 19, 2014	Would increase size standards for 46 industries in NAICS Sector 42, and 1 industry in NAICS Sector 44-45	81 *Federal Register* 3941-3949, Jan. 25, 2016 (effective Feb. 26, 2016)	Increased size standards for 46 industries in NAICS Sector 42, and 1 industry in NAICS Sector 44-45
Industries with Employee Based Size Standards not Part of Manufacturing, Wholesale Trade, or Retail Trade (primarily within NAICS Sectors 51 and 54)	78 *Federal Register* 1639, Jan. 8, 2013	79 *Federal Register* 53646-53666, Sept. 10, 2014	Would increase size standards for 30 industries and 3 sub-industries, eliminate 2 sub-industry exceptions, and decrease size standards	81 *Federal Register* 4436-4469, Jan. 26, 2016 (effective Feb. 26, 2016)	Increased size standards for 30 industries and 3 sub-industries, eliminated 2 sub-industry exceptions, and decreased size

Table A-1. (Continued)

NAICS Sectors	Notice of Intent to Review the Standard	Notice of Proposed Rulemaking	Recommended Change	Final Rule	Final Change
			for 3 industries "to exclude dominant firms"		standards for 3 industries to exclude dominant firms
Manufacturing (NAICS Sector 31-33)	78 *Federal Register* 1639, Jan. 8, 2013	79 *Federal Register* 54146-54177, Sept. 10, 2014	Would increase size standards for 209 industries in NAICS Sector 31-33 Would also increase the refining capacity component for Petroleum Refiners from no more than 125,000 barrels per calendar day to no more than 200,000 barrels per calendar day	81 *Federal Register* 4469-4492, Jan. 26, 2016 (effective Feb. 26, 2016)	Increased size standards for 209 industries in NAICS Sector 31-33, and increased the refining capacity component for Petroleum Refiners from no more than 125,000 barrels per calendar day to no more than 200,000 barrels per calendar day

Source: *Federal Register* as cited in the table.

[a] Also increased one size standard (Computer and Office Machine Repair and Maintenance) in NAICS Sector 81, Other Services, which was not reviewed during the SBA's review of that sector in 2010.

In: Business Trends in the 21st Century ISBN: 978-1-53614-260-0
Editor: C. O. Clemente Escamilla

Chapter 3

BUSINESS INVESTMENT SPENDING SLOWDOWN*

Marc Labonte

ABSTRACT

Business capital investment spending is composed of private spending on nonresidential structures (e.g., factories), equipment (e.g., machinery), and intellectual property products (e.g., software). Business investment is a key determinant of economic growth. When businesses add to the capital stock, the value of goods and services (i.e., gross domestic product [GDP]) the economy can produce increases. One reason that economic growth has been lower in the last decade is because business investment spending has grown more slowly. Boosting investment spending was one of the key goals of the 2017 tax cuts.

---

* This is an edited, reformatted and augmented version of a CRS Insight report, IN10882, dated April 9, 2018.

THE SLOWDOWN

Average annual business investment spending from 2008 to 2017 was lower than the average for the previous six 10-year periods, going back to 1948. During the financial crisis, investment spending declined by 8.2% per year in 2008 and 2009, as shown in Figure 1. It has grown since then, but by a relatively low annual average of 4.5%, compared with about 6% from 1946 to 2000. In 2017, investment spending increased by 4.7%.

The equipment category declined the most during the crisis, but has increased at the fastest pace in the recovery. The slowdown during the current expansion has been greatest within structures. Within the structures category, growth has recently been whipsawed from year to year by large swings in the subcategory "mining exploration, shafts, and wells," declining by 43% in 2016 and rising by 58% in 2017. This pattern reflects the sensitivity of investment spending for resource extraction to commodity prices, generally, and to the growth of U.S. shale production, in particular.

The investment slowdown is not limited to the United States; it has also occurred across advanced and developing economies, suggesting that plausible explanations for the slowdown are not U.S. specific.

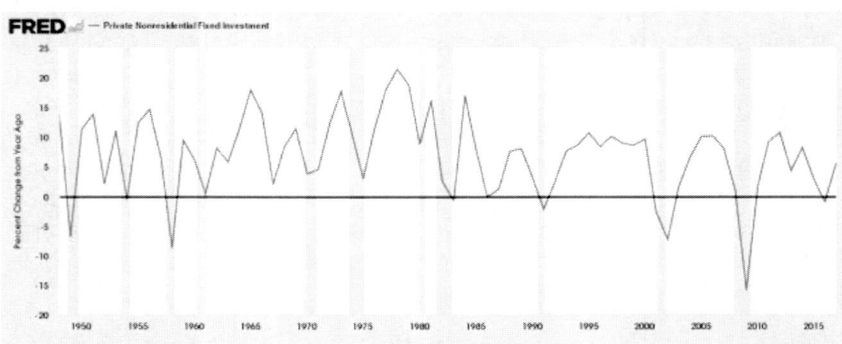

Source: Bureau of Economic Analysis, downloaded from FRED.

Figure 1. Annual Percentage Change in Business Investment. 1948-2017.

Causes of the Slowdown

Investment spending growth and economic growth are *endogenous*, meaning that at the same time that changes in investment spending cause changes in economic growth, changes in economic growth also cause changes in investment spending. Economists have debated whether the slowdown in business investment has exceeded what would be expected given the slowdown in growth. Economist Larry Summers *attributes* 48% of the decline in potential GDP to the decline in investment and 11% to the decline in productivity. One *study*, by contrast, argues that "weak investment...growth does not appear to have been an important independent contributor to weak [GDP] growth." The study attributes the investment slowdown to the slowdown in underlying economic growth, which stems from a structural slowdown in *productivity growth* and labor force growth, the latter due to the aging of the population. If capital and labor are complements instead of substitutes, a slowdown in labor force growth would reduce investment growth—as firms add fewer workers, less capital is needed for those workers to use.

Investment could be low because of low investment demand (firms' willingness to invest) or supply (a dearth of available savings to finance investment). The fact that real interest rates have been persistently low points to the former explanation. Therefore, most explanations for the slowdown focus on why investment demand has been low.

Cyclical and structural reasons are distinguishable for the slowdown in business investment and economic growth. Cyclical reasons relate to the *business cycle*—when overall business conditions are poor, as in a recession, firms are likelier to postpone investment spending, and when conditions are booming, firms are more likely to invest. From 2007 to 2009, the economy was in the longest and deepest recession since the Great Depression. From 2009 to 2013, the economic recovery was unusually sluggish, excess capacity remained elevated, and unemployment remained unusually high. One *study* attributes over 80% of the investment slowdown to weak demand across advanced economies. Beyond normal cyclical effects, the financial crisis may have temporarily disrupted some businesses' access to capital. The International Monetary Fund *found* that decreased credit availability limited investment during the recovery for euro-crisis countries, but not for the United States.

Cyclical factors have been less important since the economy recently returned to a more *normal state.* Given that the business investment slowdown *predated the financial crisis*—the annual average increase in investment from 2001 to 2007 was 2.5%—there are also a number of possible structural reasons for the slowdown. Hypotheses include the following:

- One *study* attributed the slowdown to reduced competition and business dynamism in U.S. markets due to increased industry concentration.
- Heightened uncertainty could cause businesses to delay investment projects. The IMF *found evidence* across advanced economies of a greater decline in investment at firms that are more sensitive to policy uncertainty. Policy uncertainty could come from a variety of sources, including regulatory policy and rising debt levels.
- One question is why business investment is low when rates of return on equity have been high. Jason Furman, then-chair of the Council of Economic Advisers, *noted* it could be because high rates of return are being earned by a smaller share of companies that are making large payouts to shareholders through dividends and share buybacks instead of investing. Another *theory* is that this could be caused by "short-termism" among investors and managers in publicly traded companies. But it is unclear why payouts are not being recycled into investments by other companies.
- Furman argues that the decline could be partly caused by mismeasurement if official statistics are underestimating IT quality improvements, because investment has fallen less in nominal than real terms.
- One study attributed the slowdown to the shift in GDP from capital-intensive industries, such as manufacturing, to services and knowledge-intensive industries, such as high tech. Summers argues

that large tech companies, "awash in cash," require less capital investment than traditional companies.

The behavior of investment spending as the economic expansion progresses will shed more light on the relative merits of these various theories. If investment spending picks up as the economy reaches full employment, it would indicate that the weakness was mainly cyclical. If it does not, that would support the structural explanations.

In: Business Trends in the 21st Century ISBN: 978-1-53614-260-0
Editor: C. O. Clemente Escamilla

Chapter 4

SBA'S OFFICE OF INSPECTOR GENERAL: OVERVIEW, IMPACT, AND RELATIONSHIP WITH CONGRESS*

Robert Jay Dilger

ABSTRACT

Congress created offices of inspector general (OIGs) to assist in its oversight of the executive branch. OIGs provide independent, nonpartisan analysis, conducted in accordance with generally accepted government auditing standards, to identify and recommend ways to limit waste, fraud, and abuse in federal programs and enhance program and operational efficiency and effectiveness. OIGs' activities supplement and complement those of the Government Accountability Office (GAO), which serves a similar, though not identical, role in assisting congressional oversight of the executive branch. Together, OIGs and GAO provide Congress with information and analysis needed to conduct effective oversight and, in the process, help Congress maintain its balance of power with the presidency.

---

* This is an edited, reformatted and augmented version of a Congressional Research Service report, R44589, dated April 5, 2018.

OIGs exist in more than 70 federal agencies, including all departments and larger agencies, numerous boards and commissions, and other entities. The U.S. Small Business Administration's Office of Inspector General (SBA OIG) was created under authority of the Inspector General Act of 1978 (P.L. 95-452, as amended). Its three primary statutory purposes are to

- conduct and supervise audits and investigations of the SBA's programs and operations;
- recommend policies designed to promote the economy, efficiency, and effectiveness of the SBA's programs and operations and to prevent and detect fraud and abuse; and
- keep both the SBA Administrator and Congress "fully and currently informed about problems and deficiencies relating to the administration of such programs and operations and the necessity for and progress of corrective action."

During FY2017, the SBA OIG issued 19 audit reports containing 72 recommendations for improving the SBA's programs and operations, and its investigations resulted in 35 indictments or informations and 25 convictions. The SBA OIG claimed that its recommendations resulted in monetary savings and recoveries of nearly $82.1 million in FY2017. In addition, the SBA OIG's annual *Report on the Most Serious Management and Performance Challenges Facing the SBA* focuses attention "on areas that are particularly vulnerable to fraud, waste, error, and mismanagement, or otherwise pose a significant risk and generally have been subject to one or more OIG or GAO reports."

This chapter examines the SBA OIG's statutory authorities; reporting requirements; funding ($26.9 million in FY2018, including $7 million in supplemental appropriations for overseeing SBA disaster assistance); staffing and organizational structure; and recent activities (audits, investigations, etc.). It also examines the SBA OIG's impact on monetary savings, SBA programs and operations, and legislation affecting the agency. The chapter concludes with observations concerning the SBA OIG's relationship with Congress.

Some areas of possible congressional interest, other than SBA OIG funding and staffing issues, include exploring ways to more accurately quantify the SBA OIG's claims of monetary savings and to determine if the SBA OIG should undertake additional tracking and monitoring activities to more accurately quantify the office's impact on SBA programs, operations, and legislation.

INTRODUCTION

Congress created offices of inspector general (OIGs) in 1978 (via P.L. 95-452, the Inspector General Act of 1978, or the IG Act) to assist in its oversight of the executive branch. At that time, Congress determined that there were serious deficiencies in the executive branch's auditing and investigative activities designed to curb waste, fraud, and abuse and promote agency operational and program efficiency.[1] For example, the House and Senate reports accompanying the bill that became the IG Act argued that

- auditing and investigative activities were scattered throughout the various federal departments and were often conducted in response to a complaint as opposed to having in place "affirmative programs to look for possible fraud or abuse,"
- investigators in some agencies (including the Small Business Administration, SBA) were not allowed to initiate investigations without clearance from officials responsible for the programs involved,
- many agency representatives engaged in auditing and investigative activities (including those within the SBA) reported that their office lacked sufficient budgets to do its job, many of the auditing

---

[1] Definitions of program efficiency vary. For example, the German sociologist Max Weber argued that organizations operate most efficiently when they are organized in a hierarchical fashion with established rules for making decisions and dividing the labor of the organization accordingly. The Government Accountability Office (GAO) incorporates in its definition of government efficiency how an agency spends money: a ratio of inputs (the cost of operating the government agency or program) to outcomes (the desired results of the program, such as events, occurrences, or changes in conditions, behaviors, or attitudes). See GAO, *Streamlining Government: Opportunities Exist to Strengthen OMB's Approach to Improving Efficiency*, GAO-10-394, May 7, 2010, p. 3, at http://www.gao.gov/assets/310/304231.pdf. A congressional staff member (now-retired) suggested a hybrid of these definitions: "a government agency is efficient if it is properly structured to produce accountable decisions and desired results ...[that] use the least amount of federal tax dollars to achieve desired outcomes, i.e., are cost-effective in ensuring that performance objectives are achieved." See Barry Pineles, chief counsel, House Committee on Small Business, "Hearing Memorandum: Reducing Duplication and Promoting Efficiency at the SBA: The Inspector General's View," June 3, 2013, at http://smallbusiness.house.gov/uploadedfiles/6-5-2013__final_hearing_memo.pdf.

and investigative offices (including those at the SBA) often reported to those who were responsible for the program being audited or investigated, and
- some auditors and investigators were unable to devote full time to their audit or investigative responsibilities.[2]

The House report concluded that independent OIGs "are urgently needed."[3] The Senate report concluded that "with rare exceptions, the agencies have not adequately policed their own operations and programs."[4]

OIGs were designed to provide Congress and federal agency heads independent, nonpartisan analysis, conducted in accordance with generally accepted government auditing standards, to identify and recommend ways to limit waste, fraud, and abuse in federal programs and enhance operational and program efficiency and effectiveness.

OIGs' activities were to supplement and complement those of the Government Accountability Office (GAO), which serves a similar, though not identical, role in assisting Congress fulfill its oversight function.[5]

---

[2] U.S. Congress, House Committee on Government Operations, *Establishment of Offices of Inspector General in Certain Executive Departments and Agencies*, 95th Cong., 1st sess., August 5, 1977, H.Rept. 95-584 (Washington: GPO, 1977), pp. 5-7; and U.S. Congress, Senate Committee on Governmental Affairs, *Establishment of Offices of Inspector and Auditor General in Certain Executive Departments and Agencies*, 95th Cong., 2nd sess., August 8, 1978, S.Rept. 95- 1071 (Washington: GPO, 1978), pp. 4-6.

[3] U.S. Congress, House Committee on Government Operations, *Establishment of Offices of Inspector General in Certain Executive Departments and Agencies*, 95th Cong., 1st sess., August 5, 1977, H.Rept. 95-584 (Washington: GPO, 1977), p. 11.

[4] .S. Congress, Senate Committee on Governmental Affairs, *Establishment of Offices of Inspector and Auditor General in Certain Executive Departments and Agencies*, 95th Cong., 2nd sess., August 8, 1978, S.Rept. 95-1071 (Washington: GPO, 1978), p. 9.

[5] Offices of Inspector General (OIGs) are independent entities focusing on the programs and activities of their federal agency. GAO is a congressional agency whose work spans across all federal agencies and "is done at the request of congressional committees or subcommittees ... is mandated by public laws or committee reports ... [or is undertaken] under the authority of the Comptroller General." GAO's focus is on supporting "congressional oversight by auditing agency operations to determine whether federal funds are being spent efficiently and effectively; investigating allegations of illegal and improper activities; reporting on how well government programs and policies are meeting their objectives; performing policy analyses and outlining options for congressional consideration; and issuing legal decisions and opinions, such as bid protest rulings and reports on agency rules." GAO advises "Congress and the heads of executive agencies about ways to make government more efficient, effective, ethical, equitable and responsive." See GAO, "About GAO," at http://www.gao.gov/about/index.html.

Together, OIGs and GAO (along with the Congressional Research Service [CRS] and the Congressional Budget Office [CBO]) provide Congress with information and analysis needed to conduct effective oversight and, in the process, help Congress maintain its balance of power with the presidency.

OIGs currently exist in more than 70 federal agencies, including all departments and larger agencies, numerous boards and commissions, and other entities.[6] They are predominantly located in executive branch agencies, but several legislative branch entities—for example, the Library of Congress (LOC), GAO, and the Government Publishing Office (GPO)—also have OIGs.

The overwhelming majority of OIGs, including the U.S. Small Business Administration OIG (SBA OIG), are governed by the IG Act. It structures inspector general (IG) appointments and removals, powers and authorities, and duties and responsibilities. Other laws have established or amended IG powers and authorities in specified agencies or programs. As a result, IG statutory powers and authorities are not identical across the federal government and, in certain cases, these differences are significant. Nonetheless, in general, statutory OIGs follow the IG Act's standards, guidelines, and directives.

For example, the IG Act provides IGs five statutory duties and responsibilities as follows:

1. Conduct, supervise, and coordinate audits and investigations of their agency's programs and operations.[7]

---

[6] For additional information and analysis concerning OIGs see CRS Report R43814, *Federal Inspectors General: History, Characteristics, and Recent Congressional Actions*, by Wendy Ginsberg and Michael Greene.

[7] OIG audits are conducted in accordance with federal audit standards established by the Comptroller General, and other reviews generally are conducted in accordance with standards established by the Council of the Inspectors General for Integrity and Efficiency (CIGIE). In addition, OIGs coordinate their activities with GAO to avoid duplicating federal audits. See U.S. Congress, House Committee on Small Business, *SBA Management and Performance Challenges: The Inspector General's Perspective*, 114th Cong., 2nd sess., March 16, 2016, H. Hrg. 114- 049 (Washington: GPO, 2016), p. 22.
GAO-issued Generally Accepted Government Auditing Standards (GAGAS) require that audit organizations performing audits and attestation engagements in accordance with

2. Review existing and proposed legislation and regulations relating to their agency and make recommendations in mandated semiannual reports concerning the impact of such legislation or regulations on their agency's programs and operations or on the prevention and detection of fraud and abuse in those programs and operations.
3. Recommend policies to improve their agency's administration of its programs and operations and prevent and detect fraud and abuse in those programs and operations.
4. Recommend policies to facilitate relationships between their agency and other federal, state, and local government agencies and nongovernmental entities to promote the economy and efficiency of their agency's administration of its programs and operations and prevent and detect of fraud and abuse in those programs and operations.
5. Keep both their agency head and Congress fully and currently informed concerning fraud and other serious problems, abuses, and deficiencies relating to their agency's administration of its

GAGAS must have an external peer review performed by reviewers independent of the audit organization being reviewed (another OIG or GAO) at least once every three years.
In September 2014, the U.S. Department of Interior's OIG reviewed the Small Business Administration OIG's (SBA OIG's) Investigations Division. "The final report, dated November 13, 2014, found the system of internal safeguards and management procedure for the investigative function of SBA OIG complied with CIGIE's quality standards and the applicable Attorney General Guidelines. (OIGs can be assessed as either 'compliant' or 'noncompliant'.)" See U.S. Small Business Administration (SBA), OIG, "Semiannual Report to Congress, Spring 2016," p. 61, at https://www.sba.gov/sites/default/files/oig/SBA_OIG_SAR_Spring_2016.pdf.
On December 10, 2015, the SBA OIG's audit division received a peer review rating of pass (audit organizations can receive a rating of pass, pass with deficiencies, or fail) from the Smithsonian Institution's Office of Inspector General. A sample of the SBA OIG's audits were reviewed to determine if the SBA OIG's "system of quality control" in effect for the period of April 1, 2012, through March 31, 2015, met governmental auditing standards ("A system of quality control encompasses SBA OIG's organizational structure and the policies adopted and procedures established to provide it with reasonable assurance of conforming to *Government Auditing Standards*.") See Smithsonian Institution, Office of Inspector General, "System Review Report," at https://www.sba.gov/sites/default/files/oig/SBA_OIG_Peer_Review_System_Report_FINAL_signed_508.pdf.

programs and operations and to report on the progress made in implementing recommended corrective action.[8]

This chapter examines the SBA OIG's statutory authorities; reporting requirements; funding; staffing and organizational structure; and recent activities (audits, investigations, etc.). The SBA OIG's impact on monetary savings, SBA programs and operations, and legislation affecting the agency is also examined. The chapter concludes with some observations concerning the SBA OIG's relationship with Congress.

Some areas of possible congressional interest, other than SBA OIG funding and staffing issues, include exploring ways to more accurately quantify the SBA OIG's claims of monetary savings and to determine if the SBA OIG should undertake additional tracking and monitoring activities to more accurately quantify the office's impact on SBA programs, operations, and legislation.

SBA's OIG

The SBA OIG is a separate, independent office that provides "independent, objective oversight to improve the integrity, accountability, and performance of the SBA and its programs for the benefit of the American people."[9] The SBA's IG (currently filled on an acting basis by Hannibal "Mike" Ware) directs the office and is "appointed by the President, by and with the advice and consent of the Senate, without regard to political affiliation and solely on the basis of integrity and demonstrated ability in accounting, auditing, financial analysis, law, management analysis, public administration, or investigations."[10]

---

[8] IG Act of 1978, Section 4(1)-(5); and 5 U.S.C. Appendix §4(1)-(5).

[9] SBA, "Office of Inspector General," at https://www.sba.gov/office-of-inspector-general.

[10] P.L. 95-452, the Inspector General Act of 1978 (IG Act of 1978), Section 3(a); and 5 U.S.C. Appendix §3(a). Peggy Elizabeth Gustafson was sworn in as the SBA's IG on October 2, 2009, and became the Department of Commerce's OIG on January 9, 2017. Mike Ware had been the SBA Deputy Inspector General since April 2016, and had served various roles within the Department of Interior's OIG prior to joining the SBA's OIG.

The SBA is a Cabinet-level agency. Although the SBA is one of the smaller Cabinet-level agencies (with an annual budget of $2.359 billion in FY2018, including $1.659 billion in supplemental appropriations for disaster assistance), it administers a relatively wide range of programs to support small businesses, including loan guaranty and venture capital programs to enhance small business access to capital; contracting programs to increase small business opportunities in federal contracting; direct loan programs for businesses, homeowners, and renters to assist their recovery from natural disasters; and small business management and technical assistance training programs to assist business formation and expansion.[11] The SBA expects to "support more than $44 billion in small business loans, help facilitate 23 percent of all federal contracting dollars to small businesses, counsel and train more than one million small business owners and entrepreneurs, support more than $1 billion in loans to disaster survivors, and nurture thousands of high-growth companies through $4 billion in long-term capital" in FY2018.[12] The SBA OIG is responsible for examining these programs and the various SBA offices that administer them.

IGs report to the head of their agency or establishment, but are provided various powers and protections that support their independence. For example, the SBA's IG reports to the SBA Administrator, but

- may be removed from office only by the President, or through the impeachment process in Congress.[13]
- has the authority to hire staff.[14]

---

[11] For additional information concerning these SBA programs, see CRS Report RL33243, *Small Business Administration: A Primer on Programs and Funding*, by Robert Jay Dilger and Sean Lowry.

[12] SBA "FY2018 Congressional Budget Justification and FY2016 Annual Performance Report," p. 19, at https://www.sba.gov/sites/default/files/aboutsbaarticle/FINAL_SBA_FY_2018_CBJ_May_22_2017c.pdf.

[13] In addition, the President may transfer an inspector general (IG) to another position or location within the IG's agency. If an IG is removed from office or transferred to another position or location "the President shall communicate in writing the reasons for any such removal or transfer to both Houses of Congress, not later than 30 days before the removal or transfer." See, IG Act of 1978, Section 3(b); and 5 U.S.C. Appendix §3(b).

[14] IG Act of 1978, Section 6(a)(7); and 5 U.S.C. Appendix §6(a)(7).

- determines priorities and projects (e.g., audits, reviews and investigations) without outside direction.[15]
- cannot be prevented or prohibited "from initiating, carrying out, or completing any audit or investigation, or from issuing any subpoena during the course of any audit or investigation."[16]
- must be provided "access to all records, reports, audits, reviews, documents, papers, recommendations, or other material available ... which relate to programs and operations with respect to which [the SBA] Inspector General has responsibilities under this Act."[17]
- must be provided "appropriate and adequate office space" and "such equipment, office supplies, and communications facilities and services as may be necessary for the operation of" the SBA OIG, including any "necessary maintenance services for such offices and the equipment and facilities located therein."[18]

STATUTORY AUTHORITIES

The IG Act provides all IGs nine statutory authorities:

1. Access to all records, reports, audits, reviews, documents, papers, recommendations, or other material available relating to the IG's responsibilities under the IG Act.[19]

---

[15] IG Act of 1978, Section 6(a)(2); and 5 U.S.C. Appendix §6(a)(2). The SBA Administrator, President, Members of Congress, SBA employees, and members of the public may request that a project take place, but, unless otherwise required by law, the SBA's IG is not obligated to do so.

[16] IG Act of 1978, Section 3(a); and 5 U.S.C. Appendix §3(a).

[17] IG Act of 1978, Section 6(a)(1); and 5 U.S.C. Appendix §6(a)(1).

[18] IG Act of 1978, Section 6(c); and 5 U.S.C. Appendix §6(c).

[19] Access to records, reports, etc. may be limited under specified circumstances (e.g., if such access limits "the exercise of law enforcement powers established under any other statutory authority, including United States Marshals Service special deputation"). See IG Act of 1978, Section 6(e)(8); and 5 U.S.C. Appendix §6(e)(8). There have also been instances where the executive branch has redacted information citing authority provided in other statutes. This practice is often challenged by OIGs and Congress as circumventing the IG Act's intent for access to all records, reports, etc.

2. Make such investigations and reports relating to their agency's administration of its programs and operations as are, in the judgment of the IG, necessary or desirable.
3. Request such information or assistance as may be necessary for carrying out the duties and responsibilities provided by the IG Act from any federal, state, or local governmental agency or unit thereof.
4. Require by subpoena the production of all information, documents, reports, answers, records, accounts, papers, and other data in any medium necessary in the performance of the functions assigned by the IG Act; provided that procedures other than subpoenas shall be used by the IG to obtain documents and information from federal agencies.
5. Administer to or take from any person an oath, affirmation, or affidavit, whenever necessary in the performance of the functions assigned by the IG Act.
6. Have direct and prompt access to their agency head when necessary for any purpose pertaining to the performance of functions and responsibilities under the IG Act.
7. Select, appoint, and employ such officers and employees as may be necessary for carrying out the functions, powers, and duties of the Office subject to the provisions of title 5, *United States Code*, governing appointments in the competitive service, and the provisions of chapter 51 and subchapter III of chapter 53 of such title relating to classification and General Schedule pay rates.
8. Obtain services as authorized by Section 3109 of title 5, *United States Code*, at daily rates not to exceed the equivalent rate prescribed for grade GS–18 of the General Schedule by Section 5332 of title 5, *United States Code*.
9. To the extent and in such amounts as may be provided in advance by appropriations acts, to enter into contracts and other arrangements for audits, studies, analyses, and other services with public agencies and with private persons, and to make such

payments as may be necessary to carry out the provisions of the IG Act.[20]

In addition, the IG Act provides 25 OIGs, including the SBA OIG, direct law enforcement authority.[21] It also authorizes the U.S. Attorney General to delegate law enforcement authority to other OIGs under specified circumstances.[22]

REPORTING REQUIREMENTS

The IG Act requires IGs to prepare and transmit semiannual reports (two per year) to their agency's head, not later than April 30 and October 31 of each year, summarizing the OIG's activities during the immediately preceding six-month periods ending on March 31 and September 30. Agency heads are to transmit these reports to the appropriate committees or subcommittees of Congress in unaltered form within 30 days after receipt. Agency heads may provide any additional comments deemed appropriate. Agency heads must also provide specified information, such as statistical tables showing the total number of audit reports, inspection reports, and evaluation reports for which final action had not been taken by the commencement of the reporting period; on which management decisions were made during the reporting period; and for which no final

---

[20] IG Act of 1978, Section 6(a); and 5 U.S.C. Appendix §6(a).

[21] IG Act of 1978, Section 6(e)(3); and 5 U.S.C. Appendix §6(e)(3). Five other OIGs have been provided law enforcement authority by other federal statutes.

[22] See IG Act of 1978, Section 6(e)(1)-(2); and 5 U.S.C. Appendix §6(e)(1)-(2). Law enforcement authority is generally defined as providing certain OIG employees the legal authority to carry a firearm while engaged in official duties, make an arrest without a warrant while engaged in official duties, and seek and execute warrants for arrest, search of premises, or seizure of evidence. See IG Act of 1978, Section 6(e)(1); and 5 U.S.C. Appendix §6(e)(1). The specified circumstances are "(A) the affected OIG is significantly hampered in the performance of responsibilities established by this Act as a result of the lack of such powers; (B) available assistance from other law enforcement agencies is insufficient to meet the need for such powers; and (C) adequate internal safeguards and management procedures exist to ensure proper exercise of such powers." See IG Act of 1978, Section 6(e)(2); and 5 U.S.C. Appendix §6(e)(2).

action had been taken by the end of the reporting period.[23] Copies of the semiannual reports must be made available to the public upon request and at a reasonable cost within 60 days of their transmission to Congress.[24]

The OIG's semiannual reports are required to include, but not limited to, 16 informational items. For example, the SBA OIG's report must include, among other items, the following:

- A description of significant problems, abuses, and deficiencies relating to the SBA's administration of programs and operations identified during the reporting period.
- A description of the SBA OIG's recommendations for corrective action.
- An identification of each significant recommendation described in previous semiannual reports on which corrective action has not been completed.
- A summary of matters referred to prosecutive authorities and the prosecutions and convictions that have resulted.
- A summary of each report made to the SBA Administrator relating to instances when information or assistance requested has, in the IG's judgment, been unreasonably refused or not provided during the reporting period.
- A listing of each audit report, inspection report, and evaluation report issued during the reporting period and for each report, where applicable, the total dollar value of questioned costs (including a separate category for the dollar value of unsupported costs) and the dollar value of recommendations that funds be put to better use.
- A summary of each audit report, inspection report, and evaluation report issued before the commencement of the reporting period for which no management decision has been made by the end of the reporting period (including the date and title of each such report), an explanation of the reasons such management decision has not

[23] IG Act of 1978, Section 5(b); and 5 U.S.C. Appendix §5(b).

[24] The SBA OIG's semiannual reports can be accessed online at https://www.sba.gov/oig/category/oig-navigationstructure/reading-room/semi-annual-reports-congress.

been made, and a statement concerning the desired timetable for achieving a management decision on each such report.

- Information concerning any significant management decision with which the SBA's IG is in disagreement.[25]

IGs are also required to report suspected violations of federal criminal law directly and expeditiously to the U.S. Attorney General, and any "particularly serious or flagrant problems, abuses, or deficiencies" relating to their agency's operations and administration of programs immediately to the agency's head.[26]

In addition, pursuant to P.L. 106-531, the Records Consolidation Act of 2000,[27] and the Office of Management and Budget (OMB) Circular A-136,[28] the SBA OIG issues an annual *Report on the Most Serious Management and Performance Challenges Facing the SBA*. This chapter is, arguably, the SBA OIG's signature oversight document, focusing attention "on areas that are particularly vulnerable to fraud, waste, error, and mismanagement, or otherwise pose a significant risk and generally have been subject to one or more OIG or GAO reports."[29]

FUNDING

The IG Act provides presidentially appointed IGs a separate appropriations account, known colloquially as a "line item," for their offices. This provision prevents federal administrators from limiting, transferring, or otherwise reducing OIG funding once it has been specified

---

[25] IG Act of 1978, Section 5(a); and 5 U.S.C. Appendix §5(a).

[26] IG Act of 1978, Section 4(d) and 5(d); and 5 U.S.C. Appendix §4(d) and §5(d).

[27] P.L. 106-531 authorizes federal agency heads to consolidate any statutorily required reports (including financial and performance management reports) into an annual report and submit the consolidated report not later than 150 days after the end of the agency's fiscal year. Not all OIGs are required to author this report.

[28] OMB Circular 1-136, Financial Reporting Requirements-Revised (8/4/2015), at https://www.whitehouse.gov/omb/circulars_default.

[29] SBA, OIG, "FY2018 Congressional Budget Justification," p. 20, at https://www.sba.gov/sites/default/files/aboutsbaarticle/Office_ofjnspector_General_-_FY_2018_CBJ.pdf.

in law.[30] IGs are authorized to transmit a budget estimate and request to their respective agency head each fiscal year. Each IG's request must include amounts for operations, training, and for the support of the Council of the Inspectors General on Integrity and Efficiency (CIGIE).[31] The agency's budget request to the President must include the OIG's original budget request and any comments the affected IG has regarding the proposal.[32] The President is required to include in the Administration's budget submission to Congress the IG's original request; the amount requested by the President for the OIG's operations, training, and support for CIGIE; and any comments the affected IG has regarding the proposal if the IG concludes that the President's budget would substantially inhibit the IG from performing the duties of the office.[33]

Each year, the SBA OIG transmits a budget justification document to the SBA Administrator, which is available online.[34] That document includes the SBA OIG's budget request, an overview of the SBA OIG's mission and authorities, a list of critical risks facing the SBA, an accounting of the office's oversight activities during the previous fiscal year, areas of emphasis for the coming fiscal year, and a table of statistical highlights and accomplishments for the previous fiscal year (such as the number of reports and recommendations issued, estimated amounts saved or recouped, number of indictments and convictions).

---

[30] For additional information and analysis concerning OIG budgeting, see CRS Report R43814, *Federal Inspectors General: History, Characteristics, and Recent Congressional Actions*, by Wendy Ginsberg and Michael Greene.

[31] IG Act of 1978, Section 6(f)(1); and 5 U.S.C. Appendix §6(f)(1). The Council of the Inspectors General on Integrity and Efficiency (CIGIE) is "an independent entity established within the executive branch to address integrity, economy and effectiveness issues that transcend individual Government agencies and aid in the establishment of a professional, well-trained and highly skilled workforce in the Offices of Inspectors General." See CIGIE, "What is CIGIE?" at https://www.ignet.gov/. CIGIE also oversees the conduct of high-ranking employees in the inspector general community and investigates wrongdoing against those employees. For additional information and analysis concerning CIGIE, see CRS Report R44198, *Oversight of the Inspector General Community: The IG Council's Integrity Committee*, by Wendy Ginsberg.

[32] IG Act of 1978, Section 6(f)(2); and 5 U.S.C. Appendix §6(f)(2).

[33] IG Act of 1978, Section 6(f)(3); and 5 U.S.C. Appendix §6(f)(3).

[34] The SBA OIG's budget justification documents for FY2010-FY2017 are available on the SBA's website. See SBA, "Congressional Budget Justification/Annual Performance Report," at https://www.sba.gov/about-sba/sba-performance/performance-budget-finances/congressional-budget-justification-annual-performance-report.

Table 1. SBA OIG's Appropriations, FY2010-FY2019 ($ in millions)

Fiscal Year	New Budget Authority	Transfer from the Disaster Loan Program Account	Other Adjustments	Other Account
2019 (request)	$21.900	$1.000	$0.000	$22.900
2018	$19.900	$0.000	$7.000[a]	$26.900
2017	$19.900	$1.000	$0.000	$20.900
2016	$19.900	$1.000	$0.000	$20.900
2015	$19.400	$1.000	$0.000	$20.400
2014	$19.000	$1.000	$0.000	$20.000
2013	$16.267	$1.000	$5.000 ($1.101)[b]	$21.166
2012	$16.267	$1.000	$0.000	$17.267
2011	$16.300	$1.000	($0.033)[c]	$17.267
2010	$16.300	$1.000	$0.000	$17.300

Sources: P.L. 111-117, the Consolidated Appropriations Act, 2010; P.L. 112-10, the Department of Defense and Full-Year Continuing Appropriations Act, 2011; P.L. 112-25, the Budget Control Act of 2011; P.L. 112-74, the Consolidated Appropriations Act, 2012; P.L. 112-175, the Continuing Appropriations Resolution, 2013; P.L. 113- 2, the Disaster Relief Appropriations Act, 2013; P.L. 113-6, the Consolidated and Further Continuing Appropriations Act, 2013; P.L. 113-76, the Consolidated Appropriations Act, 2014; P.L. 113-235, the Consolidated and Further Continuing Appropriations Act, 2015; P.L. 114-113, the Consolidated Appropriations Act, 2016; P.L. 115-56, the Continuing Appropriations Act, 2018 and Supplemental Appropriations for Disaster Relief Requirements Act, 2017; P.L. 115-123, the Bipartisan Budget Act of 2018; P.L. 115-141, the Consolidated Appropriations Act, 2018; and U.S Small Business Administration, Office of Inspector General, "FY2019 Congressional Budget Justification," p. 219, at https://www.sba.gov/sites/default/files/aboutsbaarticle/FY_2019_CBJ_Office_of_Inspector_General.pdf.

Notes:

[a] In FY2018, P.L. 115-123, the Bipartisan Budget Act of 2018 provided the SBA OIG $7.0 million for investigative costs related to supplemental funding for SBA disaster loans.

[b] In FY2013, P.L. 113-2 provided the SBA OIG $5.0 million to remain available until expended for expenses related to oversight of disaster loans following Hurricane Sandy. In addition, P.L. 112-25 and P.L. 113-6 imposed a federal government-wide sequestration process and a required 0.2% across-the-board rescission, resulting in a $1.101 million reduction from the SBA OIG's budget.

[c] In FY2011, P.L. 112-10 imposed a 0.2% rescission on federal agencies, resulting in a reduction of $0.033 million from the SBA OIG's budget.

Table 1 shows the SBA OIG's appropriations over the FY2010-FY2019 period. The SBA OIG received an appropriation of $26.9 million for FY2018: $19.9 million in new budget authority (including $160,000 for training and $42,000 for CIGIE) and $7 million in supplemental appropriations (provided by P.L. 115-123, the Bipartisan Budget Act of 2018) for investigative costs related to supplemental funding for SBA disaster loans.[35]

The SBA OIG has requested $22.9 million for FY2019: $21.9 million in new budget authority (including $160,000 for training and $51,000 for CIGIE) and a $1 million transfer from the SBA Disaster Loan Program account for investigative costs related to SBA disaster loans.[36]

STAFFING AND ORGANIZATIONAL STRUCTURE

As shown in *Table 2*, the SBA OIG's FTEs have remained relatively stable since FY2000, ranging from a low of 93 FTEs in FY2014 to a high of 112 FTEs in FY2000. The SBA OIG had 101 FTEs in FY2017, anticipates having 107 FTEs in FY2018, and has requested funding to support 114 FTEs in FY2019.[37] Approximately 85% of the SBA OIG's expenditures are attributed to payroll expenses.[38]

In 2013, then-SBA IG Peggy Gustafson testified that "resource constraints do sometime preclude us from initiating or continuing a number of investigations" and if she were provided additional resources, she would "target early defaulted loans, fraud, and lender negligence, and ... increase the capacity of our existing investigative personnel."[39]

---

[35] For the FY2018 training and CIGIE funding request, see SBA, OIG, "FY2018 Congressional Budget Justification," p. 22, at https://www.sba.gov/sites/default/files/oig/SBAOIG_FY_2018_CBJ_5-17-17.pdf.

[36] SBA, OIG, "FY2019 Congressional Budget Justification," p. 219, at https://www.sba.gov/sites/default/files/aboutsbaarticle/FY_2019_CBJ_Office_of_Inspector_General.pdf.

[37] SBA, "FY2019 Congressional Budget Justification and FY2017 Annual Performance Report," p. 17, at https://www.sba.gov/sites/default/files/aboutsbaarticle/SBA_FY_2019_CBJ_APR_2_12_post.pdf.

[38] SBA, OIG, "FY2019 Congressional Budget Justification," p. 198, at https://www.sba.gov/sites/default/files/aboutsbaarticle/FY_2019_CBJ_Office_of_Inspector_General.pdf.

[39] U.S. Congress, House Committee on Appropriations, Subcommittee on Financial Services and General Government, *Financial Services and General Government Appropriations for 2014, Part 6*, 113th Cong., 1st sess., April 10, 2013, p. 195.

Table 2. SBA OIG's Full-Time Equivalent Employees, FY2000-FY2019

Fiscal Year	Full-Time Equivalent Employees	Fiscal Year	Full-Time Equivalent Employees
2019	114	2009	104
(Request)			
2018 est.	107	2008	106
2017	101	2007	103
2016	96	2006	95
2015	103	2005	95
2014	93	2004	98
2013	106	2003	100
2012	110	2002	108
2011	110	2001	108
2010	110	2000	112

Source: U.S. Small Business Administration, Office of Inspector General, "Correspondence with the author," June 23, 2016, and February 1, 2017; U.S Small Business Administration, Office of Inspector General, "FY2018 Congressional Budget Justification," p. 3, at https://www.sba.gov/ sites/default/ files/aboutsbaarticle/ Office_of_Inspector_General_-_FY_2018_CBJ.pdf; and U.S. Small Business Administration, "FY2019 Congressional Budget Justification and FY2017 Annual Performance Report," p. 17, at https://www.sba.gov/sites/default/files/aboutsbaarticle/ SBA_FY_2019_CBJ_APR_2_12_post.pdf.

The SBA OIG's staff is organized into three divisions and several support offices

- The *Auditing Division* performs and oversees audits and reviews of SBA programs and operations, focusing on SBA business and disaster loans, business development and government contracting programs, as well as mandatory and other statutory audit requirements involving computer security, financial reporting, and other work.
- The *Investigations Division* manages a program to detect and deter illegal and improper activities involving SBA's programs, operations, and personnel. The Division has *criminal investigations staff* who carry out a full range of traditional law

enforcement functions and *security operations staff* who conduct name checks and, where appropriate, fingerprint checks on program applicants to prevent known criminals and wrongdoers from participating in SBA programs. Security operations staff also conduct required employee background investigations.

- The *Management and Administration Division* provide business support (e.g., budget and financial management, human resources, IT, and procurement) for the various OIG functions and activities.
- The *Office of Counsel* provides legal and ethics advice to all OIG components; represents the OIG in litigation arising out of or affecting OIG operations; assists with the prosecution of criminal, civil, and administrative enforcement matters; processes subpoenas; responds to Freedom of Information and Privacy Act requests; and reviews and comments on proposed policies, regulations, legislation, and procedures.
- The *OIG Hotline,* under the purview of the *Chief of Staff,* reviews allegations of waste, fraud, abuse, or serious mismanagement within the SBA or its programs from employees, contractors, and the public.[40]

The SBA OIG's headquarters is located in Washington, DC. The SBA OIG's Investigations Division has 12 field offices located across the United States.[41]

The SBA OIG's structure is shown in its organizational chart (see *Figure 1*).

---

[40] SBA, OIG, "FY2019 Congressional Budget Justification," p. 222, at https://www.sba.gov/sites/default/files/aboutsbaarticle/FY_2019_CBJ_Office_of_Inspector_General.pdf.

[41] The SBA's Investigations Division has 12 field offices: five in its eastern region: Atlanta, Georgia; Melville, New York; Miami, Florida; Philadelphia, Pennsylvania; and Washington, DC; four in its central region: Chicago, Illinois; Detroit, Michigan; Houston, Texas; and Kansas City, Missouri; and three in its western region: Federal Way, Washington; Lakewood, Colorado; and Norwalk, California. See SBA, "OIG Directory," at https://www.sba.gov/oig/oig-directory.

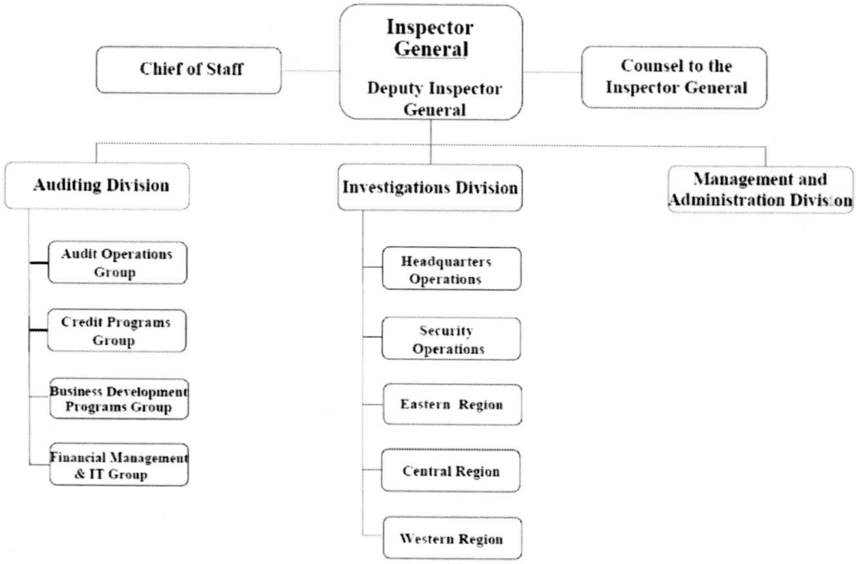

Source: U.S. Small Business Administration, Office of Inspector General, "General Organizational Chart," at https://www.sba.gov/sites/default/files/oig/OIG_Organi zation_Chart.pdf.

Figure 1. SBA OIG's Organizational Chart, FY2018.

RECENT ACTIVITIES

As mentioned previously, the SBA OIG conducts and supervises audits and investigations of the SBA's programs and operations. As a complement to its criminal and civil fraud investigations, the SBA OIG also recommends to the SBA suspensions, debarment, and other administrative enforcement actions against SBA lenders, borrowers, contractors, and others who have engaged in fraud or have otherwise exhibited a lack of business integrity.[42] The SBA OIG also conducts, supervises, and participates in various training activities to counter fraud in SBA programs.

---

42 SBA, OIG, "Semiannual Report to Congress, Fall 2016," p. 17, at https://www. sba.gov/sites/default/files/oig/ SAR_Fall_2016_Publication_Draft_-_508.pdf

Audit Reports

During FY2017, the SBA OIG issued 19 audit reports containing 72 recommendations for improving the SBA's operations. The SBA's OIG provided several examples in its congressional budget justification document of what it considered to be among its more noteworthy audits, including the following:

Business Loans and Oversight

> A review of SBA's Microloan Program performed in FY 2017 determined that SBA management did not effectively implement all prior audit recommendations made as a result of a review conducted in 2009 to improve oversight. Furthermore, SBA management did not conduct adequate program oversight to measure program performance and ensure program integrity. In our review of a statistical sample of 52 microloan files from 14 intermediaries, we found that data contained in SBA's information system for 27 of the loans did not match the information included in the intermediaries' loan files. In addition, we found that intermediaries did not have sufficient documentation to support that it originated and closed 44 of the 52 microloans, or 85 percent, totaling approximately $910,000, in accordance with SBA's requirements. These deficiencies affect the reliability of the data reported to SBA by the intermediaries.[43]
>
> An OIG report presented the results of our ongoing High Risk 7(a) Loan Review program from March 2017 to August 2017 and an overall summary of our work to date. To accomplish our objective, we used an internal loan scoring system to prioritize loans for review based on known risk attributes. A review of five early-defaulted loans identified material lender origination and closing deficiencies that justified denial of the guaranty for one loan totaling $917,107. We also identified suspicious activity on two purchased loans totaling $1.9 million, resulting in formal referrals to our Investigations Division. OIG recommended that SBA require the lender to bring the loan into compliance and, if not possible,

---

43 SBA, OIG, "FY2019 Congressional Budget Justification," p. 210, at https://www.sba.gov/sites/default/files/aboutsbaarticle/FY_2019_CBJ_Office_of_Inspector_General.pdf.

seek recovery of $917,107, plus interest, on the guaranty paid by SBA. SBA agreed with the recommendation and has contacted the lender to obtain additional information to bring the loan into compliance.

Disaster Loans

Hurricane Sandy struck the East Coast of the United States in October 2012, causing approximately $67 billion in damage. As of November 2013, SBA had approved and disbursed 19,295 loans, totaling approximately $758 million; 501 of these loans had defaulted by April 2015. A review of early defaulted Hurricane Sandy disaster loans found that despite the relatively low early default rate of Hurricane Sandy loans compared to other disasters, 17 of the 21 loans reviewed were approved without verifying borrowers' eligibility or were made to borrowers that lacked creditworthiness or repayment ability. OIG considers loans that default within 18 months of initial disbursement as defaulting early. OIG statistically projected sample results to the universe of early-defaulted loans and determined with 95 percent confidence that at least 361 of the 501 early-defaulted loans, valued at $4.3 million, were not approved in accordance with SBA or other Federal requirements. The most prevalent area of concern OIG observed was borrower creditworthiness, as the majority of loans in the sample were made to borrowers with unsatisfactory credit histories. OIG also determined that the Office of Disaster Assistance could improve its disaster loan portfolio risk analysis process to reduce the early default rate. OIG made recommendations to clarify creditworthiness guidance; train employees to adequately determine borrower eligibility, creditworthiness, and repayment ability; and improve portfolio risk.[44]

Entrepreneurial Development

In 2012, SBA provided Syracuse University $450,000 to develop a new, pilot veteran's assistance program, called the Boots to Business (B2B) program. In February 2014, SBA announced the B2B program as a full program and posted the announcement on Grants.gov. SBA staff

[44] Ibid., p. 211.

retrieved 10 eligible applications from the system and eventually selected Syracuse University for the $3 million grant. We found that SBA's program announcement included a process to evaluate B2B grant applications. However, reviewers responsible for evaluating and scoring applications did not consistently follow this evaluation guidance. Additionally, although officials in the Office of Veterans Business Development (OVBD) met with the reviewers to discuss which applicant should be selected to receive the $3 million award, SBA has no documentation rationalizing its final selection of Syracuse University. Because SBA lacked such documentation, it could not demonstrate that it made a merit-based selection in awarding the grant. Overall, these issues may have been prevented if officials in the Office of Grants Management and OVBD had provided effective oversight, and SBA had a current Standard Operating Procedure for grants management that (1) provided clear guidance on how to develop program-specific review criteria, (2) clearly defined the roles and responsibilities of grants and program personnel involved in the evaluation process, and (3) ensured grants and program personnel maintained a record of the evaluation process. SBA implemented our four recommendations.[45]

Improving IT Systems and Controls

FISMA [the Federal Information Security Management Act] requires that OIG review SBA's information security program. This review found that SBA continues to progress in certain FISMA evaluation categories, but still needs to implement 28 longstanding open recommendations and related unresolved vulnerabilities in the FISMA reporting areas. The results of the FISMA report indicates that until SBA takes steps to address longstanding weaknesses in its IT systems and control structures, the Agency will be at risk of data loss or system penetration.[46]

Preventing and Reducing Improper Payments

OIG annually evaluates SBA's compliance with the Improper Payments Elimination and Recovery Act (IPERA) requirements. OIG

[45] Ibid., p. 212.
[46] Ibid., pp. 212, 213.

objectives were to (1) assess progress made by SBA to remediate improper payment-related recommendations, and (2) determine whether SBA complied with IPERA reporting requirements using guidelines outlined in the Office of Management and Budget (OMB) Memorandum M-15-02, Appendix C to Circular No. A-123, Requirements for Effective Estimation and Remediation of Improper Payments. Our overall qualitative review showed that SBA continued to make progress in its efforts to prevent and reduce improper payments. SBA published and posted an Agency Financial Report (AFR) on its website, conducted program-specific risk assessments, published improper payment estimates for all programs and activities identified as susceptible to significant improper payments, published extracts from the applicable programmatic corrective action plans in the AFR, reported a gross improper payment rate of less than 10 percent for six of seven areas tested for FY 2016 reporting, and published and met the annual reduction target for six of the applicable seven areas tested. However, SBA was not compliant with IPERA reporting requirements because disbursements for goods and services had an improper payment rate that exceeded the 10 percent threshold; and 7(a) loan guaranty purchases did not meet their annual reduction target.[47]

Investigations, Debarment Referrals, and Training Activities

In FY2017, the SBA OIG's investigations resulted in 35 indictments or informations and 25 convictions.[48] For example,

- The owner of a Denver, Colorado, real estate investment firm was ordered to pay $951,571 in restitution and $3,745 in prosecutorial costs. He had previously been sentenced in state court to 24 years

[47] Ibid., p. 213.

[48] An *information* is a sworn written statement that charges that a particular individual has done a criminal act or is guilty of a criminal omission. Because the Fifth Amendment to the U.S. Constitution expressly creates a constitutional right to be indicted by a grand jury, an information is used in federal criminal procedure only when a defendant voluntarily pleads guilty (often as part of a plea bargain) and waives the right to an indictment. See The Free Dictionary, "Information," at http://legal-dictionary.thefreedictionary.com/Information; and The Law Dictionary, "Information," at http://thelawdictionary.org/information/.

of incarceration and 5 years of parole. This sentence will run consecutively to his earlier sentence of 24 years of incarceration for domestic violence. In June 2016, a jury had found the man guilty on 11 counts, including violating the Colorado Organized Crime Control Act; making forged (false) statements to SBA, a California bank, and the state of Colorado; criminal impersonation; and theft of funds from various lenders. He and five other family members had been originally indicted on 37 total counts. Those family members have pled guilty and have been sentenced. The investigation showed that the owner obtained a $2.323 million SBA-guaranteed loan to refinance his office building and other existing debt. To obtain the loan, he concealed his extensive criminal history and the fact that he was on probation. He also falsified documents related to his debts. This was a joint investigation with the Colorado Attorney General's Office, Colorado Bureau of Investigation, Federal Bureau of Investigation, and Federal Housing Finance Agency OIG.[49]

- A Department of Defense account manager for an information technology firm was sentenced in the U.S. District Court in the District of Maryland to 60 months in prison after pleading guilty to conspiracy to commit wire fraud. He must pay $9.440 million in restitution. His firm was one of two subcontractors to an SBA Section 8(a) company. The investigation revealed that he participated in the three companies' scheme to defraud the government by submitting fraudulent invoices that double-billed against the contract. He also submitted false claims for work not correctly performed or that was performed with the contractor or subcontractors not complying with contractual or regulatory requirements. The investigation is being jointly conducted with the

[49] SBA, OIG, "FY2019 Congressional Budget Justification," pp. 215, 216, at https://www.sba.gov/sites/default/files/aboutsbaarticle/FY_2019_CBJ_Office_of_Inspector_General.pdf.

U.S. Air Force Office of Special Investigations, Defense Criminal Investigative Service, and Naval Criminal Investigative Service.[50]

The SBA OIG also sent 106 suspension and debarment referrals to the SBA and made 5 referrals to other agencies that resulted in 26 proposed debarments and 33 final debarments by the SBA, 2 administrative agreements entered into by the SBA in lieu of debarment, and 5 present responsibility actions (investigations) by other agencies.[51] The SBA OIG also annually provides training and outreach sessions, attended by over a thousand government employees, lending officials, and law enforcement representatives, on topics related to fraud in government lending and contracting programs.[52]

MONETARY SAVINGS AND RECOVERIES

The SBA OIG reports that its audits and investigations resulted in monetary savings and recoveries of nearly $82.1 million in FY2017 ($53.7 million from potential investigative recoveries and fines, $12.7 million from asset forfeitures, $0.53 million for loans or contracts not approved or canceled, $12.9 million from loans not made as a result of name checks, and $2.1 million in disallowed costs agreed to by management).[53]

Most OIGs, including the SBA OIG, quantify their monetary savings by identifying and reporting amounts affected by their activities. This methodological approach, arguably, provides a fairly good overview of the

---

[50] Ibid., p. 216.

[51] Ibid., p. 221. Debarred contractors, lenders, and borrowers are generally ineligible for new federal contracts or SBA loans for a fixed period of time, while suspended contractors, lenders, and borrowers are generally ineligible for the duration of any investigation or litigation involving their conduct. See U.S. Congress, House Committee on Small Business, SBA Management and Performance Challenges: The Inspector General's Perspective, 114th Cong., 2nd sess., March 16, 2016, H. Hrg. 114-049 (Washington: GPO, 2016), p. 29.

[52] U.S. Congress, House Committee on Small Business, *SBA Management and Performance Challenges: The Inspector General's Perspective*, 114th Cong., 2nd sess., March 16, 2016, H. Hrg. 114-049 (Washington: GPO, 2016), p. 29.

[53] SBA, OIG, "FY2019 Congressional Budget Justification," p. 220, at https://www.sba.gov/sites/default/files/aboutsbaarticle/FY_2019_CBJ_Office_of_Inspector_General.pdf.

OIG's activities' scope, nature, and impact. However, this approach has limitations. For example, precise data concerning monetary savings are not always readily available. Also, from a budgetary perspective, the monetary savings identified is sometimes less than the actual monetary savings realized. For example,

- Savings from potential recoveries and fines ($53.7 million in FY2017) is derived from the actual amount imposed by courts in criminal sentencings (including fines and restitution), criminal settlements, and civil settlements. These recoveries are deemed "potential" because the court ordered them in FY2017, but they may not have been collected yet. The SBA OIG does not track collections resulting from these orders. As a result, the SBA OIG is not able to report the final amount of money actually recovered.[54]
- Savings from loans or contracts not approved or cancelled ($0.53 million in FY2017) is "comprised of the sum of the amounts that would have been borrowed as loans or awarded via contracts had there been no involvement by the OIG Investigations Division."[55] From a budgetary perspective, the actual monetary savings generated by these actions is less than the amount cited.[56] When a SBA loan is not approved, no funds are returned to the SBA because the loan amount has not been issued yet. When a SBA business loan is cancelled, the loan amount is ultimately returned to the lender, not to the SBA, because the SBA did not make the loan, it guaranteed a portion of it. When a small business contract is not approved, no funds are returned to the agency sponsoring the contract because the contracted amount has not been awarded yet. When a small business contract is cancelled, the contracted amount is typically made available to other contractors.

---

[54] SBA, OIG, "Correspondence with the author," June 23, 2016.
[55] Ibid.
[56] By promoting program efficiency, it could be argued that these actions cumulatively result in administrative cost savings. However, it is difficult to quantify these savings.

- Savings from loans not made as a result of name checks ($12.9 million in FY2017) is the amount that would have been borrowed by ineligible applicants "based on the amount applied for by each applicant denied; then calculated by the percentage of ownership or stock owned or to be owned in the small business or development company."[57] Once again, from a budgetary perspective, the actual monetary savings generated by these actions is less than the amount cited.
- Savings from disallowed costs agreed to by management ($2.1 million in FY2017) could result in actual budgetary savings, but the recovery process typically takes time. As a result, the final savings for disallowed costs is often not known during the fiscal year in which it is reported.

Finally, estimating the monetary savings from the SBA OIG's activities is challenging because it is difficult, if not impossible, to determine what changes the SBA might have made to its programs and operations if the SBA OIG did not exist.

Perhaps indicative of these methodological challenges, the SBA OIG's semiannual reports and annual congressional budget justification document's statistical highlights sections refer to these figures as "office-wide dollar accomplishments" as opposed to monetary savings.[58]

MOST SERIOUS MANAGEMENT AND PERFORMANCE CHALLENGES FACING THE SBA

Pursuant to P.L. 106-531, the Records Consolidation Act of 2000, and OMB Circular A-136, the SBA OIG issues an annual *Report on the Most Serious Management and Performance Challenges Facing the SBA*. This

---

[57] SBA, OIG, "Correspondence with the author," June 23, 2016.

[58] For example, see SBA, OIG, "FY2019 Congressional Budget Justification," p. 220, at https://www.sba.gov/sites/default/files/aboutsbaarticle/FY_2019_CBJ_Office_of_Inspector_General.pdf.

chapter is, arguably, the SBA OIG's signature oversight document, focusing attention "on areas that are particularly vulnerable to fraud, waste, error, and mismanagement, or otherwise pose a significant risk and generally have been subject to one or more OIG or GAO reports."[59]

The FY2018 *Report on the Most Serious Management and Performance Challenges Facing the SBA* lists the following eight challenges:

1. Weaknesses in small business contracting programs and inaccurate procurement data undermine the reliability of contracting goals achievements.
2. SBA's information technology leadership capabilities need strengthening to address operational risks and challenges.
3. SBA needs effective human capital strategies to carry out its mission successfully and become a high-performing organization.
4. SBA needs to improve its risk management and oversight practices to ensure its loan programs operate effectively and continue to benefit small businesses.
5. SBA needs to ensure that the Section 8(a) business development program identifies and addresses the needs of program participants, only eligible firms are admitted into the program, and standards for determining economic disadvantage are justifiable.
6. SBA can improve its loan programs by ensuring quality deliverables and reducing improper payments at SBA loan operation centers.
7. Disaster assistance must balance competing priorities to deliver timely assistance and reduce improper payments.
8. SBA needs to effectively manage its acquisition program.[60]

The SBA OIG provides a series of recommended actions within each of the reported challenges to enhance the effectiveness of the SBA's

[59] Ibid., p. 207.

[60] SBA, OIG, *Report on the Most Serious Management and Performance Challenges in Fiscal Year 2018*, Report Number 18-01, October 12, 2017, at https://www.sba.gov/sites/default/files/oig/SBA_OIG_Report_18-01.pdf.

programs and operations. The management challenges are "driven by SBA's current needs" and based on the SBA OIG's understanding of the SBA's programs and operations, as well as challenges presented in other agency reports, principally GAO reports. Accordingly, the challenges presented each year may change based the SBA's actions or inactions "to remedy past weaknesses."[61]

For example, in its FY2018 report, the SBA OIG reported that the SBA's Office of the Chief Information Officer made significant progress in improving its oversight of information technology investments (Challenge 2) and the SBA's Office of Capital Access improved the quality control program for its loan centers and took actions to accurately report and reduce improper payments (Challenge 6). However, the SBA has still not implemented two of the three private lender disaster loan programs mandated by the Small Business Disaster Response and Loan Improvement Acts of 2008 (Challenge 7).[62]

Impact on Program Efficiency and Effectiveness

OIGs are, arguably, best known for investigations addressing waste, fraud, and abuse and audits containing recommendations to enhance programmatic and operational efficiencies. However, a full and complete assessment of an OIG's impact should address all of the office's statutory responsibilities, including its efforts to

- enhance programmatic and operational efficiencies and the OIG's agency's effectiveness in achieving program goals through audits;
- reduce waste, fraud, and abuse through investigations;

[61] U.S. Congress, House Committee on Small Business, *SBA Management and Performance Challenges: The Inspector General's Perspective*, 114th Cong., 2nd sess., March 16, 2016, H. Hrg. 114-049 (Washington: GPO, 2016), pp. 23-24.

[62] SBA, OIG, *Report on the Most Serious Management and Performance Challenges in Fiscal Year 2018*, Report Number 18-01, October 12, 2017, pp. 4, 14, 17, at https://www.sba.gov/sites/default/files/oig/SBA_OIG_Report_18- 01.pdf.

- assist Congress and the OIG's agency by making recommendations concerning the impact of legislation and regulations on programmatic and operational efficiencies and waste, fraud, and abuse;
- assist the OIG's agency by making recommendations to facilitate the agency's relationships with other governmental and nongovernmental entities; and
- keep the OIG's agency head and Congress fully and currently informed of its findings and the agency's progress in implementing recommended corrective actions.

Enhancing Programmatic and Operational Efficiency and the Achievement of Program Goals through Audits

As shown in *Table 3*, over the past eight fiscal years, the SBA OIG reports that it

- issued 178 audit reports (an average of 22.25 audit reports per fiscal year);
- provided 900 recommendations for improving SBA operations, identifying improper payments, and strengthening controls to reduce fraud and unnecessary losses in SBA programs (an average of 112.5 recommendations per fiscal year), with the SBA taking action on 873 recommendations (an average of 109.1 recommendations addressed per fiscal year);
- generated $226.9 million in savings and efficiencies (an average of $28.4 million per fiscal year) in disallowed costs agreed to by SBA management and recommendations that funds be put to better use agreed to by SBA management;

- questioned $384.7 million in costs (an average of $48.1 million per fiscal year);[63] and
- recommended that $141.1 million be put to better use (an average of $17.6 million per fiscal year).

In terms of impact, the data presented in *Table 3* suggest that the SBA has made hundreds of changes to its internal operating procedures and programs as a direct result of the SBA OIG's audits.[64] In addition, comments by Members of the House Committee on Small Business and Senate Committee on Small Business and Entrepreneurship during congressional oversight hearings suggest that they view the SBA OIG's audits helpful in their oversight of the SBA, especially in terms of identifying management weaknesses and recommending solutions to remedy those weaknesses.[65] For example, in his opening remarks at a March 2016 congressional oversight hearing concerning the SBA's management and performance challenges, Representative Steve Chabot, chair of the House Committee on Small Business, stated

> It is clear that the Inspector General plays a critical role in ensuring effective management of the SBA. By conducting audits to identify program mismanagement, by investigating fraud or other wrongdoing, or by recommending changes to increase the efficiency of SBA operations, she has provided independent and objective reviews of agency actions.[66]

---

[63] The SBA views questioned costs as those that are found to be improper. Unsupported costs may be proper, but lack documentation. The SBA considers unsupported costs a subset of questioned costs. See SBA, OIG, "Semiannual Report to Congress, Fall 2016," p. 25, at https://www.sba.gov/sites/default/files/oig/SAR_Fall_2016_Publication_Draft_-_508.pdf.

[64] For additional information concerning the SBA OIG's impact on the SBA's 7(a) loan guarantee program, see CRS Report R41146, *Small Business Administration 7(a) Loan Guaranty Program*, by Robert Jay Dilger.

[65] For example, see U.S. Congress, House Committee on Small Business, *SBA Management and Performance Challenges: The Inspector General's Perspective*, 114th Cong., 2nd sess., March 16, 2016 (Washington: GPO, 2016); and U.S. Congress, House Committee on Small Business, Committee Staff, "Memorandum, Full Committee Hearing: SBA Management and Performance Challenges: The Inspector General's Perspective," March 14, 2016, at http://smallbusiness.house.gov/uploadedfiles/3-16-2016_hearing_memo.pdf.

[66] .S. Congress, House Committee on Small Business, *SBA Management and Performance Challenges: The Inspector General's Perspective*, 114th Cong., 2nd sess., March 16, 2016 (Washington: GPO, 2016), pp. 1-2.

Table 3. SBA OIG's Audits, FY2010-FY2017 ($ in millions)

Fiscal Year	Number of Audit Reports	Number of Recommendations Issued/Acted Upon[a]	Dollar Amount in Accomplishments[b]	Value of Costs Questioned	Value of Recommendations that Funds be Put to Better Use
2017	19	72/72	$2.1	$138.6	$0.0
2016	23	81/84	$3.2	$8.0	$1.3
2015	17	80/84	$15.0	$2.4	$9.1
2014	20	100/137	$93.7	$4.4	$4.8
2013	19	129/109	$42.8	$45.9	$40.7
2012	22	126/113	$8.8	$172.1	$50.7
2011	24	136/168	$60.2	$12.3	$0.0
2010	34	176/106	$1.1	$1.0	$34.5
Total	178	900/873	$226.9	$384.7	$141.1

Sources: U.S. Small Business Administration, Office of Inspector General, "Congressional Budget Justification, FY2012," pp. 1, 12, at https://www.sba. gov/sites/default/files/aboutsbaarticle/FINAL%20FY%202012%20CBJ%20FY%202010%20APR_0.pdf; U.S. Small Business Administration, Office of Inspector General, "Congressional Budget Justification, FY2013," p. 11, at https://www.sba.gov/sites/default/files/files/4-508%20Compliant%20FY%202013%20Office%20of%20Inspector%20General%20CBJ2(1).pdf; U.S. Small Business Administration, Office of Inspector General, "FY2014 Congressional Budget Justification," p. 16, at https://www.sba.gov/sites/default/files/files/4-508%20Compliant%20OIG%20FY%202014%20CBJ.PDF; U.S. Small Business Administration, Office of Inspector General, "FY201S Congressional Budget Justification," pp. 1, 17, at https://www.sba.gov/sites/default/files/files/SBA%20OIG%20FY%202015%20Congressional%20Submission%20508%20FINAL%20post.pdf; U.S. Small Business Administration, Office of Inspector General, "FY2016 Congressional Budget Justification," pp. 1, 22, at https://www.sba.gov/sites/default/files/files/4-Office_of_the_Inspector_General_FY_2016_CBJ_508.pdf; U.S. Small Business Administration, Office of Inspector General, "FY2017 Congressional Budget Justification," pp. 1, 21, at https:// www.sba.gov/sites/default/files/FY17-CBJ-oig.pdf; U.S. Small Business Administration, Office of Inspector General, "FY2018 Congressional Budget Justification," p. 23, at https://www.sba.gov/sites/default/files/aboutsbaarticle/Office_of_Inspector_General_-_FY_2018_CBJ.pdf; and U.S. Small Business Administration, Office of Inspector General, "FY2019 Congressional Budget Justification," p. 220, at https://www.sba.gov/sites/default/files/aboutsbaarticle/FY_2019_CBJ_Office_of_Inspector_General.pdf.

Notes:

[a] The number of the SBA OIG's recommendations acted upon by the SBA in a fiscal year may exceed the number of recommendations issued by the SBA OIG because the number acted upon may include recommendations issued in previous fiscal years.

[b] Sum of disallowed costs agreed to by management and recommendations that funds be put to better use agreed to by management.

However, some Members have also noted that the SBA OIG's impact is limited because the SBA OIG has no enforcement authority and the SBA has chosen to ignore many of its recommendations. As Representative Nydia Velazquez noted during that March 2016 congressional oversight hearing, some of the management challenges reported in the SBA OIG's annual *Report on the Most Serious Management and Performance Challenges Facing the SBA* "were first highlighted over a decade ago."[67] In addition, Peggy Gustafson (SBA's IG from October 2, 2009-January 9, 2017) testified at that hearing that the SBA currently "has 144 open OIG recommendations pertaining to reviews conducted in recent years and not so recent years across SBA programs."[68] She also testified that the SBA

> did demonstrate positive progress in resolving recommendations associated with five of the identified challenges [in the annual report on the most serious challenges facing the SBA]. However, they remained at status quo on four of the challenges and demonstrated no progress on one recommendation in an area related to information technology. Now, clearly these results I would say paint a mixed picture relative to SBA's commitment to addressing these challenges in earnest and their ability to overcome these challenges.
>
> Having said that, I think it also has to be acknowledged that SBA has shown that with a sustained, committed effort over time, they can achieve successful results in these challenges. For example, they moved to green [implemented the SBA OIG's recommendations concerning] ... the very large challenge related to their LMAS [Loan Management and Accounting System Modernization] IT system. So I think that really shows that these are challenges that with the right effort can really be conquered and met.[69]

Others have suggested that OIGs in general, including the SBA OIG, focus their auditing efforts on identifying and addressing programmatic

---

[67] Ibid., p. 1.
[68] Ibid., p. 4.
[69] Ibid.

and operational inefficiencies and spend less time addressing "whether the agency program operations were providing the outputs intended by Congress."[70] In their view, Congress passed P.L. 103-62, the Government Performance and Results Act of 1993, and P.L. 111-352, the Government Performance and Results Act Modernization Act of 2010, to provide mechanisms to assess the effectiveness of federal programs in a way that supplements the efforts of OIGs (e.g., by establishing statutory requirements for most agencies to set goals, measure performance, and submit related plans and reports to Congress for its potential use).[71]

In sum, the evidence suggests that the SBA OIG's audits have helped to increase the efficiency of the SBA's programs and operations. However, it could also be argued that the SBA OIG's impact is muted because OIGs lack enforcement authority, meaning that the SBA may proceed with, or without, taking into account the recommendations presented in the SBA OIG's audits.

Reducing Waste, Fraud, and Abuse through Investigations

As shown in *Table 4*, over the past eight fiscal years, the SBA OIG reports that it

- opened 599 cases (an average of 74.9 cases opened per fiscal year);
- issued 508 indictments or informations (an average of 63.5 indictments or informations per fiscal year), with 388 convictions (an average of 48.5 convictions per fiscal year);

---

[70] Barry Pineles, chief counsel, House Committee on Small Business, "Hearing Memorandum: Reducing Duplication and Promoting Efficiency at the SBA: The Inspector General's View," June 3, 2013, at http://smallbusiness.house.gov/uploadedfiles/6-5-2013__final_hearing_memo.pdf.

[71] Ibid., pp. 6-8. For additional information and analysis concerning P.L. 103-62, the Government Performance and Results Act of 1993, and P.L. 111-352, the Government Performance and Results Act Modernization Act of 2010, see CRS Report R42379, *Changes to the Government Performance and Results Act (GPRA): Overview of the New Framework of Products and Processes*, by Clinton T. Brass.

- generated $978.4 million in investigative recoveries and fines, asset forfeitures attributed to OIG investigations, loans or contracts not approved or cancelled as a result of investigations, and loans not made as a result of name checks (an average of $122.3 million per fiscal year); and
- recommended 487 suspensions or disbarments (an average of 60.9 per fiscal year), with the SBA suspending or disbarring 256 of these firms or owners (an average of 32.0 firms/owners per fiscal year).

The SBA OIG also reported that it has an active, annual caseload of about 255 criminal and civil fraud investigations of potential loan and contracting fraud and other wrongdoing and that "many of these investigations involve complex, multi-million-dollar fraudulent financial schemes perpetrated by multiple suspects."[72]

The data presented in *Table 4* suggest that the SBA OIG's investigations have resulted in hundreds of criminal convictions and millions of dollars in recovered funds. In addition, comments by Members of the House Committee on Small Business and Senate Committee on Small Business and Entrepreneurship suggest that, generally speaking, they acknowledge and value the SBA OIG's investigations as a means to identify and reduce waste, fraud, and abuse.[73] However, the SBA's former IG, Peggy Gustafson, has testified that the SBA OIG's investigative efforts, in initiating and continuing investigations, are constrained by resource limitations.

---

[72] SBA, OIG, "FY2019 Congressional Budget Justification," p. 196, at https://www.sba.gov/sites/default/files/aboutsbaarticle/FY_2019_CBJ_Office_of_Inspector_General.pdf.

[73] For example, see U.S. Congress, House Committee on Small Business, SBA Management and Performance Challenges: The Inspector General's Perspective, 114th Cong., 2nd sess., March 16, 2016 (Washington: GPO, 2016), pp. 2, 7-8, 12; and U.S. Congress, House Committee on Small Business, Committee Staff, "Memorandum, Full Committee Hearing: SBA Management and Performance Challenges: The Inspector General's Perspective," March 14, 2016, at http://smallbusiness.house.gov/uploadedfiles/3-16-2016_hearing_memo.pdf.

Table 4. SBA OIG's Investigations, FY2010-FY2017 ($ in millions)

Fiscal Year	Number of Cases Opened	Number of Indictments and Informations	Number of Convictions[a]	Recoveries and Management Avoidances[b]	Number of Suspensions & Debarments Recommended/ Issued[c]
2017	86	35	25	$79.9	106/33
2016	104	45	41	$141.5	75/32
2015	78	52	57	$118.8	74/46
2014	51	103	67	$76.2	50/42
2013	50	64	51	$348.2	65/26
2012	65	59	59	$81.8	45/31
2011	85	69	47	$60.7	41/30
2010	80	81	41	$71.3	31/16
Total	599	508	388	$978.4	487/256

Sources: U.S. Small Business Administration, Office of Inspector General, "Semiannual Report to Congress, Spring 2010," p. 24, at https://www.sba. gov/sites/default/files/oig/oig%20spring% 20 2010%20sar.pdf; U.S. Small Business Administration, Office of Inspector General, "Semiannual Report to Congress, Fall 2010," p. 24, at "https://www.sba.gov/sites/default/files/oig/Semiannual%20Report%20to%20Congress%20-%20Fall%20 2010_0.pdf; U.S. Small Business Administration, Office of Inspector General, "Congressional Budget Justification FY2012," pp. 1, 12, 13, at https://www.sba.gov/sites/default/files/aboutsbaarticle/FINAL% 20FY%202012%20CBJ% 20FY%202010%20APR_0.pdf; U.S. Small Business Administration, Office of Inspector General, "Congressional Budget Justification, FY2013," pp. 11-12, at https://www.sba.gov/ sites/default/files/files/4-508%20Compliant%20FY%202013%20Office%20of%20Inspector%20General% 20CBJ2(1).pdf; U.S. Small Business Administration, Office of Inspector General, "FY2014 Congressional Budget Justification," pp. 2, 16, 17, at https://www.sba.gov/sites/default/ files/ files/4-508%20Compliant %20OIG%20FY%202014%20CBJ.PDF; U.S. Small Business Administration, Office of Inspector General, "FY2015 Congressional Budget Justification," pp. 1, 15, 17, 18, at https://www.sba.gov/sites/default/files/files/ SBA%20OIG%20FY%202015%20 Congressional%20Submission%20508%20FINAL%20post.pdf; U.S. Small Business Administration, Office of Inspector General, "FY2016 Congressional Budget Justification," pp. 1, 22, 23, at https://www.sba.gov/sites/default/files/files/4-Office_of_the_Inspector_General_FY_2016_CBJ_ 508. pdf; U.S. Small Business Administration, Office of Inspector General, "FY2017 Congressional Budget Justification," pp. 1, 22, 23, at https://www.sba.gov/sites/default/files/ FY17-CBJ-oig.pdf; U.S. Small Business Administration, Office of Inspector General, "FY2018 Congressional Budget Justification," pp. 23, 24, at https://www.sba.gov/sites/default/files/aboutsbaarticle/Office_ of_Inspector_General_-_FY_2018_CBJ.pdf; and U.S. Small Business Administration, Office of Inspector General, "FY2019 Congressional Budget Justification," pp. 220, 221, at https://www.sba.gov/sites/default/files/aboutsbaarticle/FY_2019_CBJ_Office _of_ Inspector_General.pdf.

Notes:

[a] The number of convictions may exceed the number of indictments and informations in a fiscal year because a conviction in any fiscal year could result from an indictment or information issued in that fiscal year or a previous fiscal year.

[b] Sum of potential investigative recoveries and fines, asset forfeitures attributed to OIG investigations, loans or contracts not approved or cancelled as a result of investigations, and loans not made as a result of name checks.

[c] The number of suspensions and debarments issued by the SBA in response to a recommendation from the SBA OIG does not include the number of recommended suspensions and debarments pending at the end of the fiscal year.

Recommendations Concerning the Impact of Legislation and Regulations

The SBA OIG reports that it routinely reviews and comments on proposed changes to the SBA's program directives.[74] These changes "include regulations, internal operating procedures, agency policy notices, and SBA forms completed by the public."[75]

The SBA OIG also tracks, reviews, and comments on legislation affecting the SBA and participates in OMB's Legislative Referral Memoranda (LRM) process for reviewing and coordinating agency recommendations on proposed, pending, and enrolled legislation.[76] The SBA OIG also "receives, through the SBA Office of Congressional and Legislative Affairs, congress-related documents being circulated by OMB, including pending legislation for consideration of Administration views and perspectives."[77]

When the SBA OIG identifies "material weaknesses" in changes proposed by the SBA, it "works with the Agency to implement recommended revisions to promote controls that are more effective and deter waste, fraud, or abuse."[78] The SBA OIG provides the SBA with both formal and informal comments. Formal comments are provided "through the Agency's internal document control process, the Correspondence Management System (CMS),[79] and as a reviewing party in the Agency's

---

[74] SBA, OIG, "Semiannual Report to Congress, Spring 2016," p. 18, at https://www.sba.gov/sites/default/files/oig/SBA_OIG_SAR_Spring_2016.pdf.

[75] Ibid.

[76] See U.S. Office of Management and Budget, "Circular No. A-19, Legislative Coordination and Clearance (9/20/1979)," at https://www.whitehouse.gov/omb/circulars_a019/.

[77] SBA, OIG, "Correspondence with the author," July 5, 2016.

[78] SBA, OIG, "Semiannual Report to Congress, Spring 2016," p. 18, at https://www.sba.gov/sites/default/files/oig/SBA_OIG_SAR_Spring_2016.pdf.

[79] The SBA's CRM-Correspondence Management (CRM-CM) system "will efficiently manage, organize, search, track, and report on correspondence and action plans... The CRM-CM will store and manage correspondence from the members of the U.S. House of Representatives and the U.S. Senate, the President, and SBA's Administrator or Deputy Administrator." See SBA, "Privacy Impact Assessment: Name of System/Application: CRM-Correspondence Management Program Office: Office of the Executive Secretariat," at https://www.sba.gov/sites/default/files/files/CRM_Correspondence_Management.pdf.

Paperwork Reduction Act (PRA) process."[80] Informal comments "occur in the context of program officials seeking SBA OIG guidance when preparing new guidance."[81]

In terms of legislation, the SBA OIG provides comments and suggestions "directly with congressional stakeholders" and shares its views with SBA officials and OMB if the legislation is being "circulated for solicited views by OMB through its LRM process, or if determined by the OIG to be a necessary course of action."[82]

As shown in *Table 5*, over the past eight fiscal years, the SBA OIG reports that it

- conducted 921 reviews of legislation, regulations, standard operating procedures, and other issuances (an average of 115.1 reviews per fiscal year);[83] and
- submitted comments on 472 of these initiatives (an average of 59.0 initiatives commented on per fiscal year).

The data in *Table 5* suggest that the SBA OIG actively reviews and comments on legislation and SBA program directives.

---

[80] SBA, OIG, "Correspondence with the author," July 5, 2016. "OIRA [the Office of Information and Regulatory Affairs] was created within OMB [the Office of Management and Budget] by Section 3503 of the Paperwork Reduction Act (PRA) of 1980 (44 U.S.C. Chapter 35) ...With regard to paperwork reduction, the act generally prohibited agencies from conducting or sponsoring a collection of information until they had submitted their proposed information collection requests to OIRA and the office had approved those requests. The PRA's requirements cover rules issued by virtually all agencies, including Cabinet departments, independent agencies, and independent regulatory agencies and commissions. Although the PRA gave OIRA substantive responsibilities in many areas, the bulk of the office's day-to-day activities under the act were initially focused on reviewing and approving agencies' proposed information collection requests." For additional information and analysis concerning the PRA see CRS Report RL32397, *Federal Rulemaking: The Role of the Office of Information and Regulatory Affairs*, coordinated by Maeve P. Carey and CRS Report RL32240, *The Federal Rulemaking Process: An Overview*, coordinated by Maeve P. Carey.

[81] SBA, OIG, "Correspondence with the author," July 5, 2016.

[82] Ibid.

[83] Other issuances include policy notices, procedural notices, the SBA Administrator's action memoranda, and other SBA initiatives, which frequently involve the implementation of new programs or policies.

Table 5. Legislation, Regulations, Standard Operating Procedures (SOPs), and Other Issuances Reviewed and Comments Provided, FY2010-FY2017

Fiscal Year	Legislation, Regulations, SOPs, and Other Issuances Reviewed	Number of Initiatives for Which Comments Were Provided
2017	101	36
2016	119	52
2015	129	72
2014	93	46
2013	115	60
2012	136	79
2011	133	80
2010	95	47
Total	921	472

Sources: U.S. Small Business Administration, Office of Inspector General, "Semiannual Report to Congress, Spring 2010," p. 22, at https://www.sba. gov/sites/default/files/oig/oig%20spring%202010%20sar.pdf; U.S. Small Business Administration, Office of Inspector General, "Semiannual Report to Congress, Fall 2010," p. 21, at "https://www.sba.gov/sites/default/files/oig/Semiannual%20Report%20to%20Congress%20-%20Fall%20201 0_0.pdf; U.S. Small Business Administration, Office of Inspector General, "Congressional Budget Justification FY2012," p. 12, at https://www.sba.gov/sites/ default/files/aboutsbaarticle/INAL%20FY%202012%20CBJ% 20FY%202010%20APR_0.pdf; U.S. Small Business Administration, Office of Inspector General, "Semiannual Report to Congress, Spring 2011," p. 17, at https://www.sba. gov/sites/default/files/oig/Semi-Annual% 20Report%20to%20Congress%20-%20Spring%202011.pdf; U.S. Small Business Administration, Office of Inspector General, "Semiannual Report to Congress, Fall 2011," p. 17, at https://www.sba.gov/sites/ default/files/oig/Fall%202011%20SBA%20OIG%20SAR.pdf; U.S. Small Business Administration, Office of Inspector General, "Congressional Budget Justification, FY2013," p. 11, at https://www.sba.gov/sites/default/ files/files/4-508%20Compliant%20FY%202013%20Office%20of% 20Inspector% 20General%20CBJ2(1).pdf; U.S. Small Business Administration, Office of Inspector General, "Semiannual Report to Congress, Spring 2012," p. 20, at https://www.sba.gov/sites/default/files/oig/SBA%20OIG%20SAR%20Spring%202012% 20.pdf; U.S. Small Business Administration, Office of Inspector General, "Semiannual Report to Congress, Fall 2012," p. 20, at https://www.sba. gov/sites/default/files/oig/FINAL_FALL%202012_SAR.pdf; U.S. Small Business Administration, Office of Inspector General, "FY2014 Congressional Budget Justification," p. 17, at https://www.sba.gov/sites/ default/files/files/4-508%20 Compliant%20OIG%20FY%202014%20CBJ.PDF; U.S. Small Business Administration, Office of Inspector General, "Semiannual Report to Congress, Spring 2013," p. 19, at https://www.sba.gov/sites/default/files/oig/ SBA% 20OIG%20_Spring_%202013_SAR.pdf; U.S. Small Business Administration, Office of Inspector General, "Semiannual Report to Congress, Fall 2013," p. 18, at https://www.sba.gov/sites/default/files/oig/Fall_2013_-_SBA_OIG_SAR_0.pdf; U.S. Small Business Administration, Office of Inspector General, "FY2015 Congressional Budget Justification," p. 15, at https://www.sba.gov/sites/default/files/files/SBA%20OIG%20FY%202015%20Congressional%20Submission %20508%20FINAL%20post.pdf; U.S. Small Business Administration, Office of Inspector General, "FY2016 Congressional Budget Justification," p. 23, at https://www.sba.gov/sites/default/files/files/4-Office_of_the_ Inspector_General _FY_2016_CBJ_508.pdf; U.S. Small Business Administration, Office of Inspector General, "FY2017 Congressional Budget Justification," p. 22, at https://www.sba.gov/sites/default/files/FY17-CBJ-oig.pdf; U.S. Small Business Administration, Office of Inspector General, "FY2018 Congressional Budget Justification," p. 24, at https://www.sba.gov/sites/ default/files/aboutsbaarticle/ Office_of_Inspector_General_-_FY_2018_CBJ.pdf; and U.S. Small Business Administration, Office of Inspector General, "FY2019 Congressional Budget Justification," p. 221, at https://www.sba.gov/ sites/ default/files/aboutsbaarticle/ FY_2019_CBJ_Office_of_Inspector_General.pdf.

Note: Other issuances include policy notices, procedural notices, the SBA Administrator's action memoranda, and other SBA initiatives, which frequently involve the implementation of new programs or policies.

However, it is difficult to determine the impact of these reviews and comments because the SBA OIG does not track or report data concerning the SBA's response to these comments. The SBA OIG indicated that neither the dynamic nature of the informal comment process nor the collaborative follow-up procedures from formal comments are conducive to quantification.... Our sense of these comments is that the Agency will generally act upon SBA OIG comments. Typically, the Agency modifies clearances and PRA packages in response to material SBA OIG concerns. An accurate tracking and quantification of these clearances, however, is unlikely to yield particularly useful data relative to the resource expenditure necessary for that collection.[84]

Facilitating the SBA's Relationships with Other Governmental and Nongovernmental Entities

The SBA OIG provides training and outreach sessions on topics related to fraud in government lending and contracting programs. These training and outreach sessions are designed to facilitate the SBA's relationships with other governmental and nongovernmental entities in identifying and ameliorating fraud.

The SBA OIG's outreach and training sessions are attended by over 1,000 people each year, including SBA and other government employees, lending officials, and law enforcement representatives.[85] Topics include "types of fraud, fraud indicators and trends; how to report suspicious activity that may be fraudulent; suspension and debarment, the Program Fraud Civil Remedies Act, and other topics related to deterring and detecting fraud in government lending and contracting programs."[86]

---

[84] SBA, OIG, "Correspondence with the author," July 5, 2016.

[85] SBA, OIG, "FY2017 Congressional Budget Justification," p. 19, at https://www.sba.gov/sites/default/files/FY17- CBJ-oig.pdf.

[86] Ibid.

Table 6. Outreach and Training Sessions, FY2010-FY2017

Fiscal Year	Number of Sessions	Number of Attendees
2017	220	3,556
2016	74	1,717
2015	28	1,067
2014	25	1,370
2013	19	900
2012	24	1,100
2011	24	1,130
2010	11	505
Total	425	11,345

Sources: U.S. Small Business Administration, Office of Inspector General, "Semiannual Report to Congress, Spring 2010," p. 22, at https://www.sba.gov/ sites/default/files/oig/oig%20spring%202010%20sar.pdf; U.S. Small Business Administration, Office of Inspector General, "Semiannual Report to Congress, Fall 2010," p. 21, at "https://www.sba.gov/sites/default/files/oig/Semiannual%20Report%20to%20 Congress %20-%20Fall%202010_0.pdf; U.S. Small Business Administration, Office of Inspector General, "Semiannual Report to Congress, Spring 2011," p. 17, at https://www.sba.gov/sites/default/files/ oig/Semi-Annual%20Report%20to%20Congress%20-%20Spring%202011.pdf; U.S. Small Business Administration, Office of Inspector General, "Semiannual Report to Congress, Fall 2011," p. 16, at https://www.sba.gov/sites/default/files/oig/ Fall%202011%20SBA%20OIG%20SAR.pdf; U.S. Small Business Administration, Office of Inspector General, "Semiannual Report to Congress, Spring 2012," p. 21, at https://www.sba.gov/sites/default/files/oig/SBA%20OIG%20SAR%20Spring% 202012%20. pdf; U.S. Small Business Administration, Office of Inspector General, "Semiannual Report to Congress, Fall 2012," p. 17, at https://www.sba.gov/sites/default/files/oig/FINAL_FALL%20 2012_SAR.pdf; U.S. Small Business Administration, Office of Inspector General, "FY2014 Congressional Budget Justification," p. 15, at https://www.sba.gov/sites/default/files/files/4-508%20Compliant%20OIG%20 FY%202014%20CBJ. PDF; U.S. Small Business Administration, Office of Inspector General, "FY2015 Congressional Budget Justification," p. 16, at https://www.sba.gov/sites/default/files/files/SBA% 20OIG%20FY%202015%20Congressional%20Submission%20508%20FINAL%20post.pdf; U.S. Small Business Administration, Office of Inspector General, "FY2016 Congressional Budget Justification," pp. 3, 20, at https://www.sba.gov/sites/default/files/files/4-Office_of_the_Inspector_General_FY_ 2016_CBJ_508.pdf; U.S. Small Business Administration, Office of Inspector General, "FY2017 Congressional Budget Justification," pp. 2, 19, at https://www.sba.gov/sites/default/ files/FY17-CBJ-oig.pdf; and U.S. Small Business Administration, Office of Inspector General, "FY2019 Congressional Budget Justification," p. 197, at https://www.sba.gov/sites/default/files/aboutsbaarticle/FY_2019_CBJ_ Office_of_Inspector_General.pdf.

As shown in *Table 6*, the SBA OIG provided 425 outreach and training sessions over the past eight fiscal years (an average of 53.1 sessions per fiscal year) to 11,345 attendees (an average of 1,418 attendees per fiscal year).

The SBA OIG also cosponsors and/or participates in roundtable discussions, procurement training seminars, and various small business award ceremonies; and is an active participant in the Emerging Leaders program.[87]

The data presented in *Table 6* suggest that the SBA OIG actively provides training and outreach sessions related to identifying and addressing fraud. The office also participates in a number of activities involving federal agencies and others with an interest in fraud prevention activities. It is difficult to measure the impact of these training and outreach activities on the SBA's interaction with other federal agencies. The SBA OIG reports that these sessions are well-attended, and receive high ratings from attendees.

Keeping the SBA Administrator and Congress Fully and Currently Informed

As mentioned previously, the IG Act requires IGs to keep their agency's administrator and Congress fully and currently informed concerning fraud and other serious problems, abuses, and deficiencies relating to the agency's administration of its programs and operations and to report on the progress made in implementing recommended corrective action. The SBA OIG's informational role is conducted through both formal and informal communication.

Formal communication occurs through (1) the publication of audits, investigations, semiannual reports, and the annual *Report on the Most Serious Management and Performance Challenges Facing the SBA*; (2) correspondence with SBA officials, congressional staff, and Members of Congress; (3) briefings with SBA officials, congressional staff, and Members of Congress (as needed or as requested); (4) press releases; and

---

[87] The Emerging Leaders program provides "executives of businesses poised for growth in historically challenged communities" with "the organizational framework, resource network, and motivation required to build sustainable businesses and promote the economic development within urban communities." The program "is open to small business owners and executives that: have annual revenues of at least $400,000; have been in business for at least 3 years; have at least one employee, other than self." See SBA, "SBA Emerging Leaders Initiative," at https://www.sba.gov/about-sba/sba-initiatives/sba-emerging-leaders-initiative.

occasionally (5) congressional testimony.[88] Informal communication occurs primarily through telephone consultation or by email with SBA officials, congressional staff, and Members of Congress (often facilitated by the SBA OIG's chief of staff).[89]

In terms of communication with the SBA, the SBA OIG reports that it has "immediate and direct access to the Administrator and her staff. As such, there are meetings that occur as needed with the Administrator. There are more frequent meetings with Deputy Administrator [Douglas J.] Kramer."[90]

In 2014, then-SBA Administrator Maria Contreras-Sweet testified before the Senate Committee on Small Business and Entrepreneurship that she tried to visit with the SBA's IG "on a monthly basis" and to have a proactive relationship with the OIG by receiving feedback "in advance of promulgating something" to help the agency "to be more efficient" and to avoid getting "caught up in messy quagmires at the end of the process."[91]

In terms of communication with Congress, the SBA OIG reports that it "has regular communications and meetings (as needed or requested) to keep the Congress apprised of significant findings or issues identified during our oversight of SBA" and that the "OIG has a staff member that is responsible for congressional relations."[92] In addition, because its semiannual reports to Congress are published every six months, the SBA OIG finds that those reports' "utility as a viable means to make a recommendation for legislation advancing through the legislative process is limited in the context of current legislative affairs."[93] As a result, because "the legislative process is very dynamic," the SBA OIG often relies on "frequent and informal" communication with congressional staff

---

[88] The SBA IG testified before Congress six times in 2011, once in 2012, three times in 2013, three times in 2014, none in 2015, and once in 2016. See SBA, "Congressional Testimony," at https://www.sba.gov/oig/category/oig-navigationstructure/reading-room/congressional-testimony.

[89] SBA, OIG, "Correspondence with the author," June 23, 2016.

[90] Ibid.

[91] U.S. Congress, Senate Committee on Small Business and Entrepreneurship, *The Fiscal Year Budget Request for the Small Business Administration*, 113th Cong., 1st sess., April 17, 2013, S. Hrg. 113-176 (Washington: GPO, 2014), p. 10.

[92] SBA, OIG, "Correspondence with the author," June 23, 2016.

[93] SBA, OIG, "Correspondence with the author," July 5, 2016.

and Members of Congress to provide its input on legislation and other matters affecting the SBA, often by telephone and email.[94]

The SBA OIG reports frequent and, in its view, meaningful consultation with both the SBA and Congress in an attempt to keep them fully informed of its activities and recommendations. It is difficult to determine the impact and/or extent of the SBA OIG's communication with SBA officials, congressional staff, and Members of Congress because much of that communication occurs through informal means, is not tracked, and data concerning the SBA's or congressional response to the provided comments and recommendations are not compiled or reported.

As mentioned previously, then-SBA Administrator Maria Contreras-Sweet testified before Congress that she believed that her relationship with the SBA OIG was "proactive" and "helps us to be more efficient."[95] Also, in his opening remarks at the aforementioned March 2016 congressional hearing on the SBA's management and performance challenges, Representative Steve Chabot, chair of the House Committee on Small Business, stated that,

> By clarifying the specific areas in which improvement is needed and highlighting possible paths forward for the agency, the insights offered by the Inspector General are invaluable as the Committee continues to work with the SBA to develop meaningful solutions to its management and performance challenges.[96]

RELATIONSHIP WITH CONGRESS

Generally speaking, OIGs' relationships with Congress tend to ebb and flow over time, varying with the personalities, interests, needs, and actions

---

[94] Ibid.

[95] U.S. Congress, Senate Committee on Small Business and Entrepreneurship, *The Fiscal Year Budget Request for the Small Business Administration*, 113th Cong., 1st sess., April 17, 2013, S. Hrg. 113-176 (Washington: GPO, 2014), p. 10.

[96] U.S. Congress, House Committee on Small Business, *SBA Management and Performance Challenges: The Inspector General's Perspective*, 114th Cong., 2nd sess., March 16, 2016 (Washington: GPO, 2016), p. 2.

of the principals involved. One constant has been a genuine interest from Members of Congress of both political parties in OIGs' efforts to identify and reduce waste, fraud, and abuse and enhance program efficiency and effectiveness. The congressional interest in these issues can take on a partisan, contentious tone, especially during periods of divided government. The House and Senate Committees on Small Business, however, have traditionally tried to avoid partisanship. For example, at a potentially contentious Senate Committee on Small Business and Entrepreneurship hearing in 2007, then-Senate Committee Chair John Kerry stated, "Senator Snowe [then-ranking Member] and I and all Members of this Committee manage a Committee that works in a very bipartisan way and try very hard to keep the politics off the table."[97] More recently, House Small Business Committee Chair Steve Chabot stated during House floor consideration of H.R. 208, the Recovery Improvements for Small Entities After Disaster Act of 2015

> I want to offer a special thanks to our committee's ranking member, Ms. Velazquez, for her insight and leadership on this issue and for working in a bipartisan, bicameral manner, as she does. I have seen that as chair of the Small Business Committee that I chair now, but I have also been the ranking member under her when she was chair, and it was always bipartisan. We have worked together in a very collegial manner, and I thank her for that.[98]

The extent to which the small business committees have been able to avoid partisan conflict has varied somewhat over time, reflecting the personalities of committee leaders and the nature of the issues that have presented themselves at any given time. Nonetheless, the small business committees' tradition of valuing bipartisanship has served to reduce the potential for conflict with the SBA OIG, primarily because committee

---

[97] U.S. Congress, Senate Committee on Small Business and Entrepreneurship, *SBA Lender Oversight: Preventing Loan Fraud and Improving Regulation of Lenders*, 110th Cong., 1st sess., November 13, 2007, S.Hrg. 110-504 (Washington: GPO, 2008), p. 1.

[98] Rep. Steve Chabot, "Superstorm Sandy Relief and Disaster Loan Program Improvement Act of 2015," House debate, *Congressional Record*, vol. 161, part 168 (November 16, 2015), p. H8226.

members generally do not feel a need to question the SBA OIG's motives when its investigations and audits find perceived weaknesses in the Administration's implementation of the SBA's programs or in the Administration's efforts to identify and address waste, fraud and abuse. The expectation that both committee members and the SBA's IG do not, and should not, pursue a political agenda may help to explain why small business committee members rarely ask the SBA OIG to undertake specific studies.[99] In their view, the SBA's IG is expected to aggressively pursue perceived weaknesses in the SBA's programs and operations regardless of potential political consequences. Requesting specific studies could be seen as suggesting that the SBA OIG is not doing its job well, or as a partisan effort to embarrass the Administration.

The SBA OIG's relationship with Congress has not always been without controversy. For example, in October 2008, then-Senator John Kerry, chair of the Senate Committee on Small Business and Entrepreneurship, criticized the SBA OIG on the Senate floor for issuing what he described as "a heavily redacted report" concerning the SBA's oversight of one of the agency's largest 7(a) lenders. Speaking on behalf of himself and then-Ranking Member Senator Olympia Snowe, he accused the SBA OIG of not exercising "independent authority on what was redacted and instead let the agency it was investigating dictate that large sections of the chapter be redacted ... contrary to the usual process that occurs with SBA OIG reports."[100] He argued that the SBA OIG's action had "the potential to render the OIG useless," and "prevented accountability in Government by keeping from the public information

[99] In FY2014, none of the 20 reports issued by the SBA OIG were undertaken due to a request from a Member of Congress or congressional staff, or a member of the public. One report was undertaken in response to a hotline complaint from SBA program officials. In FY2015, none of the 17 reports issued by the SBA OIG were undertaken due to a request from a Member of Congress or congressional staff, an SBA employee, or a member of the public. SBA, OIG, "Correspondence with the author," June 23, 2016.

[100] Sen. John Kerry, "Report of the SBA Inspector General," remarks in the Senate, *Congressional Record*, vol. 154, part 160 (October 2, 2008), pp. S10468-S10470. Also, see U.S. Congress, Senate Committee on Small Business and Entrepreneurship, *SBA Lender Oversight: Preventing Loan Fraud and Improving Regulation of Lenders*, 110th Cong., 1st sess., November 13, 2007, S.Hrg. 110-504 (Washington: GPO, 2008), pp. 1-6, 31-45, 109-112.

about the oversight capabilities of an agency that, though comparatively small, can have a huge impact on our economy."[101]

Senator Kerry's comments illustrate how quickly an OIG's relationship with Congress can change. Prior to the publication of that redacted report, the SBA OIG was generally praised by Members of both political parties for its efforts concerning the oversight of the SBA's response to the 2005 Gulf Coast hurricanes, audits of the SBA's oversight of lenders, and investigations leading to numerous indictments and convictions of fraudulent SBA lenders and borrowers.

In sum, comments by House and Senate small business committee leaders seem to suggest that they view the SBA OIG and GAO as two valuable assets that can assist and enhance the committees' oversight role. However, history has shown that an apparent harmonious relationship between an OIG and congressional committees can change quickly as circumstances change.

Some areas of possible congressional interest concerning the SBA OIG, other than funding and staffing issues, include exploring ways to more accurately quantify the SBA OIG's claims of monetary savings and determining if the SBA OIG should undertake additional tracking and monitoring activities to more accurately quantify the office's impact on SBA programs and operations and legislation.

---

101 Sen. John Kerry, "Report of the SBA Inspector General," remarks in the Senate, *Congressional Record*, vol. 154, part 160 (October 2, 2008), p. S10469.

In: Business Trends in the 21st Century
Editor: C. O. Clemente Escamilla
ISBN: 978-1-53614-260-0

Chapter 5

SMALL BUSINESS ADMINISTRATION MICROLOAN PROGRAM (UPDATED)*

Robert Jay Dilger

ABSTRACT

The Small Business Administration's (SBA's) Microloan program provides direct loans to qualified nonprofit intermediary lenders who, in turn, provide "microloans" of up to $50,000 to small businesses and nonprofit child care centers. It also provides marketing, management, and technical assistance to microloan borrowers and potential borrowers. Authorized in 1991 as a five-year demonstration project, it became operational in 1992, and was made permanent, subject to reauthorization, in 1997.

The Microloan program is designed to assist women, low-income, veteran, and minority entrepreneurs and small business owners by providing them small-scale loans for working capital or the acquisition of materials, supplies, or equipment. In FY2017, Microloan intermediaries provided 4,992 microloans totaling $69.3 million. The average Microloan was $13,884 and had a 7.5% interest rate.

* This is an edited, reformatted and augmented version of a Congressional Research Service report, R41057, dated March 30, 2018.

Critics of the SBA's Microloan program argue that it is expensive relative to alternative programs, duplicative of the SBA's 7(a) loan guaranty program, and subject to administrative shortfalls. The program's advocates argue that it assists many who otherwise would not be served by the private sector and is an important source of capital and training assistance for low-income, women, and minority business owners.

Congressional interest in the Microloan program has increased in recent years, primarily because microloans are viewed as a means to assist very small businesses, especially women- and minority-owned startups, to get loans that enable them to create and retain jobs. Job creation, always a congressional interest, has taken on increased importance given continuing concerns about job growth during the current economic recovery.

This chapter opens with a discussion of the rationale provided for having a Microloan program, describes the program's eligibility standards and operating requirements for lenders and borrowers, and examines the arguments presented by the program's critics and advocates. It then discusses P.L. 111-240, the Small Business Jobs Act of 2010, which increased the Microloan program's loan limit for borrowers from $35,000 to $50,000, and the aggregate loan limit for intermediaries after their first year of participation in the program from $3.5 million to $5 million.

It also discusses P.L. 115-141, the Consolidated Appropriations Act, 2018, which, among other provisions, relaxed requirements on Microloan intermediaries that prohibited them from spending more than 25% of their technical assistance grant funds on prospective borrowers and more than 25% of those grant funds on contracts with third parties to provide that technical assistance. The act increased those percentages to 50% (originally in H.R. 2056, the Microloan Modernization Act of 2017, and S. 526, its companion bill in the Senate).

Small Business Microloans and Training Assistance

The Small Business Administration (SBA) administers programs that support small businesses, including loan guarantees to lenders to encourage them to provide loans to small businesses "that might not otherwise obtain financing on reasonable terms and conditions" and grants to nonprofit organizations to provide marketing, management, and technical training assistance to small business owners.[1] Historically, one of the justifications presented for funding the SBA's loan guarantee programs has been that small businesses can be at a disadvantage, compared with other businesses, when trying to obtain access to sufficient capital and credit.[2] It has been argued that this disadvantage is particularly acute for startups and microbusinesses (firms with fewer than five employees):

> Traditional lending institutions, such as banks and investors, are unlikely to offer loans and investment capital to microfirms due to a variety of reasons. One barrier to microlending is a concern that startups and smaller enterprises are risky investments since growing businesses typically exhibit erratic bursts of growth and downturn. The perceived risk of these types of companies reduces the chances of a microbusiness to obtain financing. Another issue is that microbusinesses by and large require smaller amounts of capital, and thus banks or investment companies often believe that it is not efficient use of their time or resources, nor will they receive a substantive return on investment from such a small loan amount.[3]

An Urban Institute survey of SBA 7(a), 504/Certified Development Company (504/CDC), Small Business Investment Company (SBIC), and Microloan borrowers conducted in 2007 found that Microloan borrowers reported having the most difficulty in finding acceptable financing elsewhere. Less than one-third (31%) of Microloan borrowers reported that they would have been able to find acceptable financing elsewhere,

---

[1] U.S. Small Business Administration (SBA), "Fiscal Year 2010 Congressional Budget Justification," pp. 29-30, at https://www.sba.gov/sites/default/files/aboutsbaarticle/Congressional_Budget_Justification_2010.pdf.

[2] Veronique de Rugy, *Why the Small Business Administration's Loan Programs Should Be Abolished*, American Enterprise Institute for Public Policy Research, AEI Working Paper #126, April 13, 2006, at http://www.aei.org/files/2006/04/13/20060414_wp126.pdf. Also, see U.S. Government Accountability Office, *Small Business Administration: 7(a) Loan Program Needs Additional Performance Measures*, GAO-08-226T, November 1, 2007, pp. 3, 9-11, at http://www.gao.gov/new.items/d08226t.pdf.

[3] U.S. Congress, House Committee on Small Business, *Full Committee Legislative Hearing on the SBA's Microloan and Trade Programs*, 110th Cong., 1st sess., July 12, 2007, H.Hrg. 110-35 (Washington: GPO, 2007), p. 6.

compared with 35% of SBIC borrowers, 40% of 7(a) borrowers, and 48% of 504/CDC borrowers.[4]

Since its inception in 1953, the SBA has provided loan guarantees to encourage lenders to issue small businesses loans.[5] Interest in creating a separate loan program to address the specific needs of startups and microbusinesses increased during the 1980s, primarily due to the growth and experience of microlending institutions abroad and evidence concerning private lending practices that led Congress to conclude that a new loan program was necessary "to reach very small businesses that were not being served by traditional lenders of SBA's credit programs."[6]

To address the perceived disadvantages faced by very small businesses in gaining access to capital, Congress authorized the SBA's Microloan lending program in 1991 (P.L. 102-140, the Departments of Commerce, Justice, and State, the Judiciary, and Related Agencies Appropriations Act, 1992). The program became operational in 1992. Its stated purpose is

> to assist women, low-income, veteran ... and minority entrepreneurs and business owners and other individuals possessing the capability to operate successful business concerns; to assist small business concerns in those areas suffering from a lack of credit due to economic downturns; ... to make loans to eligible intermediaries to enable such intermediaries to provide small-scale loans, particularly loans in amounts averaging not more than $10,000, to start-up, newly established, or growing small business concerns for working capital or the acquisition of materials, supplies, or equipment; [and] to make grants to eligible intermediaries

---

[4] Christopher Hayes, *An Assessment of the Small Business Administration's Loan and Investment Programs: Survey of Assisted Businesses* (Washington: The Urban Institute, January 2008), p. 5, at http://www.urban.org/UploadedPDF/411599_assisted_business_survey.pdf.

[5] The SBA also provided direct loans to small businesses until 1994. For further analysis, see CRS Report R40985, *Small Business: Access to Capital and Job Creation*, by Robert Jay Dilger.

[6] Robert Cull, Asli Demiriguc-Kunt, and Jonathan Morduch, "Microfinance Meets the Market," *Journal of Economic Perspectives*, vol. 23, no. 1 (Winter 2009), pp. 169-172; and U.S. Congress, Senate Committee on Small Business and Entrepreneurship, *Microloan Program Improvement Act of 2001*, report to accompany S. 174, 107th Cong., 1st sess., May 26, 2001, S.Rept. 107-18 (Washington: GPO, 2001). About 3.54 million employer firms in the United States in 2012 had fewer than five employees. See U.S. Census Bureau, *Statistics of U.S. Businesses: U.S. & States, Totals*, at http://www2.census.gov/econ/susb/data/2012/us_state_totals_2012.xls.

that, together with non-Federal matching funds, will enable such intermediaries to provide intensive marketing, management, and technical assistance to microloan borrowers.[7]

The SBA's Microloan lending program was authorized initially as a five-year demonstration project. It was made permanent, subject to reauthorization, in 1997 (P.L. 105-135, the Small Business Reauthorization Act of 1997).[8]

Congressional interest in the Microloan program has increased in recent years, primarily because microloans are viewed as a means to assist very small businesses, especially women- and minority-owned startups, obtain loans that enable them to create jobs. Job creation and preservation,

---

[7] 15 U.S.C. §636(m)(1)(A).

[8] Prior to the Microloan program, the SBA temporarily established, in 1964, the "6 on 6" pilot lending program, which provided up to $6,000 for a term of up to 6 years "aimed specifically at disadvantaged potential entrepreneurs." See U.S. Congress, House Select Committee on Small Business, Subcommittee on Minority Small Business Enterprise, *Government Minority Small Business Programs*, hearing pursuant to H. Res. 5 and 19, 92nd Cong., 1st sess., July 27, 1971 (Washington: GPO, 1972), p. 6. Also, in 1964, P.L. 88-452, the Economic Opportunity Act of 1964 (Title IV-Employment and Investment Incentives), authorized the director of the Office of Economic Opportunity, through the SBA, to provide what were subsequently called Economic Opportunity Loans (EOL). The EOL program became operational in January 1965 and continued through 1992 (the final EOL loan disbursement took place in 1996). P.L. 93-386, the Small Business Amendments (approved August 23, 1974) transferred authority for the EOL program from the Office of Economic Opportunity to the SBA. Initially, the EOL program provided direct loans (of up to $25,000, with loan terms of up to 15 years) to assist small businesses promote employment of the long-term unemployed. Starting in 1968, EOL loans increasingly were issued as guaranteed loans. The program's loan limits were increased, by law, from $25,000 to $50,000 in 1972 and to $100,000 in 1976. The EOL program's requirements and operations evolved over time, but remained focused on providing loans to low-income, minority-owned, very small businesses. The EOL program also emphasized the provision of management and technical training assistance to disadvantaged entrepreneurs. See U.S. Congress, House Committee on Education and Labor, *Economic Opportunity Act Amendments of 1967*, hearing on H.R. 8311, 90th Cong., 1st sess., June 23, 1967 (Washington: GPO, 1967), pp. 1356-1362. U.S. Congress, House Committee on Appropriations, Subcommittee on Commerce, Justice, State, and Judiciary, *Departments of Commerce, Justice, and State, the Judiciary and Related Agencies Appropriations for 1993*, 102nd Cong., 2nd sess., February 19, 1992 (Washington: GPO, 1992), pp. 503-504; and U.S. General Accounting (now Government Accountability) Office, *Most Borrowers of Economic Opportunity Loans Have Not Succeeded in Business*, CED-81-3, December 8, 1980, pp. 1-8, at http://www.gao.gov/assets/140/131190.pdf.

always a congressional interest, has taken on increased importance given continuing concerns about job growth.[9]

This chapter describes the Microloan program's eligibility standards and operating requirements for lenders and borrowers and examines the arguments presented by the program's critics and advocates. It also examines changes to the program authorized by P.L. 111-240, the Small Business Jobs Act of 2010.

P.L. 111-240 authorized the Secretary of the Treasury to establish a $30 billion Small Business Lending Fund (SBLF) to encourage community banks to provide small business loans ($4.0 billion was issued), a $1.5 billion State Small Business Credit Initiative to provide funding to participating states with small business capital access programs, and about $12 billion in tax relief for small businesses.[10] It also authorized changes to the SBA's loan guaranty programs, including increasing the Microloan program's loan limit for borrowers from $35,000 to $50,000, and the aggregate loan limit for intermediaries after their first year of participation in the program from $3.5 million to $5 million. It also authorized the SBA to waive, in whole or in part through FY2012, the nonfederal share requirement for loans to the Microloan program's intermediaries and for grants made to Microloan intermediaries for small business marketing, management, and technical assistance for up to a fiscal year.

P.L. 115-141, the Consolidated Appropriations Act, 2018, among other provisions, relaxed requirements on Microloan intermediaries that prohibited them from spending more than 25% of their technical assistance grant funds on prospective borrowers and more than 25% of those grant funds on contracts with third parties to provide that technical assistance. The act increased those percentages to 50% (originally in H.R. 2056, the

---

[9] SBA, Office of Advocacy, *Small Business Economic Indicators for 2003*, August 2004, p. 3; and Brian Headd, "Small Businesses Most Likely to Lead Economic Recovery," *The Small Business Advocate*, vol. 28, no. 6 (July 2009), pp. 1, 2.

[10] For further information and analysis concerning the Small Business Lending Fund, see CRS Report R42045, *The Small Business Lending Fund*, by Robert Jay Dilger. For further information and analysis concerning the State Small Business Credit Initiative, see CRS Report R42581, *State Small Business Credit Initiative: Implementation and Funding Issues*, by Robert Jay Dilger.

Microloan Modernization Act of 2017, and S. 526, its companion bill in the Senate).

This chapter also discusses several bills introduced during the 114th and 115th Congresses. For example, during the 114th Congress,

- S. 1445, the Microloan Act of 2015, would have removed the requirements that no more than 25% of Microloan technical assistance grant funds may be used to provide information and technical assistance to prospective borrowers or on third-party contracts to provide that assistance. It would have also eliminated the Microloan program's minimum state allocation formula.[11]
- H.R. 2670, the Microloan Modernization Act of 2015, and S. 1857, the Senate companion bill, would have increased the Microloan program's aggregate loan limit for intermediaries after their first year of participation in the program from $5 million to $6 million, increased the program's repayment terms from not more than 6 years to not more than 10 years for loans greater than $10,000, and required the SBA Administrator to establish a rule enabling intermediaries to apply for a waiver of the requirement that no more than 25% of Microloan technical assistance grant funds may be used to provide information and technical assistance to prospective borrowers. The House passed H.R. 2670 on July 13, 2015.[12]

---

[11] The Microloan program's minimum allocation formula is "Subject to the availability of appropriations, of the total amount of new loan funds made available for award under this subsection in each fiscal year, the Administration shall make available for award in each State (including the District of Columbia, the Commonwealth of Puerto Rico, the United States Virgin Islands, Guam, and American Samoa) an amount equal to the sum of (I) the lesser of – (aa) $800,000; or (bb) 1/55 of the total amount of new loan funds made available for award under this subsection for that fiscal year; and (II) any additional amount, as determined by the Administration." See 15 U.S.C. 636 (m)(7)(B)(i). The Obama Administration supported the elimination of the Microloan program's minimum state allocation formula and the 25% restriction on the use of Microloan technical assistance funds to provide information and technical assistance to prospective borrowers and on third-party contracts to provide that assistance. See SBA, "Fiscal Year 2017 Congressional Budget Justification and FY2015 Annual Performance Report," p. 100, at https://www.sba.gov/sites/default/files/FY17-CBJ_FY15-APR.pdf.

[12] H.R. 2670 was reported by the House Committee on Small Business on June 25, 2015. Amendments to remove the requirement that no more than 25% of Microloan technical

- S. 2850, the Microloan Program Modernization Act of 2016, would have increased the Microloan program's aggregate loan limit for intermediaries after their first year of participation in the program from $5 million to $6 million and, among other provisions, eliminated the requirements that intermediaries spend no more than 25% of Microloan technical assistance grant funds on technical assistance to prospective borrowers and no more than 25% of those funds on third party contracts for technical assistance.

During the 115th Congress,

- H.R. 2056, the Microloan Modernization Act of 2017, and S. 526, its companion bill in the Senate would, as introduced, increase the Microloan program's aggregate loan limit for intermediaries after their first year of participation in the program from $5 million to $6 million and, among other provisions, eliminate the requirement that intermediaries spend no more than 25% of Microloan technical assistance grant funds on technical assistance to prospective borrowers and no more than 25% of those funds on third-party contracts for technical assistance.

H.R. 2056 and S. 526 were amended in committee to require intermediaries to spend no more than 50% of Microloan technical assistance grant funds on technical assistance to prospective borrowers and no more than 50% of those funds on third-party contracts for technical assistance. The House bill, as amended, was favorably reported by the House Committee on Small Business on July 12, 2017, and agreed to by the House on July 24, 2017, by voice vote.[13] The Senate bill was favorably

assistance grant funds may be used on third-party contracts to provide technical assistance and to eliminate Microloan program's minimum state allocation formula were not agreed to during committee markup. S. 1857 was reported by the Senate Committee on Small Business and Entrepreneurship on September 15, 2015.

[13] The Trump Administration supports the elimination of the Microloan program's minimum state allocation formula and increasing to 50% the 25% restriction on the use of Microloan

reported by the Senate Committee on Small Business and Entrepreneurship on March 19, 2018. As mentioned previously, the 50% thresholds were included in P.L. 115-141.

THE SBA MICROLOAN PROGRAM: FUNDING, ELIGIBILITY STANDARDS, PROGRAM REQUIREMENTS, AND STATISTICS

Unlike the SBA's 7(a) and 504/CDC loan guarantee programs, the SBA Microloan program does not guarantee loans.[14] Instead, it provides direct loans to qualified nonprofit intermediary Microloan lenders who, in turn, provide "microloans" of up to $50,000 to small business owners, entrepreneurs, and nonprofit child care centers.[15] There are currently 144 active Microloan intermediaries serving 49 states, the District of Columbia, and Puerto Rico.[16]

Funding

The Microloan program's administrative costs (anticipated to be $47.66 million in FY2018) are funded through the SBA's salaries and

---

technical assistance funds to provide information and technical assistance to prospective borrowers and on third-party contracts to provide that assistance. See SBA, "Fiscal Year 2018 Congressional Budget Justification and FY2016 Annual Performance Report," p. 92, at https://www.sba.gov/sites/default/files/aboutsbaarticle/FINAL_SBA_FY_2018_CBJ_May_22_2017c.pdf.

[14] For information and analysis concerning the SBA's 7(a) and 504/CDC programs, see CRS Report R41146, *Small Business Administration 7(a) Loan Guaranty Program*, by Robert Jay Dilger and CRS Report R41184, *Small Business Administration 504/CDC Loan Guaranty Program*, by Robert Jay Dilger.

[15] P.L. 111-240, the Small Business Jobs Act of 2010, increased the loan limit for borrowers from $35,000 to $50,000.

[16] SBA, "Fiscal Year 2019 Congressional Budget Justification and FY2017 Annual Performance Report," p. 37, at https://www.sba.gov/sites/default/files/aboutsbaarticle/SBA_FY_19_508 Final5_1.pdf. For a list of all Microloan intermediaries, regardless of lending volume, see SBA, *Microloan Program: Partner Identification & Management System Participating Intermediary Microlenders Report*, June 21, 2017, at https://www.sba.gov /sites/default/ files/articles/microlenderrpt5_20170621.pdf.

expenses and business loan administration accounts. In addition, each year the SBA receives an appropriation for credit subsidies for its direct lending (Microloan) program.

Business loan credit subsidies represent the net present value of cash flows to and from the SBA over the life of the loan portfolio. For guaranteed loans, the net present value of cash flows is primarily affected by the difference between the cost of purchasing loans that have defaulted and the revenue generated from fees and collateral liquidation. For direct (Microloan) lending, the net present value of cash flows is primarily affected by the cost of offering below market interest rates to intermediaries because the cost of purchasing loans that have defaulted is typically relatively small because intermediaries are required to maintain a loan loss reserve. In addition, the SBA does not charge intermediaries fees.[17]

In FY2018, the SBA was provided $3.438 million, to remain available until expended, for direct (Microloan) business loan credit subsidies. This appropriation was expected to support about $36.0 million in lending to intermediaries.[18]

---

[17] The SBA's Office of Financial Analysis and Modeling is responsible for ensuring that the computation of subsidy rates for the SBA's credit programs are in compliance with the Federal Credit Reform Act of 1990 (FCRA). As indicated on its website: "The FCRA requires all credit agencies, including the SBA, to budget and account for the cost of credit programs by determining the net present value of cash flows to and from the Government over the life of the portfolio and expressing the net amount as a credit subsidy rate. The process to develop a subsidy rate is lengthy and complex, requiring unique data collection techniques and analysis efforts. SBA develops its subsidy rates by creating models that incorporate data on loan maturity, borrowers' interest rates, fees, grace periods, interest subsidies, delinquencies, purchases or defaults, recoveries, prepayments, advances and borrower characteristics. See SBA, Office of Financial Analysis and Modeling, "Summary of Responsibilities," at https://www.sba.gov/offices/headquarters/ocfo/resources/13299. Also, see U.S. Congress, Senate Committee on Small Business and Entrepreneurship, *Small Business Reauthorization and Improvements Act of 2006*, report to accompany S. 3778, 109th Cong., 2nd sess., November 16, 2006, S.Rept. 109-361 (Washington: GPO, 2006), p. 6; and U.S. Government Accountability Office, *Participants in SBA's Microloan Program Could Provide Additional Information to Enhance the Public's Understanding of Recovery Act Fund Uses and Expected Outcomes,* GAO-10-1032R, September 29, 2010, p. 2, at http://www.gao.gov/assets/100/97128.pdf.

[18] SBA, "Fiscal Year 2018 Congressional Budget Justification and FY2016 Annual Performance Report," p. 92, at https://www.sba.gov/sites/default/files/aboutsbaarticle/FINAL_SBA_FY_2018_CBJ_May_22_2017c.pdf; and P.L. 115-141, the Consolidated Appropriations Act, 2018.

The SBA received an appropriation of $31.0 million in FY2018 for grants to selected Microloan intermediaries and qualified "non-lending technical assistance providers" to provide Microloan borrowers and prospective borrowers marketing, management, and technical training assistance.[19]

As shown in *Table 1*, Microloan intermediaries provided counseling services to 19,600 small businesses in FY2017. The data indicate that the number of small businesses served by the Microloan technical assistance program has generally increased in recent years.

Table 1. Microloan Technical Assistance Program Counseling Services, FY2010-FY2017

Fiscal Year	Number of Small Businesses Provided Microloan Technical Assistance Counseling Services
2010	14,916
2011	15,900
2012	15,892
2013	19,368
2014	15,668
2015	17,200
2016	17,948
2017	19,600

Sources: U.S. Small Business Administration, "Fiscal Year 2017 Congressional Budget Justification and FY2015 Annual Performance Report," p. 99, at https://www.sba.gov/sites/default/files/FY17-CBJ_FY15-APR.pdf; and U.S. Small Business Administration, "Fiscal Year 2019 Congressional Budget Justification and FY2017 Annual Performance Report," p. 37, at https://www.sba.gov/sites/default/files/aboutsbaarticle/SBA_FY_19_508Final5_1.pdf.

Intermediary Microloan Lender Eligibility Standards

To become a qualified intermediary Microloan lender, an applicant must

- be organized as a nonprofit community development corporation or other entity, a consortium of nonprofit community development

---

[19] P.L. 115-141.

corporations or other entities, a quasigovernmental economic development corporation, or an agency established by a Native American Tribal Government;

- be located in the United States, including the Commonwealth of Puerto Rico, the U.S. Virginia Islands, Guam, and American Samoa;
- have made and serviced short-term, fixed rate loans of not more than $50,000 to newly established or growing small businesses for at least one year; and
- have at least one year of experience providing technical assistance to its borrowers.[20]

If accepted into the program by the SBA, it can borrow no more than $750,000 from the SBA during its first year of participation, no more than $1.25 million each year thereafter, and no more than an aggregate of $5 million.[21]

As mentioned previously, legislation was introduced during the 114th Congress (H.R. 2670, S. 1857, and S. 2850) and the 115th Congress (H.R. 2056 and S. 526) to increase the Microloan program's aggregate loan limit for Microloan intermediaries after their first year of participation in the program from $5 million to $6 million.

Intermediary Microloan Lender Program Requirements

Intermediaries are not required to make any interest payments on the Microloan during the first year, but interest accrues from the date that the SBA disburses the loan proceeds to the intermediary. After that, the SBA

---

[20] 13 C.F.R §120.701; and 13 C.F.R §120.702. P.L. 111-240, the Small Business Jobs Act of 2010, increased the loan limit for borrowers from $35,000 to $50,000.

[21] 13 C.F.R §120.706; and SBA, "SOP 52 00 A: Microloan Program," (effective April 28, 2016), p. 20, at https://www.sba.gov/sites/default/files/sops/SOP-52-00-A-Microloan.pdf. P.L. 111-240, the Small Business Jobs Act of 2010, increased the aggregate loan limit for intermediaries after their first year of participation in the program from $3.5 million to $5 million.

determines the schedule for periodic payments. Loans must be repaid within 10 years.[22]

The SBA charges intermediaries an interest rate that is based on the five-year Treasury rate, adjusted to the nearest one-eighth percent (called the Base Rate), less 1.25% if the intermediary maintains an historic portfolio of Microloans averaging more than $10,000, and less 2.0% if the intermediary maintains an historic portfolio of Microloans averaging $10,000 or less. The Base Rate, after adjustment, is called the Intermediary's Cost of Funds. The Intermediary's Cost of Funds is initially calculated one year from the date of the note and is reviewed annually and adjusted as necessary (called recasting). The interest rate cannot be less than zero.[23]

Intermediaries are required to contribute not less than 15% of the loan amount in cash from nonfederal sources and, as security for repayment of the loan, must provide the SBA first lien position on all notes receivable from any microloans issued under the program.[24] Unlike the SBA's 7(a) and 504/CDC loan guarantee programs, the SBA does not charge intermediaries upfront or ongoing service fees under the Microloan program.[25]

As mentioned previously, P.L. 111-240 temporarily allowed the SBA to waive, in whole or in part through FY2012, the intermediary's 15% nonfederal share requirement under specified circumstances (e.g., the economic conditions affecting the intermediary and the intermediary's performance) for up to a fiscal year.[26]

Intermediaries are required to deposit the proceeds from the SBA's loans, their 15% contribution, and payments from their Microloan borrowers into a Microloan Revolving Fund. Intermediaries may only

---

[22] 13 C.F.R §120.706.

[23] 15 U.S.C. §636(m)(3)(F)(iii); and SBA, "SOP 52 00 A: Microloan Program," (effective April 28, 2016), p. 20, at https://www.sba.gov/sites/default/files/sops/SOP-52-00-A-Microloan.pdf. In recent years, the Intermediary's Cost of Funds has been either zero or close to zero.

[24] 13 C.F.R §120.706. Note: The 15% contribution must be from nonfederal sources and may not be borrowed. For purposes of this program, Community Development Block Grants are considered nonfederal sources.

[25] Ibid.

[26] P.L. 111-240, the Small Business Jobs Act of 2010, §1401. Matching Requirements Under Small Business Programs.

withdraw from this account funds necessary to make microloans to borrowers, repay the SBA, and establish and maintain a Loan Loss Reserve Fund to pay any shortage in the Microloan Revolving Fund caused by delinquencies or losses on its microloans.[27] They are required, until they have been in the program for at least five years, to maintain a balance in the Loan Loss Reserve Fund equal to 15% of the outstanding balance of the notes receivable from their Microloan borrowers.[28] After five years, if the intermediary's average annual loss rate during the preceding five years is less than 15% and no other factors exist that may impair the intermediary's ability to repay its obligations to the SBA, the SBA Administrator may reduce the required balance in the intermediary's Loan Loss Reserve Fund to the intermediary's average annual loss rate during the preceding five years, but not less than 10% of the portfolio.[29] Intermediaries are required to maintain their Loan Loss Reserve Fund until they have repaid all obligations owed to the SBA.

The SBA does not maintain detailed data necessary to determine an aggregate default rate for Microloan borrowers. However, in 2007, the SBA estimated that the borrower default rate for the Microloan program was about 12%.[30] Because the Loan Loss Reserve Fund is used to contribute toward the cost of borrower defaults, and is often sufficient to cover the entire cost of such defaults, the SBA's loss rate for intermediary repayment is typically less than 3% each year.[31]

---

[27] 13 C.F.R §120.709.

[28] 13 C.F.R §120.710.

[29] Ibid.

[30] U.S. Congress, House Committee on Small Business, *Full Committee Hearings on the Small Business Administration's Microloan Program*, 110th Cong., 1st sess., June 14, 2007, H.Hrg. 110-30 (Washington: GPO, 2007), p. 15. Note: A study released on December 28, 2009 by the SBA's Office of the Inspector General concluded that Microloan intermediaries may be under-reporting the default rate. See SBA, Office of the Inspector General, "SBA's Administration of the Microloan Program under the Recovery Act," December 28, 2009, at http://www.sba.gov/officeof-inspector-general/868/12427.

[31] In FY2016, the Microloan program's intermediary default rate was 1.6%. See SBA, *Agency Financial Report, Fiscal Year 2016*, p. 68, at https://www.sba.gov/sites/default/files/aboutsbaarticle/Agency_Financial_Report_FY_2016.pdf. At the end of FY2016, $9.46 million in loans to intermediaries had been charged off. This represents 1.96% of total funds disbursed to intermediaries ($9.46 million of $483.59 million) and 6.54% of the current outstanding principal balance of loans to intermediary lenders ($9.46 million of $144.67

An intermediary may be suspended or removed from the Microloan program if it fails to comply with a specified list of program performance standards. For example, intermediaries are required to close and fund at least 10 microloans per year, cover the service territory assigned by the SBA, honor the SBA determined boundaries of neighboring intermediaries and non-lender technical assistance providers, fulfill reporting requirements, maintain a loan currency rate of 85% or more (where loans are no more than 30 days late in scheduled payments), maintain a default rate of 15% or less, and "satisfactorily provide" in-house technical assistance to microloan clients and prospective microloan clients.[32]

Intermediary Marketing, Management, and Technical Training Assistance

As mentioned previously, in FY2018, the SBA received $31.0 million for grants to Microloan intermediaries and qualified "non-lending technical assistance providers" to provide Microloan borrowers and prospective borrowers marketing, management, and technical training assistance (see Appendix for previous funding levels).

Intermediaries are eligible to receive a Microloan technical assistance grant "of not more than 25% of the total outstanding balance of loans made to it under this subsection."[33] Grant funds may be used only to provide marketing, management, and technical assistance to Microloan borrowers, except that no more than 50% of the funds may be used to provide such assistance to prospective Microloan borrowers. Grant funds may also be used to attend training required by the SBA.[34] Also, intermediaries must contribute, solely from nonfederal sources, an amount equal to 25% of the

---

million). SBA, Office of Congressional and Legislative Affairs, "Correspondence with the author," December 2, 2016.

[32] 13 C.F.R §120.716. A new Microloan intermediary is not required to meet the minimum loan requirement during the year it enters the program.

[33] 15 U.S.C. §636(m)(4)(A). Note: The SBA's Program for Investment in Microentrepreneurs Act (PRIME) program also provides nonprofit organizations grant funding to assist low-income entrepreneurs with training assistance. See, SBA, "PRIME Program," at https://www.sba.gov/offices/headquarters/oca/resources/11416.

[34] 13 C.F.R §120.712.

grant amount. In addition to cash or other direct funding, the contribution may include indirect costs or in-kind contributions paid for under nonfederal programs.[35] Intermediaries may expend no more than 50% of the grant funds on third-party contracts for the provision of technical assistance.[36]

In addition, as mentioned earlier, P.L. 111-240 temporarily allowed the SBA to waive, in whole or in part through FY2012, the 25% nonfederal share requirement for grants made to Microloan intermediaries for small business marketing, management, and technical assistance under specified circumstances (e.g., the economic conditions affecting the intermediary and the intermediary's performance) for up to a fiscal year.[37]

The SBA does not require Microloan borrowers to participate in the marketing, management, and technical assistance program. However, intermediaries typically require Microloan borrowers to participate in the training program as a condition of the receipt of a microloan. Combining loan and intensive training assistance is one of the Microloan program's distinguishing features.

Intermediaries that have a portfolio of loans made under the program "that averages not more than $10,000 during the period of the intermediary's participation in the program" are eligible to receive an additional training grant equal to 5% of "the total outstanding balance of loans made to the intermediary."[38] Intermediaries are not required to make a matching contribution as a condition of receiving these additional grant funds.

Non-lending Technical Assistance Providers

Each year, the SBA is authorized to select qualified nonprofit, non-lending technical assistance providers to receive grant funds to provide

---

[35] 13 C.F.R §120.712. Intermediaries may not borrow their contribution.

[36] Ibid.

[37] P.L. 111-240, the Small Business Jobs Act of 2010, §1401. Matching Requirements Under Small Business Programs.

[38] 13 C.F.R §120.712; and 15 U.S.C. §636(m)(4)(C)(i).

marketing, management, and technical assistance to Microloan borrowers. Any nonprofit entity that is not an intermediary may apply for these funds.[39]

The SBA may award up to 55 grants each year to qualified non-lending technical assistance providers to deliver marketing, management, and technical assistance to Microloan borrowers. The grants may be for terms of up to five years and may not exceed $200,000.[40] The nonprofit entity must contribute, solely from nonfederal sources, an amount equal to 20% of the grant. In addition to cash or other direct funding, the contribution may include indirect costs or in-kind contributions paid for under nonfederal programs.[41]

The SBA stopped awarding these grants at the beginning of FY2005. The SBA determined at that time that the non-lending technical assistance providers duplicated much of what was already being provided by Microloan intermediaries and other SBA entrepreneurial development programs.[42]

Microloan Borrower Eligibility Standards

With one exception, Microloan borrowers must be an eligible, for-profit small business as defined by the Small Business Act. P.L. 105-135, the Small Business Reauthorization Act of 1997, expanded the Microloan program's eligibility to include borrowers establishing a nonprofit childcare business.

Microloan Borrower Program Requirements

Intermediaries are directed by legislative language to provide borrowers "small-scale loans, particularly loans in amounts averaging not

---

[39] 13 C.F.R §120.714.

[40] Ibid.

[41] Ibid.

[42] SBA, Office of Congressional and Legislative Affairs, "Correspondence with the author," August 2, 2012.

more than $10,000."[43] They are also directed, "to the extent practicable ... to maintain a microloan portfolio with an average loan size of not more than $15,000."[44] Microloans for more than $20,000 are allowed "only if such small business concern demonstrates that it is unable to obtain credit elsewhere at comparable interest rates and that it has good prospects for success."[45] The maximum loan amount is $50,000 and no borrower may owe an intermediary more than $50,000 at any one time.[46]

Microloan proceeds may be used only for working capital and acquisition of materials, supplies, furniture, fixtures, and equipment. Loans cannot be made to acquire land or property, and must be repaid within six years.[47] Within these parameters, loan terms vary depending on the loan's size, the planned use of funds, the requirements of the intermediary lender, and the needs of the small business borrower. During the 114th Congress, H.R. 2670 would have increased the program's repayment terms from not more than 6 years to not more than 10 years for loans greater than $10,000.

On loans of more than $10,000, the maximum interest rate that can be charged to the borrower is the interest rate charged by the SBA on the loan to the intermediary, plus 7.75 percentage points. On loans of $10,000 or less, the maximum interest rate that can be charged to the borrower is the interest charged by the SBA on the loan to the intermediary, plus 8.5 percentage points.[48] Rates are negotiated between the borrower and the

[43] 15 U.S.C. §636(m)(1)(A)(iii)(I).

[44] 15 U.S.C. §636(m)(6)(B).

[45] 15 U.S.C. §636(m)(3)(E).

[46] 13 C.F.R §120.707. P.L. 111-240, the Small Business Jobs Act of 2010, increased the loan limit for borrowers from $35,000 to $50,000.

[47] Ibid.

[48] 15 U.S.C. §636(m)(6)(C)(i) and 15 U.S.C. §636(m)(6)(C)(ii) indicate that the threshold average loan amount for determining the maximum interest rate charged to borrowers is $7,500. The SBA increased the threshold average loan amount used to determine the maximum interest rate charged to borrowers from $7,500 to $10,000 in 2001, citing authority provided in P.L. 106-554, the Consolidated Appropriations Act, 2001 (2000 legislation–Small Business Reauthorization Act of 2000): "SBA is amending § 120.707(c) [the section in the U.S. Code of Federal Regulations concerning the threshold average loan amount for determining the maximum interest rate charged to borrowers] to reflect the statutory change which increased the dollar amount to $10,000 up from $7,500." See SBA, "Microloan Program," 66 *Federal Register* 47877, September 4, 2001. However, P.L. 106-554 included language amending Section 7(m) of the Small Business Act (15 U.S.C. 636(m)) "in paragraphs (1)(A)(iii)(I), (3)(A)(ii), and (4)(C)(i)(II), by striking "$7,500" each place it appears and inserting "$10,000." The three sections cited in P.L. 106-554 referred to

intermediary, and typically range from 6.5% to 9%. In FY2017, the average interest rate charged was 7.5%.[49]

Each intermediary establishes its own lending and credit requirements. However, borrowers are generally required to provide some type of collateral (consistent with prudent lending practices), and a personal guarantee to repay the loan.[50] The SBA does not review the loan for creditworthiness.[51]

Intermediaries are allowed to charge borrowers reasonable application and origination fees up to 2% of the Microloan, and actual out-of-pocket closing expenses, such as collateral appraisals and credit reports. These fees may be added to the loan amount and financed over the life of the loan.[52]

---

encouraging intermediaries to make "loans in amounts averaging not more than $7,500;" directing the Administration to "give priority to those applicants that provide loans in amounts averaging not more than $7,500;" and eligibility for technical assistance grants "the intermediary has a portfolio of loans made under this subsection that averages not more than $7,500 during the period of the intermediary's participation in the program." According to the SBA, "at the time of the change in the law, SBA staff believed that Congress intended to raise all of the microloan thresholds to $10,000 from $7,500, as evidenced by the fact that Congress revised the general purpose language in §7(m)(1)(A)(iii). That provision was revised to state that one of the purposes of the Microloan program is to enable intermediaries to provide small-scale loans, 'particularly in amounts averaging not more than $10,000.' In addition, the legislative history indicates that the loan amounts were increased to reflect inflation, but does not explain why only some loan amounts were adjusted and not others.... Furthermore, it would be confusing to have different thresholds in the several provisions that incentivize intermediaries to make small loans, especially when those thresholds had been the same prior to the changes implemented by P.L. 106-554.... For these reasons, SBA staff believed that increasing all of the microloan thresholds to $10,000 from $7,500 would achieve the Congressional purpose in making more small loans available. The regulations implemented the legislative changes in 2001. There is Congressional awareness of these longstanding microloan program regulations, which have never been challenged or questioned. There is also Congressional awareness of the discrepancies in the statute, as evidenced by the 13 bills that have been introduced since 2001 to correct them." SBA, Office of Congressional and Legislative Affairs, "Correspondence with the author," November 14, 2013.

[49] SBA, "Nationwide Loan Report, October 1, 2016 through September 30, 2017," March 13, 2018.

[50] The SBA urges intermediaries in its Microloan SOP "to temper collateral requirements with strong technical assistance and to be creative in their definition of acceptable collateral." See SBA, "SOP 52 00 A: Microloan Program," (effective April 28, 2016), p. 50, at https://www.sba.gov/sites/default/files/sops/SOP-52-00-AMicroloan.pdf.

[51] SBA, "Microloan Program," at https://www.sba.gov/content/microloan-program.

[52] SBA, "SOP 52 00 A: Microloan Program," (effective April 28, 2016), p. 51, at https://www.sba.gov/sites/default/files/sops/SOP-52-00-A-Microloan.pdf.

Microloan Program Statistics

As of the end of FY2017, the SBA had disbursed 1,167 loans to Microloan intermediaries totaling $524.8 million. About 43% (504) of these loans, with an unpaid principal balance of $157.3 million, were still active.[53]

In FY2017, the SBA disbursed 29 loans totaling $13.6 million to intermediaries and intermediaries provided 4,992 microloans totaling $69.3 million to small businesses.[54] The average loan to an intermediary was $469,828, and the average microloan to a small business was $13,884.[55]

Table 2 provides the number and amount of loans to intermediaries and the number and amount of Microloans to small businesses from FY2010 to FY2017. The data indicate that the amount of Microloans provided to small businesses has generally increased in recent years.

The Microloan program is open to all small business entrepreneurs, but targets new and early-stage businesses in "underserved markets, including borrowers with little to no credit history, low-income borrowers, and women and minority entrepreneurs in both rural and urban areas who generally do not qualify for conventional loans or other, larger SBA guaranteed loans."[56] An analysis conducted by the Urban Institute found that about 9.9% of conventional small business loans are issued to minority-owned small businesses and about 16% of conventional small business loans are issued to women-owned businesses.[57] In FY2017, of those reporting their race, minority-owned or -controlled firms received

---

[53] SBA, Office of Congressional and Legislative Affairs, "Correspondence with the author," November 22, 2017.

[54] SBA, "Nationwide Loan Report, October 1, 2016 through September 30, 2017," March 13, 2018; and SBA, Office of Congressional and Legislative Affairs, "Correspondence with the author," November 22, 2017.

[55] SBA, "Nationwide Loan Report, October 1, 2016 through September 30, 2017," March 13, 2018; and SBA, Office of Congressional and Legislative Affairs, "Correspondence with the author," November 22, 2017.

[56]

[57] Kenneth Temkin, Brett Theodos, with Kerstin Gentsch, *Competitive and Special Competitive Opportunity Gap Analysis of the 7(A) and 504 Programs* (Washington: The Urban Institute, 2008), p. 13, at http://www.urban.org/ UploadedPDF/411596_504_gap_analysis.pdf.

46.4% of the number of microloans issued and 33.3% of the amount issued.[58] Women-owned or -controlled firms received 46.7% of the number of microloans issued and 38.4% of the amount issued.[59]

More than three-quarters of all Microloan borrowers (81.5%) in FY2017 were located in an urban area. Also, startup companies received 37.7% of the number of microloans issued in FY2017, and 37.1% of the total amount of microloans issued in FY2017.[60]

As mentioned previously, the Microloan program's estimated borrower default rate is about 12%.[61] Because the Loan Loss Reserve Fund is used to contribute toward the cost of borrower defaults, and is often sufficient to cover the entire cost of such defaults, the SBA's loss rate for intermediary repayment is typically less than 3% annually. For example, the Microloan program's intermediary default rate was 2.36% in FY2015, 1.60% in FY2016, and 2.26% in FY2017.[62]

Microloans are often used for more than one purpose. In FY2017, they were most commonly used for working capital (70.0%), new equipment (25.8%), inventory (21.6%), and supplies (7.9%).[63]

---

[58] SBA, "Nationwide Loan Report, October 1, 2016 through September 30, 2017," March 13, 2018. 814 of 4,992 Microloan borrowers (16.3%) did not report their race. These borrowers received $9.6 million in loans. Because the race of these borrowers is unknown, their borrowing was removed from the calculation of the proportional share percentage figures provided for minority-owned or -controlled firms.

[59] Ibid.

[60] Ibid.

[61] U.S. Congress, House Committee on Small Business, *Full Committee Hearings on the Small Business Administration's Microloan Program*, 110th Cong., 1st sess., June 14, 2007, H.Hrg. 110-30 (Washington: GPO, 2007), p. 15. Note: A study released on December 28, 2009 by the SBA's Office of the Inspector General concluded that Microloan intermediaries may be under-reporting the default rate. See SBA, Office of the Inspector General, "SBA's Administration of the Microloan Program under the Recovery Act," December 28, 2009, at http://www.sba.gov/officeof-inspector-general/868/12427.

[62] SBA, *Agency Financial Report, Fiscal Year 2015*, p. 73, at https://www.sba.gov/sites/default/files/aboutsbaarticle/4- Financial%20Reporting.pdf; SBA, *Agency Financial Report, Fiscal Year 2016*, p. 68, at https://www.sba.gov/sites/default/files/aboutsbaarticle/ Agency_Financial_Report_FY_2016.pdf; and SBA, *Agency Financial Report, Fiscal Year 2017*, p. 71, at https://www.sba.gov/sites/default/files/aboutsbaarticle/SBA_FY_2017_ AFR_.pdf.

[63] SBA, "Nationwide Loan Report, October 1, 2016 through September 30, 2017," March 13, 2018. Percentages add to more than 100% as proceeds may be used for more than one purpose.

Table 2. Microloan Program Statistics, FY2010-FY2017 ($ in millions)

FY	# of SBA Loans to Intermediaries	Amount of SBA Loans to Intermediaries	# of Microloans to Small Businesses	Amount of Microloans to Small Businesses
2010	71	$34.2	3,729	$44.1
2011	67	$32.2	4,002	$46.8
2012	42	$21.6	3,973	$44.7
2013	68	$38.3	4,426	$51.2
2014	34	$24.2	3,948	$56.1
2015	56	$30.3	3,682	$51.9
2016	44	$27.5	4,493	$60.8
2017	29	$13.6	4,992	$69.3

Sources: U.S. Small Business Administration, Office of Congressional and Legislative Affairs, "Correspondence with the author," November 22, 2017; and U.S. Small Business Administration, "Nationwide Loan Report, October 1, 2009 through September 30, 2010," January 14, 2011; "Nationwide Loan Report, October 1, 2010 through September 30, 2011," November 2, 2011; "Nationwide Loan Report, October 1, 2011 through September 30, 2012," October 15, 2012; "Nationwide Loan Report, October 1, 2012 through September 30, 2013," October 28, 2013; "Nationwide Loan Report, October 1, 2013 through September 30, 2014," June 4, 2015; "Nationwide Loan Report, October 1, 2014 through September 30, 2015," November 16, 2015; "Nationwide Loan Report, October 1, 2015 through September 30, 2016," November 28, 2016; and "Nationwide Loan Report, October 1, 2016 through September 30, 2017," March 13, 2018.

CONGRESSIONAL ISSUES

Critics of the SBA's Microloan program argue that it is duplicative of other available programs, expensive relative to alternative programs, and subject to administrative shortfalls. The program's advocates argue that it provides assistance that "reaches many who otherwise would not be served by the private sector or even the SBA's 7(a) loan program" and "has provided an important source of capital for low-income women business owners and minority borrowers."[64]

---

[64] U.S. Congress, House Committee on Small Business, *Full Committee Hearing on the Small Business Administration's Microloan Program*, 110th Cong., 1st sess., June 14, 2007, H.Hrg. 110-30 (Washington: GPO, 2007), pp. 1, 2.

Program Duplication

Critics of the SBA's Microloan program argue that its direct lending program is duplicative of the SBA's 7(a) loan guarantee program and its marketing, management, and technical training assistance grant program is duplicative of the SBA's training assistance provided through Small Business Development Centers, SCORE (Service Corps of Retired Executives), and Women Business Centers. For example, President George W. Bush proposed to eliminate all funding for the Microloan program in his FY2005, FY2006, and FY2007 budget requests to Congress, arguing that "the 7(a) program is capable of serving the same clientele through the Community Express programs for much lower cost to the Government."[65] President Bush also proposed to terminate the Microloan program's marketing, management, and technical assistance grant program in his FY2008 and FY2009 budget requests to Congress.[66]

Critics argued in 2007 that about 44% of the SBA's 7(a) program's loan guarantees at that time were for loans under $35,000 (the Microloan program's former loan limit for borrowers), representing more than 17 times the number of loans issued through the SBA's Microloan program.[67] In their view, the 7(a) program had demonstrated that it can service the needs of small businesses targeted by the SBA's Microloan program.[68] They also argued that the SBA's Microloan program's marketing, management, and technical assistance grants program was not necessary because the SBA "already supports a nationwide network of resource

---

[65] U.S. Office of Management and Budget (OMB), *Budget of the United States Government: Fiscal Year 2005*, p. 334, at http://www.gpoaccess.gov/usbudget/fy05/pdf/budget/sba.pdf; OMB, *Budget of the United States Government: Fiscal Year 2006*, p. 313, at http://www.gpoaccess.gov/usbudget/fy06/pdf/budget/sba.pdf; and OMB, *Budget of the United States Government: Fiscal Year 2007*, p. 283, at http://www.gpoaccess.gov/usbudget/fy07/pdf/budget/sba.pdf.

[66] OMB, *Budget of the United States Government: Fiscal Year 2008*, pp. 139, 140, at http://www.gpoaccess.gov/ usbudget/fy08/pdf/budget/sba.pdf; and OMB, *Budget of the United States Government: Fiscal Year 2009*, p. 130, at http://www.gpoaccess gov/usbudget/fy09/pdf/budget/sba.pdf. The Bush Administration also proposed to increase the interest rate charged to intermediaries.

[67] .S. Congress, House Committee on Small Business, *Full Committee Legislative Hearing on the SBA's Microloan and Trade Programs*, 110th Cong., 1st sess., July 12, 2007, H.Hrg. 110-35 (Washington: GPO, 2007), p. 37.

[68] Ibid.

partners who provide counseling and training to entrepreneurs, including Small Business Development Centers, Women's Business Centers, and SCORE."[69] They argued that about 94% of Microloan intermediaries are located within 20 miles of a Small Business Development Center, a Women's Business Center, or a SCORE partner.[70]

Advocates argue that the SBA's Microloan program is complementary, not duplicative, of the SBA's 7(a) loan guarantee program. They assert that Microloan borrowers are particularly disadvantaged when seeking access to capital, often having no credit history or lower credit scores than most applicants for the SBA's 7(a) loan guarantee program.[71] In their view, it is important that the SBA has a program whose sole focus is to assist Microloan borrowers in starting microbusinesses and have in place intermediaries that "have essential expertise on the needs of this key demographic."[72]

Advocates also argue that the SBA's Microloan marketing, management, and technical assistance grants program is "a crucial element which enables intermediaries to assist microbusiness owners step by step through their development and growth" and "not only increases the likelihood of full repayment of the loan, but augments business survival and success."[73] As mentioned previously, intermediaries typically require Microloan borrowers to participate in the training program as a condition of the receipt of the microloan.

Program Cost

Critics of the SBA's Microloan program argue that it is expensive relative to other SBA programs, costing about $7,506 per small business

[69] Ibid., pp. 37, 38.

[70] U.S. Congress, House Committee on Small Business, *Full Committee Hearing on the Small Business Administration's Microloan Program*, 110th Cong., 1st sess., June 14, 2007, H.Hrg. 110-30 (Washington: GPO, 2007), p. 7.

[71] U.S. Congress, House Committee on Small Business, *Full Committee Legislative Hearing on the SBA's Microloan and Trade Programs*, 110th Cong., 1st sess., July 12, 2007, H.Hrg. 110-35 (Washington: GPO, 2007), p. 27.

[72] Ibid., p. 7.

[73] Ibid.

assisted in FY2017, compared to $1,316 per small business assisted in the SBA's 7(a) loan guarantee program.[74] President George W. Bush cited the program's higher expense when he recommended in his FY2005, FY2006, and FY2007 budget requests to Congress that the program be terminated and when he recommended in his FY2008 and FY2009 budget requests to Congress that the interest rate charged to Microloan intermediaries be increased to make the program "self-financing."[75]

Advocates argue that the program's higher cost per small business assisted is unavoidable given the relatively unique nature of the program and the special needs of its borrowers. They assert that intermediaries often have to spend a significant amount of time with Microloan borrowers because those borrowers tend to have less experience with the credit application process and a more difficult time documenting their qualifications for assistance than borrowers in the SBA's loan guaranty programs. Also, in their view, raising the interest rate charged to intermediaries to make the program self-financing would reduce the program's cost, but could also defeat the program's purpose. They assert that because microloans are small, it is difficult for intermediaries to generate enough interest income to cover their costs. As a result, if the interest rate charged to intermediaries is increased, they contend that intermediaries would have to pass the increase on to Microloan borrowers. In their view, increasing the program's cost to Microloan borrowers "will create an economic hardship for them and make it more difficult for them

---

[74] SBA, "Fiscal Year 2019 Congressional Budget Justification and FY2017 Annual Performance Report," pp. 31, 36, 37, at https://www.sba.gov/sites/default/files/aboutsbaarticle/SBA_FY_19_508Final5_1.pdf.

[75] OMB, *Budget of the United States Government: Fiscal Year 2008*, pp. 139, 140, at http://www.gpoaccess.gov/ usbudget/fy08/pdf/budget/sba.pdf; OMB, *Budget of the United States Government: Fiscal Year 2009*, p. 130, at http://www.gpoaccess.gov/usbudget/fy09/pdf/budget/sba.pdf; U.S. Congress, House Committee on Small Business, *Full Committee Legislative Hearing on the SBA's Microloan and Trade Programs*, 110th Cong., 1st sess., July 12, 2007, H.Hrg. 110-35 (Washington: GPO, 2007), p. 38; and U.S. Congress, House Committee on Small Business, Subcommittee on Finance and Tax, *Subcommittee Hearing on Improving the SBA's Access to Capital Programs for our Nation's Small Businesses*, 110th Cong., 2nd sess., March 5, 2008, H.Hrg. 110-76 (Washington: GPO, 2008), p. 33.

to grow their businesses" and "lead to fewer jobs created and fewer tax dollars paid."[76]

Program Administration

On September 28, 2017, the SBA's Office of Inspector General (OIG) released an audit of the SBA's administration of the Microloan program, following up on an earlier audit released on December 28, 2009. The OIG reported a number of deficiencies that it argued needed to be addressed "to ensure effective operation of the Microloan program."[77]

In 2009, the OIG found that

- the SBA's oversight of the Microloan program was focused on the intermediaries' ability to repay their SBA loans and was limited to a cursory review of quarterly financial reports supported by only one monthly bank statement. The bank statements were used to simply verify the outstanding balances reported on the intermediaries' quarterly reports. This review process did not allow the SBA to analyze the sources and uses of funds "which is necessary to detect inappropriate fund transfers between the intermediaries' [Microloan Revolving Funds and Loan Loss Reserve Funds] accounts."[78]
- onsite reviews were conducted only when an intermediary defaulted on its SBA loan.
- the program was inadequately staffed, operating at that time "with 6 analysts who oversee more than 160 intermediaries, 460

[76] U.S. Congress, House Committee on Small Business, Subcommittee on Finance and Tax, *Subcommittee Hearing on Improving the SBA's Access to Capital Programs for our Nation's Small Businesses*, 110th Cong., 2nd sess., March 5, 2008, H.Hrg. 110-76 (Washington: GPO, 2008), p. 46.

[77] SBA, Office of the Inspector General, "SBA's Administration of the Microloan Program under the Recovery Act," p. 3, at https://www.sba.gov/sites/default/files/oig/om10-10.pdf.

[78] Ibid., p. 1.

intermediary loans, and approximately 2,500 microloans per year."[79]

- the reported Microloan borrower default rate of 12% "appeared low given the high-risk nature of the program."[80]
- the audit identified duplicate loan reporting and 92 Microloan borrowers with outstanding microloan balances exceeding the then-$35,000 limit.
- the SBA's output performance metrics "do not ensure the ultimate program beneficiaries, the microloan borrowers, are truly assisted by the program" and "without appropriate [outcome performance] metrics, SBA cannot ensure the Microloan program is meeting policy goals."[81] The OIG recommended that the SBA "develop additional performance metrics to measure the program's achievement in assisting microloan borrowers in establishing and maintaining successful small businesses."[82]

In its 2017 audit, the OIG found that the SBA had taken several actions (see footnote below) to improve its oversight of the Microloan program since the 2009 audit but that the agency still had "internal control weaknesses" that prevented it from conducting "adequate program oversight to measure program performance and ensure program integrity."[83]

---

[79] Ibid.

[80] Ibid., p. 4. The OIG found that 1 intermediary made 1,182 microloans valued at over $11 million since 1993 and only reported slightly more than a 1% historical default rate, and 39 other intermediaries that reported that none of their loans had defaulted.

[81] Ibid., p.6.

[82] Ibid., p. 7.

[83] SBA, Office of the Inspector General, "Audit of SBA's Microloan Program," executive summary, at https://www.sba.gov/sites/default/files/oig/SBA_OIG_Report_17-19.pdf. The SBA provided the OIG a list of actions taken to improve Microloan program oversight in recent years, including: ...In 2010, the program office implemented a comprehensive quarterly reporting analysis, which has been completed on a quarterly basis for each active intermediary in the Microloan Program since that time. ...This information enables SBA to understand each Intermediary's relative health by displaying historical default rate, delinquency rate, collateral coverage rate, loan loss reserve coverage rate and other valuable risk indicators. Performing this quarterly analysis on every Intermediary has enabled SBA to minimize its losses due to Intermediary non-payment by providing warning signs well before performance issues reach a non-recoverable level. Also in 2010,

Specifically, the OIG audited 14 intermediary lenders and 52 microloan files and found documentation deficiencies, or differences between the information contained in the lender's loan file versus that in the SBA Microloan Program Electronic Reporting System (MPERS) in 44 of the 52 files. The OIG also argued that the audit revealed that inadequate documentation exists to show that the "no credit elsewhere" test had been properly administered; that, in some cases, inadequate supporting documentation existed to show how the microloan funds were used by the borrower; and that, in some cases, interest rates and fees were charged that exceeded the limits allowed under the program rules and regulations.[84]

The identified internal control weaknesses

> were due to the SBA not having an overall site visit plan, an adequate information system, available funding for system improvements, or clear Standard Operating Procedures (SOPs). Additionally, SBA management focused on output-based performance measures instead of outcome measures.[85]

The OIG recommended that the SBA (1) continue efforts to improve the information system to include outcome-based performance measurements and ensure the data captured can be used to effectively monitor the Microloan Program compliance, performance, and integrity;

OEO [the Office of Economic Opportunity] implemented an annual financial statement analysis that OEO staff has completed annually for each Intermediary. This analysis also allows SBA to see potential financial issues well in advance of becoming a problem in order to limit the risk of Intermediary non-payment to SBA. Further, in 2012 OEO designed its first Site Visit Checklist to be used by SBA District Office personnel when conducting annual site visits to the Microloan intermediaries. ... In 2013 OEO published its first Microloan Standard Operating Procedure (SOP) since the Program's inception in 1992. This SOP provides guidance to both SBA staff who are involved in managing the Program and the Intermediary lenders who participate. This SOP was updated in 2015 to incorporate changes made to the Microloan Program regulations. In 2014 the Microloan Program Office designed and implemented a grant calculator spreadsheet that is used by both OEO staff and each Intermediary as a project management tool for the technical assistance grants and the Intermediary's quarterly expense billings and performance reports. ...OEO conducts monthly webinar sessions with all participating lenders in order to provide Program-related updates, ongoing training and allow for presentation of best practices. See Ibid., pp. 13, 14.

[84] Ibid., p. 14.

[85] Ibid., p. 7.

(2) develop and implement a site visit plan to comprehensively monitor microloan portfolio performance and ensure program results can be evaluated program-wide; (3) update SOP 52 00A to clarify requirements regarding evidence for use of proceeds and credit elsewhere; and (4) update the microloan reporting system manual to reflect current technology capabilities. The SBA concurred with the four recommendations and stated that the agency will target September 30, 2019, for full implementation.[86]

LEGISLATION

As mentioned previously, during the 111th Congress, P.L. 111-240, the Small Business Jobs Act of 2010, increased the Microloan program's loan limit for borrowers from $35,000 to $50,000, and increased the loan limit for Microloan intermediaries after their first year of participation in the program from $3.5 million to $5 million.[87] It also temporarily allowed the SBA to waive, in whole or in part through FY2012, the nonfederal share requirement for loans to the Microloan program's intermediaries and for grants made to Microloan intermediaries for small business marketing, management, and technical assistance under specified circumstances (e.g., the economic conditions affecting the intermediary and the intermediary's performance) for up to a fiscal year.[88]

---

[86] Ibid., p. 8.

[87] P.L. 111-240, the Small Business Jobs Act of 2010, §1113. Maximum Loan Limits Under Microloan Program.

[88] P.L. 111-240, §1401. Matching Requirements Under Small Business Programs. During the 111th Congress, H.R. 3854, the Small Business Financing and Investment Act of 2009, passed by the House by a vote of 389-32, on October 29, 2009, would have increased the Microloan program's loan funding to "such sums as may be necessary" to support $110 million in direct microloans in FY2010 and $110 million in FY2011, increased the program's technical assistance grant funding to $80 million in FY2010 and $80 million in FY2011, authorized $20 million ($10 million in FY2010 and $10 million in FY2012) for a new Microloan interest assistance grant program, broadened the eligibility requirements for Microloan intermediaries to qualify for lower interest rates, increased the program's maximum loan amount to intermediaries during their first year in the program from $750,000 to $1 million, and in later years from an aggregate of $3.5 million to $7 million, and increased the percentage of technical assistance grant funds that an intermediary can spend on prospective borrowers from 25% to 35%, and on the provision of technical assistance through third-party providers from 25% to 35%.

No bills were introduced during the 112th Congress concerning the Microloan program. During the 113th Congress,

- H.R. 3191, the Expanding Opportunities to Underserved Businesses Act, would have increased the Microloan program's loan limit for borrowers from $50,000 to $75,000.
- S. 2487, the Access to Capital, Access to Opportunity Act, would have increased that limit to $100,000.
- S. 2693, the Women's Small Business Ownership Act of 2014, and its House companion bill, H.R. 5584, would have increased the Microloan program's aggregate loan limit for intermediaries after their first year of participation in the program from $5 million to $7 million. These bills would have also removed the requirements that no more than 25% of Microloan technical assistance grant funds may be used to provide information and technical assistance to prospective borrowers or on third-party contracts to provide the assistance.

During the 114th Congress, as mentioned earlier,

- S. 1445, the Microloan Act of 2015, would have removed the requirements that no more than 25% of Microloan technical assistance grant funds may be used to provide information and technical assistance to prospective borrowers or on third-party contracts to provide the assistance. It would have also eliminated the Microloan program's minimum state allocation formula.
- H.R. 2670, the Microloan Modernization Act of 2015, and its companion bill in the Senate (S. 1857) would have increased the Microloan program's aggregate loan limit for intermediaries after their first year of participation in the program from $5 million to $6 million, increased the program's repayment terms from not more than 6 years to not more than 10 years for loans greater than $10,000, and require the SBA Administrator to establish a rule enabling intermediaries to apply for a waiver of the requirement

that no more than 25% of Microloan technical assistance grant funds may be used to provide information and technical assistance to prospective borrowers. The House passed H.R. 2670 on July 13, 2015. S. 1857 was reported by the Senate Committee on Small Business and Entrepreneurship on July 29, 2015.

- S. 2850, the Microloan Program Modernization Act of 2016, would have increased the Microloan program's aggregate loan limit for intermediaries after their first year of participation in the program from $5 million to $6 million; eliminated the requirements that intermediaries spend no more than 25% of Microloan technical assistance grant funds on technical assistance to prospective borrowers and no more than 25% of those funds on third-party contracts for technical assistance; required the SBA to study and report on the operations of a representative sample of Microloan intermediaries and other intermediaries and make recommendations on how to reduce costs associated with intermediaries' participation in the program and to increase intermediary participation in the program; and required the Government Accountability Office to study and report on the SBA's oversight of the program, SBA's processes to ensure intermediary compliance with program rules and regulations, and the program's overall performance.

During the 115th Congress,

- P.L. 115-141, the Consolidated Appropriations Act, 2018, relaxed the requirements that intermediaries spend no more than 25% of Microloan technical assistance grant funds on technical assistance to prospective borrowers and no more than 25% of those funds on third-party contracts for technical assistance by increasing those percentages to 50%. These provisions were originally in H.R. 2056, the Microloan Modernization Act of 2017, and S. 526, its companion bill in the Senate (as amended in committee).

- H.R. 2056, the Microloan Modernization Act of 2017, and S. 526, its companion bill in the Senate, would, among other provisions, increase the Microloan program's aggregate loan limit for intermediaries after their first year of participation in the program from $5 million to $6 million.

CONCLUDING OBSERVATIONS

During the 111th Congress, congressional debate concerning proposed changes to the SBA's loan guaranty programs, including the Microloan program, centered on the likely impact the changes would have on small business access to capital, job retention, and job creation. As a general proposition, some, including President Obama, argued that economic conditions made it imperative that the SBA be provided additional resources to assist small businesses in acquiring capital necessary to start, continue, or expand operations and create jobs.[89] Others worried about the long-term adverse economic effects of spending programs that increase the federal deficit. They advocated business tax reduction, reform of financial credit market regulation, and federal fiscal restraint as the best means to assist small business economic growth and job creation.[90]

In terms of specific program changes, the provisions enacted in P.L. 111-240 (allowing the SBA to temporarily waive the Microloan program's nonfederal share matching requirements, increasing the loan limit for borrowers from $35,000 to $50,000, and increasing the loan limit for intermediaries after their first year of participation in the program from

---

[89] Rep. Nydia Velázquez, Small Business Financing and Investment Act of 2009," House debate, *Congressional Record*, daily edition, vol. 155, no. 159 (October 29, 2009), pp. H12074, H12075; Senator Mary Landrieu, "Statements on Introduced Bills and Joint Resolutions," remarks in the Senate, *Congressional Record*, daily edition, vol. 155, no. 185 (December 10, 2009), p. S12910; and The White House, "Remarks by the President on Job Creation and Economic Growth," December 8, 2009, at https://obamawhitehouse.archives.gov/the-press-office/remarks-president-job-creationand-economic-growth.

[90] Susan Eckerly, "NFIB Responds to President's Small Business Lending Initiatives," October 21, 2009; and NFIB, "Government Spending," at https://www.nfib.com/content/issues/economy/government-spending-small-businesseshave-a-bottom-line-government-should-too-49051/.

$3.5 million to $5 million) and legislation introduced during recent Congresses (increasing borrower loan limits, increasing intermediary loan limits, and removing restraints on the use of technical assistance grants) are all designed to achieve the same goal: create jobs by enhancing micro borrowers' access to capital and technical training assistance.

Determining how specific changes in federal policy are most likely to lead to job creation is a challenging question. For example, a 2008 Urban Institute study concluded that differences in the term, interest rate, and amount of SBA financing "was not significantly associated with increasing sales or employment among firms receiving SBA financing."[91] However, they also reported that their analysis accounted for less than 10% of the variation in firm performance. The Urban Institute suggested that local economic conditions, local zoning regulations, state and local tax rates, state and local business assistance programs, and the business owner's charisma or business acumen also "may play a role in determining how well a business performs after receipt of SBA financing."[92]

As the Urban Institute study suggests, given the many factors that influence business success, measuring the SBA's Microloan program's effect on job retention and creation is complicated. That task is made even more challenging by the absence of performance-oriented measures that could serve as a guide.

The SBA's Office of Inspector General has recommended that the SBA adopt performance-oriented measures, specifically recommending that the SBA track the number of Microloan borrowers who remain in business after receiving a microloan to measure the extent to which the Microloan program contributed to their ability to stay in business. It has also recommended that the SBA require intermediaries to report the technical assistance provided to each Microloan borrower and "use this data to analyze the effect technical assistance may have on the success of

---

[91] Shelli B. Rossman and Brett Theodos, with Rachel Brash, Megan Gallagher, Christopher Hayes, and Kenneth Temkin, *Key Findings from the Evaluation of the Small Business Administration's Loan and Investment Programs: Executive Summary* (Washington, DC: The Urban Institute, January 2008), p. 58, at http://www.urban.org/Uploaded PDF/411602_executive_summary.pdf.

[92] Ibid.

Microloan borrowers and their ability to repay microloans."[93] Other performance-oriented measures that Congress might also consider include requiring the SBA to survey Microloan borrowers to measure the difficulty they experienced in obtaining a loan from the private sector; the ease or difficulty of finding, applying, and obtaining a microloan from an intermediary; and the extent to which the microloan or technical assistance received contributed to their ability to create jobs or expand their scope of operations.

APPENDIX. MICROLOAN TECHNICAL ASSISTANCE PROGRAM FUNDING

Table A-1. Microloan Technical Assistance Program Funding, FY2000-FY2017 (Appropriations and actual expenditures, $ in millions)

Fiscal Year	Initial Appropriation	Modifications	Final Appropriation	Actual Expenditures
2000	$23.200 $20.000	($0.088)[a]	$23.112	$19.243
2001	$17.500 $15.000	($0.044)[b]	$19.956	$18.385
2002	$15.000	—	$17.500	$17.742
2003		($0.098)[c]	$14.902	$14.899
2004		($0.089)[d]	$14.911	$14.655
2005	$14.000	($0.112)[e]	$13.888	$13.813
2006	$13.000	($0.130)[f]	$12.870	$12.792
2007	$13.000	—	$13.000	$12.800
2008	$15.000	—	$15.000	$14.816
2009	$20.000	—	$20.000	$19.813
2010	$22.000	$24.000[g]	$46.000	$43.220
2011	$22.000	($0.044)[h]	$21.956	$24.603
2012	$20.000	—	$20.000	$19.446
2013	$20.000	($0.191)[i]	$19.809	$19.985

[93] SBA, Office of the Inspector General, "SBA's Administration of the Microloan Program under the Recovery Act," pp. 6, 7, at https://www.sba.gov/sites/default/files/oig/om10-10.pdf.

Fiscal Year	Initial Appropriation	Modifications	Final Appropriation	Actual Expenditures
2014	$20.000	—	$20.000	$19.267
2015	$22.300	—	$22.300	$22.247
2016	$25.000	—	$25.000	$24.340
2017	$31.000	—	—	$23.535

Source: SBA, Congressional Budget Justification, (FY2002-FY2010), at http://archive.sba.gov/about sba/budgetsplans/BUDGET_REQ_PERF_PLAN.html; SBA, Congressional Budget Justification, [FY2011-FY2019], at http://www.sba.gov/about-sba-services/217; P.L. 109-148, the Department of Defense, Emergency Supplemental Appropriations to Address Hurricanes in the Gulf of Mexico, and Pandemic Influenza Act, 2006; P.L. 111-5, the American Recovery and Reinvestment Act of 2009; P.L. 112-10, the Department of Defense and Full-Year Continuing Appropriations Act, 2011; P.L. 112-25, the Budget Control Act of 2011; P.L. 112-74, the Consolidated Appropriations Act, 2012, P.L. 112-175, the Continuing Appropriations Resolution, 2013; P.L. 113- 6, the Consolidated and Further Continuing Appropriations Act, 2013; P.L. 113-76, the Consolidated Appropriations Act, 2014; P.L. 113-235, the Consolidated and Further Continuing Appropriations Act, 2015; P.L. 114-113, Consolidated Appropriations Act, 2016; and P.L. 115-31, the Consolidated Appropriations Act, 2017.

[a] In FY2000, P.L. 106-113, the Consolidated Appropriations Act, 2000, required a 0.38% across-the-board rescission for federal agencies in FY2000, resulting in a reduction of $0.088 million from the Microloan Technical Assistance program.

[b] In FY2001, P.L. 106-554, the Consolidated Appropriations Act, 2001, imposed a 0.22% rescission on federal agencies, resulting in a $0.044 million reduction from the Microloan Technical Assistance program.

[c] In FY2003, P.L. 108-7, the Consolidated Appropriations Resolution, 2003, imposed a rescission of 0.65% on federal agencies, resulting in a $0.098 million reduction from the Microloan Technical Assistance program.

[d] In FY2004, P.L. 108-199, the Consolidated Appropriations Act, 2004, imposed a 0.59% rescission on federal agencies, resulting in a reduction of $0.089 million from the Microloan Technical Assistance program.

[e] In FY2005, P.L. 108-447, the Consolidated Appropriations Act, 2005, imposed a 0.8% rescission on federal agencies, resulting in a reduction of $0.112 million from the Microloan Technical Assistance program.

[f] In FY2006, P.L. 109-148 imposed a 1.0% rescission on federal agencies, resulting in a reduction of $0.130 million from the Microloan Technical Assistance program.

[g] In FY2009, P.L. 111-5 provided the Microloan Technical Assistance Program an additional $24 million to remain available until September 30, 2010. The funds were awarded in FY2010.

[h] In FY2011, P.L. 112-10 imposed a 0.2% rescission on federal agencies, resulting in a reduction of $0.044 million from the Microloan Technical Assistance program.

[i] In FY2013, P.L. 112-25 and P.L. 113-6 imposed in a federal government-wide sequestration process and a required 0.2% across-the-board rescission, resulting in a $0.191 million reduction from the Microloan Technical Assistance program.

INDEX

A

B

C

D

E